The New Interpretation of Dreams: Maps for Psychotherapy
and the General Reader

by

James P. Gustafson, MD
University of Wisconsin
Medical School

Publisher: James P. Gustafson, MD, Madison, Wisconsin

Library of Congress Catalog Card Number 97-94989
ISBN 0-9662185-0-7

Back Cover Photograph by Karin Wolfe Gustafson

Printed in the United States by Omnipress, Madison, Wisconsin. To obtain this book, write
James P. Gustafson, MD, Professor of Psychiatry, University of Wisconsin, 6001 Research Park
Boulevard, Madison, Wisconsin, 53719-1179, or telephone (608) 263-6059.

Preface

It is an honor to write a preface for my classmate at Harvard College and Medical School, of whom I have seen very little since we graduated together thirty years ago. He went the way of a very unorthodox professor of psychiatry, as in this book, and his five previous books, while I went the way of the simple practitioner of medicine, who retains a trace of his liberal education.

That is why it is also so fitting that I write the preface to The New Interpretation of Dreams, for its subtitle is Maps for Psychotherapy and the General Reader, and that is my domain, and I the ideal reader, to explain to you the beauty of this book.

What is Dr. Gustafson providing us? Why maps of the territory of dreams? The answer is very simple. "The brain is a dreaming instrument" (Hilts, 1997), absolutely necessary to creatures who move about in the world, and need to predict what they are moving into, next. This is the view of the famous neuroscientist, Rodolfo Llinas, and this is the view of Dr. Gustafson. He is giving us his general theory of dreams, which is a search theory, for mapping the force fields in which the subject is moving.

What happens when people only rely on the conscious mind with its focal powers of concentration? Some of them become very good specialists, at making money, or reputation, or skill in a branch of knowledge, but they are left more or less at a loss outside their little area. I read very little anymore, but I still remember from my college days with Dr. Gustafson what Erasmus said in 1511 about the professions:

> On the contrary, the more eminent a profession, the fewer people
> in it can answer to the name. You'll find more good skippers than
> good princes, more good doctors than good bishops. That is no
> reproach to an order, but rather a tribute to a few who have conducted
> themselves nobly in the noblest of orders (p. 147)

When I read this passage in the 60s, I had no idea that he was right that mankind as a whole is in the grip of folly, for I was only a youth myself. I could only see special cases, like my professors who were not very impressive, as a group.

Now that I have been in practice over thirty years in this little town beside Lake Huron, I see how right Erasmus was about humanity. I would put it more simply that humanity remains stuck in high school. My patients remain so vulnerable to lacking money (see Henry, 1973, Chapter 5 on "Vulnerability": Sources of Man's Fear in Himself and in Society") that they run off and get a specialty for making some of it as soon as they can. They are so intent on this, that they wear down at a very great rate. They compensate themselves by eating, a great deal, and drinking, a great deal, and watching the tube, a great deal. Between their depletion and their compensation, they pretty much shoot their lives. I see all too much of this in my consulting room.

Now, reading Dr. Gustafson, I believe he is saying that one of the great powers of dreams is to get us free of such a rundown world to what he calls "a world elsewhere" to be renewed. After I read his manuscript this chill November, I dreamt:

> I throw a football from the back row of my high school to the front row, and am acclaimed a big deal. When I drive back, I find it is impossible to get to the front door, because it is locked in a sea of ice. I am going ahead on foot, and happen to look up at a place called "The Rookery," and see it is full of grizzly bears about to pounce on me. I eye them, and they hold back.

I want only to say one thing about this dream, that I learned from reading this book. When I am tired of this world of endless competitions in which numbers decide everything (my high school), I can go back into aboriginal space to find the dimensions that are lacking in the modern world. I enter here the world of bears.

Now, the bears take me back to the marvelous story on the same subject of renewal by William Faulkner called "The Bear" (1942). This is one of the annoying things about reading Dr. Gustafson, that he keeps drawing us back to whatever wisdom we once had and let pass. He seems to be saying that we cannot do without Faulkner and Erasmus and all of those other fellows. This is bad news for modern medicine and so forth. If Dr. Gustafson is right, our profession is on a hopelessly narrow path. Maybe it has always been so. Look at the doctors in Moliere (1666) and in Bergson (1901)!

I have asked Dr. Gustafson why he did not keep his book as simple as he could, so it could be published by the companies that published his previous five books. If he had kept to renewal in dreams, for example, he could have managed to get a publisher readily. Renewal in Dreams would be the kind of advertisement that the world is waiting for, another promise, for one-dimensional man. Dr. Gustafson replied that this was precisely what was wrong with all the theories of dream interpretation. They reduce the marvelous dream instrument to a single function. Like Freud reduced it to the secret gratification of wishes.

Even with this drastic curtailment of his subject, Freud could only sell 351 copies in his first six years after publication (Freud, 1900, xx). Still, he insulted his own subject, in this way of the world. The uncompromising Dr. Gustafson is going to give us "the pattern that connects" dreaming in all its ramifications. He is quite like Melville (1851) with his whale. Indeed, Dr. Gustafson wrote his first book (1986, 1997) in the grip of Melville's dream voyage.

The next day after this conversation with Dr. Gustafson about his refusal to compromise his subject, I saw a patient who is grieving over the impending death of his mother. He dreamt:

> He was trying to clean his nails, but the store where he sought an implement only had pliers and gross instruments of that kind which were also too expensive.

Now, I thought, here is a search for cleansing rebirth, but it runs right into gross instruments and expense. I decided to follow Dr. Gustafson's lead, and find out about the search to be cleansed, and its obstacles. I found myself in great emotional currents. First, he had felt dirty, even in his nationality. Second, his grandfather was so gross as to take to his warts with pliers. Third, his mother was so cheap as to buy him toys that fell apart. In very short order, we had <u>reached</u> from his search back to childhood for renewal, to the very tears and rage that blocked his way.

I understood at once why Dr. Gustafson is refusing to compromise his subject by making it come out all right. He believes, rightly, I think, that dreams are going to be filled with <u>incongruent images</u>, of things like nail cleaning and pliers that don't seem to belong together. Again, I am driven back to college and what Max Ernst said about surrealism:

> I think I would say that it amounts to the exploitation of the chance
> meeting on a non-suitable plane of two mutually distant realities
> (a paraphrase and generalization of the well-known quotation from
> Lautreamont "Beautiful as the chance meeting upon a dissecting table
> of a sewing machine and an umbrella") . . . (1952, p. 60)

This is precisely what Dr. Gustafson's search theory is trying to map for us; namely, how we must reach between opposites, if we are going to avoid foolishness. He even ends with Rabelais. I think I am going to have to go back to college after all.

One more thing, to the practical reader like myself. The very hardest thing about this book is Dr. Gustafson's theory of dimensionality, which he borrowed from Bateson (1979). By this, Dr. Gustafson means that a map must have one more dimension than the territory it is mapping (n + 1) (Gustafson, 1986, 1997, Chapter 15). He argues that an adequate map of dreaming must have at least 10 dimensions. I count more than that from his chapters which number 12.

This much I understand. The typical mind of today is in one-dimension, of maximizing something ($, reputation, etc.). The dream routinely goes into two-dimensions, like the cleaning of nails, with pliers, to complicate reality. Beyond two dimensions is beyond most of us. The Hottentots used to say, one, two and many.

But I can tell you this, that the other 8+ dimensions discussed by Dr. Gustafson are what can make us so acute with the simple incongruency of cleaning nails with pliers (2+ dimensions). We modern men do not understand how the world can radiate from polarities such as those discussed by Levi-Strauss (Dr. Gustafson, Chapter 10), so that everything, everything in the world is included. That kind of wealth of materials makes us think of catalogs. But this book is no catalog.

Indeed, I will give you your college outline of the course, in case you get lost in the wealth of materials along the way. The argument of this book is so <u>tightly constructed</u>. It is the very set of "algorithms of the heart" (Bateson, 1972, on Levi-Strauss).

Levi-Strauss argued that the aboriginal mind was profoundly logical, but not all of Levi-Strauss's modern readers had the patience to struggle with the precise and wide-ranging beauty of the instrument. The same will be true of the readership of this book because Dr. Gustafson is insisting that we adapt our minds to the dimensionality (10 D-) of the dreaming instrument, rather than that it reduce itself to our terms (1 or 2 D-). Indeed, Dr. Gustafson's book must have reached my simple mind, for I dreamt after my first draft of this preface: "I am asked to consult to a man who leaps straight into the air, uttering complex verbiage. I decline, but I have an opinion about his fate." The dream reads his fate as locked in by the 1-dimension he cannot get out of (a limit cycle attractor, with a single basin). I believe I am going to save myself a lot of trouble by reading the dimensionality of my patients in their dreams, and in my dreams about them!.

Joseph Lacherlich, MD
Bay City, Michigan
November, 1997

Author's Preface to The New Interpretation of Dreams

I am aware of the risk of putting New in front of Freud's title of 1900, and, you, the reader, will judge for yourself if I have rightly laid claim to creating a new map of this territory of dreams. A more accurate title would be The Old/New Interpretation of Dreams, but it would be too clumsy a title for a modern world on the run with little time to trouble with contradictions. What I mean is that I have built on Freud, Jung, and Levi-Strauss, and many others from the last hundred years of mapping dreams to give practical help to patients. This book is the yield of a hundred years of the work of others, for augmenting brief and long-term psychotherapy. It is a map of this royal road.

Yet it is much more, for dream is the province, not only of clinicians come lately, but it is the very being of aboriginal humanity and it is the very wellspring of all art, narrative, visual, and musical, from Homer to Shakespeare to Melville in the narrative form, with other lines in painting and music and architecture and dance and so forth. Therefore, I have taken the scope of this book as the dream-thinking of man from timeless space that is ab-original, to the time of Western man that only began about three thousand years ago at Troy in Homer's Iliad. This book is a map of the royal road of humanity's artfulness that is incomparably greater than his/her clinical work. Thus, it is a book for the general reader looking to augment his/her dream capacity.

What is then new? I can judge best by what I could glimpse before I wrote this book, and what I can see after I wrote this book. What has emerged for me is clarity about the great lines of force in the force-field that we all live in. To the right is the great pull of history into a modern time-urgency that is governed by our Puritan leaders so perfectly illustrated by the Republican party, or the men of the bottom-line of quantity. To the left is the great pull of our ancient instincts into the great vortex of nature ruled by the Virgin or the Goddess of Complete Being and so faintly represented in our time by a Democratic party that trades on looking out for all of us and all of nature and quality herself.

What is new is clarity about the collision of the old and new lines of force, and the dream as a map of what that force-field forbids and what it allows. I am much better after composing this book at sighting my patients being carried away by their Puritan projects to their ruin, like Brutus, who says to Cassius,

> There is a tide in the affairs of men
> which, taken at the flood, leads on to fortune (Julius Caesar, Shakespeare, W., IV, iii, 218-219).

I am also much better at sighting my patients, and my friends, and myself, finding their way back out of the time-urgency of these tides of history, to the great satisfactions for which we are built as a part of nature. If my readers can map these lines of force better for themselves, I will be satisfied. This is no luxury, for, as ancient humanity knew, you live by riding these currents, but you die by getting carried away by them.

I thought of dedicating this book to Lewis Carroll, for in his Alice of 1865, he foresaw this force-field of which I am writing. He knew you can go down a little hole back into the great capacity of nature, but he also knew that men would be there as pitiful or silly as always, bent on owning everything. His Cheshire Cat is the guiding spirit of the place, for he knows how to appear on these croquet grounds of the Queen // and he knows how to disappear. This is the grace of dream capacity, which is the ability to move as freely as possible from one domain to another. The Cheshire Cat is the modern fool, and modern master of transitions, like the archaic opossum, or coyote, or raven.

Then, I recalled that a nearer neighbor had achieved much the same grace in 1949 when Aldo Leopold wrote A Sand County Almanac. His old house is a few blocks from mine, if I did not reach mine until 1973 when he was long gone. But he is not gone at all in his book, especially in his essay called "Great Possessions" which is worthy of Thoreau himself. Leopold wrote of himself before dawn as a medieval king:

> Like other great landowners, I have tenants. They are negligent about rents, but very punctilious about tenures. Indeed at daybreak from April to July they proclaim their boundaries to each other, and so acknowledge, at least by inference, their fiefdom to me. (p. 44)

His piece is a choral composition that opens with the single call of a field sparrow at 3:30 AM, explodes into full cacophony, and dallies with his dog before his title to this property runs out:

> He has paid scant respect to all these vocal goings-on, for to him the evidence of tenantry is not song, but scent . . . Now he is going to translate for me the olfactory poems that who-knows-what silent creatures have written in the summer night. At the end of each poem sits the author -- if we can find him (pp. 46-47)

Having modulated from the aural to the visual to the olfactory key, Leopold returns to the dominant aural:

> A tractor roars warning that my neighbor is astir. The world has shrunk to those mean dimensions known to county clerks. We turn towards home, and breakfast. (p. 47)

Here is a neighbor to emulate, a prince of all of nature, who knows how to yield the field for the daytime hours. He will not claim too much, yet he gives us everything.

I could not have written this book, probably, if I had not been situated like Leopold, our Prospero, in my middle age of having spent a great deal of time in this modern history of psychotherapy (see Gustafson, 1986; 1997; Gustafson and Cooper, 1990; Gustafson, 1992; 1995a; 1995b), and had a great deal of space to get out of this history. Last night as I contemplated these final sentences, I realized that I live very close to the longitude of 90° west, and to the latitude of 45° north. Thus, I live half way around the western world, and half way between the equator and the north pole. Perhaps, I am best situated to write about the achievement of balance with the help of dreams.

I am most grateful to my four chief readers, friends and critics, for their thoughtfulness and responsiveness and spontaneity in reply to my text: Ruth Gustafson, Peter Miller, Michael Moran, and Vance Wilson. Also to Dee Jones for her faithful speed, accuracy and workmanship in assembling the copy, to Pam DeGolyer for her faithful tracking of the endless permissions, to Jan Martinson for much of the skillful videotaping of the cases in my Clinic, and to Lowell Cooper and Michael Wood for helpful suggestions, and to the trainees and clinicians who read and discussed the first nine chapters of this book with me in my Brief Psychotherapy Clinic at the University of Wisconsin Department of Psychiatry: Jantina Borst, Christine Costanzo, Roy Eenigenburg, Anna Flynn, Rise Futterer, Marci Gittleman, Jeanie Jundt, Barb Kelly, Lori Kuntz, Phil Lomas, Sara Long, Sarah ̶ ̶ ̶ ̶ ̶ ̶ ̶ ̶ ̶ ̶cio Martinez, Dennis Merritt, Kathy Morley, Shannon O'Connor, Molli ̶ ̶ ̶ ̶ ̶ ̶ ̶ ̶ ̶ ̶ ̶ ̶ ̶Valerie Stromquist, Steve Sutherland, and Pauline Th ̶permitted me to quote their dreams in the service of ̶ ̶ ̶ ̶ ̶ ̶ ̶ ̶ ̶ ̶ ̶errors are all my own.

. . . that <u>dream</u>-power which every night shows thee
is thine own; a power transcending all limit and privacy,
and by virtue of which a man is the conductor of the whole
river of electricity – Ralph Waldo Emerson, 1844, p. 241

Contents
The New Interpretation of Dreams: Maps for Psychotherapy
and The General Reader

Introduction -- One Hundred Years of the Unconscious

-- We have obviously been so busy with the question of what we
think that we entirely forget to ask what the unconscious psyche
thinks of us -- Jung, 1968, p. 94.

I have labored to write this book so that absolute beginners can find the skill they want to borrow, while experienced people can contemplate the entire array of the music of dreams in its full complexity. Before I note the powers to be displayed from dreams, I need for some readers to explain why we do need dreams at all in our field of psychotherapy.

Psychotherapy is in a depleted state, quite like that of the general population. On the one hand, it is full of the cognitive-behavioral activity of the conscious mind trying to harness the patient to stop things like thinking negatively, or avoiding, or drinking, and so forth. On the other hand, it plays a very passive waiting game as in a Rogerian mirror. In other words, it is highly willful, or highly receptive (Gustafson, 1995a,b).

Being highly willful with programs for the patient to follow will get some things done, and being highly receptive to follow the patient will get some patients to get up by themselves. If these activities were not of some use, they would disappear altogether.

They are better than nothing, and capable of earning a living. As I suggested, the weakness/strength of doctoring is the very weakness/strength of Western civilization, which presumes that that power comes from without, extrinsically, through technical sources, like electrical outlets. Thus, the patients that are depleted are pumped up with antidepressive programs or drugs, and patients that are wired are defused with antianxiety programs or drugs. The opposite policy of receptivity also locates the power extrinsically to the patient in the transference relationship. The doctor is the self-object that the patients must swallow, or, as we say more technically, introject.

About a hundred years ago, Freud proposed that the unconscious mind is the great source of power within, although greatly in need of modulation to be used. Like any other tremendous energy source, it is destructive in its full force, but workable when it has passed through transformations that bring it down to earth. With Breuer in 1895, Freud first proposed that this vitality was strangulated inside the patient. Later, he used less violent but political terms like repressed. Still later in his structural theory, he pictured the conscious mind as censored by a structure he called the super-ego.

In any event, Freud's therapeutics was to release the patient from the strictures of his conscious mind, to let in the repressed power of his unconscious mind. For him, the royal road to this release of power from within was the dream (Freud, 1900). Actually, his chief metaphor for this influx of vitality is not the highway, but the railroad. The trains of thought connect the veneer of the polite conscious stations of the mind, with the impolite and utterly narcissistic stations of the unconscious mind.

Imagine the retina as a little metaphor for the entire mind. In the center is the conscious focus, upon what is acceptable. Surrounding this station is a vast periphery in shadow, into which trains of thought may penetrate by what Freud called free association.

Figure 0.1

"Freud's Trains"

searching for more dimensions, out of

the focal mind of the conscious, into

the unconscious: a kind of railroad

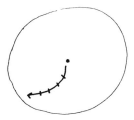

Since Freud, an array of transportations have been invented for getting from the conscious center of the mind to search the unconscious heart of darkness. Freud's railroad is but one. Unfortunately, this entire array is mostly unknown to psychotherapy in 1996. Because of its increasing conscious focus, the unconscious has become more peripheral. Knowledge of how to get there is around, but tends to be retained as dogma. Each school has its own correct way. There are a few texts (Natterson, 1980/1993; Delaney, 1993) which collect those correct ways into compendia. But there is no grasp of these routes of access to the unconscious as a set of searches in a simple relationship to each other.

So I offer in the first half of this book the powers of access to the unconscious which have been discovered in the years 1895-1995 and mostly forgotten. I suggest in simple mathematics that each is a search with its own algorithm or formula and with its own domain or typical discoveries. I take each as a kind of valid music, like a style within the canon of classical music which is performed by contemporary symphonies. Chapter 1 is Freud's search by free association. Chapter 2 is Jung's search for the compensating opposite. Chapter 3 is the existential search along the spatial, temporal and sensory dimensions. Chapters 4, 5 and 6 extend the classical triad of searches, especially into the musical inventions of Erikson, the underworld destroyers of Hillman, and the inscapes of Margulies -- these searches extend those of Freud, Jung, and the existentialists, respectively.

Yet there is much more music than this. In the second half of this book, I show dimensions of dreams that are hardly discussed at all. In Chapter 7, I show the science of dreams which takes the dream as a kind of memory search utilized by mammals when they are confronted with complex problems which cannot be fit into or assimilated to their solutions. In Chapter 8, I show the art of adding dimensions or dream screens or worlds elsewhere for projecting problems that cannot be managed in the usual two dimensions of the conscious mind. In Chapter 9, I show Winnicott's uncanny "dream dives" from the conventional world of the child into the underworld of strange, pulsating forces. In Chapter 10, I show Levi-Strauss' unconscious searches in myth between the poles of survival for the people concerned, as between the world of corn and the world of the antelope for the Zuni.

What I am preparing is a relatively simple method of reading the different kinds of unconscious music quite akin to the orchestral scoring of Levi-Strauss, which I will arrive at in Chapters 11 and 12. In Chapter 11, I will show how society forces us to orient mostly in two dimensions, which are inside our group versus outside our group. Yet this also creates the continual paradox that being an insider gets you crushed, while being an outsider fills you with urges to crush others. Gustafson (1992) mapped this two-dimensional oscillator, which is a repeating story, as a strange loop which looks like this:

Figure 0.2

an oscillator with two dimensions, that is,

a strange loop –

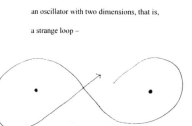

In Chapter 12, I show how individuals develop dimensions beyond the necessary in- and out- to get beyond the fate of a playing card in the deck of humanity. Like the Cheshire Cat in <u>Alice</u> (Carroll, 1865), you can only oppose the Queen if you have dimensions in which you can disappear. Otherwise, you will lose your head. The dimensions of the drawing on p. 79 of <u>Alice</u> then create a space which looks like this:

Figure 0.3

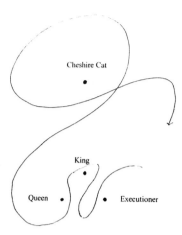

While it could be simpler to learn this tremendous subject by pretending that you perform steps one, two and three, in that kind of linear mathematics, it would distort the actual terrain we are going to be looking into. The rhetoric of the different schools make it sound as if you can penetrate the mystery of dreams by that kind of harnessing of the will.

Actually, that kind of coherence is only true of the conscious mind. The unconscious mind pulses wildly between coherence and incoherence, and only gravitates around certain basins, which are called strange attractors in chaos theory. Once a theory gravitates around a single attractor, it is essentially dying, in what is called a limit cycle attractor which looks like this (see my Chapter 5 on circles as a symbol of death, and the need to destroy dead things in dreams, as argued by Hillman (1973):

Figure 0.4

a limit cycle attractor

returns to the deadliness of

the focal mind in one dimension

This wisdom of this subject is to keep from settling, and thus going to sleep, within a dead daydream. The Zen Masters of 11th Century Japan (Sekida, 1977) knew something about blocking this huge tendency of humanity. Then there is possible a perpetual departure, from two dimensions into the hyperspace of ten dimensions, which looks like this:

Figure 0.5

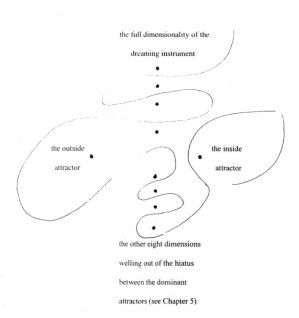

the full dimensionality of the

dreaming instrument

the outside

attractor

the inside

attractor

the other eight dimensions

welling out of the hiatus

between the dominant

attractors (see Chapter 5)

This is the full dimensionality of the brain as an oscillator for mapping the subject's territory in the world. Interestingly, it is the very same dimensionality needed to map the wave forms of a fully alert mind on the EEG (Schmid, 1991). Still it is also useful to return to the crude resting state, of two dimensions, to map whether you are in or out of the group, or to return to one-dimension, to map whether you are swallowed up as a mere function in the megamachine (Mumford, 1970) of society!

Chapter 1. Freud.

It is possible to make a simple start on Freud's method for the dissection of dreams, as if we were doing histology and had to prepare slides of cells to study under a microscope. Freud began science in just this way in Brücke's laboratory, and so we may follow in his footsteps. Dreams, after all, are composite biological structures, and Freud did dissect them to display them. In this metaphorical sense, Freud never left behind his training from the famous Brücke, a professor of physiology in Vienna.

Step one is to clarify what the dreams are reacting to from the day residue, or bothersome part of the day preceding the night of the dream. Dreams are like immunological reactions to foreign bodies:

> . . . our dream-thoughts are dominated by the same material that has occupied us during the day and we only bother to dream of things which have given us cause for reflection during the daytime (p. 207)

For example, in the "Non Vixit" dream of Freud himself which we will take apart with Freud, the disturbing cause for reflection was this:

> I had heard from my friend in Berlin, whom I have referred to as "Fl." (i.e. Fliess), that he was about to undergo an operation and that I should get further news of his condition from some of his relatives in Vienna. The first reports I received after the operation were not reassuring and made me feel anxious. I should have much preferred to go to him myself, but just at that time I was the victim of a painful complaint that made movement of any kind a torture for me. (p. 518)

Freud adds that the sister of Fliess had died in her youth after a very brief illness, and, thus, Freud fears that Fliess is going down the same deadly path.

> I must have imagined that his constitution was not much more resistant than his sister's and that, after getting much worse news of him, I should make the journey after all--and arrive too late, for which I would never cease to reproach myself. (pp. 518-519)

For Freud as a particular dreamer, potential for reproach is always an aggravating foreign body, which sets reflection in motion. He is highly allergic to reproach. A survey to his forty-seven dreams noted in the Index of Dreams, "A. Dreamt by Freud Himself," will discover a very high percentage as reflections from reproaches. A survey of "B. Dreamt by Others," will discover other motives for reflection: (excluding the footnote to Alexander the Great's dream), the first three react to painful hunger, painful comparison of self to friend getting married, and painful fear of a lack of dowry (money). (Alexander fears his siege of Tyre is faltering.)

Step two is to take apart this reflecting structure of the dream into its pieces, and subject each to a process of free association. Oddly, the dream as a coherent whole is actually a conglomerate of incoherent pieces, glued together by a coherent narrative. When each piece is subjected to free association, it turns out often to be a further conglomeration. Thus, the dream is a conglomerate of conglomerates. For example, a character in a dream is often like a composite photograph of many people at once, as if many photographic negatives were superimposed upon one another:

> As a rule the identification or construction of a composite person takes place for the very purpose of avoiding the representation of the common element. Instead of saying: "A has hostile feelings toward me and so has B," make a composite figure out of A and B in the dream. (p. 356)

Let us return to "Non Vixit" to see what is meant by the pieces of the dream, and their dissection into further pieces. I quote first the dream in its entirety:

> I had gone to Brücke's laboratory at night, and, in response to a gentle knock on the door, I opened it to (the late) Professor Fleischl, who came in with a number of strangers and, after exchanging a few words, sat down at his table.

> This was followed by a second dream. (I have spaced the two dreams apart here, which are run together in the text)

> My friend Fl. (Fliess) had come to Vienna unobtrusively in July. I met him in the street in conversation with my (deceased) friend P., and went with them to some place where they sat opposite each other as though they were at a small table. I sat in front at its narrow end. Fl. spoke about his dead sister and said that in three quarters of an hour she was dead, and added some such words as "that was the threshold." As P. failed to understand him, Fl. turned to me and asked me how much I had told P. about his affairs. Whereupon, overcome by strange emotions, I tried to explain to Fl. that P. (could not understand anything at all, of course, because he) was not alive. But what I actually said -- and I myself noticed the mistake -- was, "NON VIXIT." I then gave P. a piercing look. Under my gaze he turned pale; his form grew indistinct and his eyes a sickly blue -- and finally he melted away. I was highly delighted at this and I now realized the Ernst Fleischl, too, had been no more than an apparition, a "revenant" ("ghost" -- literally, "one who returns"); and it seemed to me quite possible that people of that kind only existed as long as one liked and could be got rid of if someone else wished it. (pp. 456-457)

Now, the pieces of this text that Freud dissects out for us are (in order of his presentation):

A)   the annihilating look at the eyes made to turn sickly blue (p. 458);
B)   the NON VIXIT phrase (pp. 458-460);
C)   the feeling of being "overcome by strange emotions" (pp. 518-519);
D)   his discussion of self-reproach in C) leads back to another day residue previously omitted! (overlooked!): "I was given a warning not to discuss the matter (of Fliess's operation) with anyone" (p. 519); this in turn leads back to the character of Professor Fleischl (pp. 519 -520);

E)   the feeling of being "highly delighted" in making P. disappear (pp. 520-525).

He rides the trains of thought from these five stations in the text. Notice, we have shifted metaphors from histology to railroads. That is typical of Freud's text itself, which has the same conglomerate structure as the dreams (Shields, 1990).

To return to the method of dissection (and stay comfortable in a linear mode of ABC), notice that Freud need not dissect every phrase in the text. Five will do, because they will double back and pick up pieces or phrases that have not been taken as starting points (like Brücke as a character, P. as a character, the idea of "revenants" (ghosts) and so forth).

Let us take these five dissections one at a time. The first is easy, because Freud quickly remembers being annihilated himself by such a look from Brücke himself for arriving late to Brücke's laboratory. He notes with satisfaction that he has reversed roles, so Freud is the annihilator, and P. is annihilated. Furthermore, the blue eyes have been taken from the annihilator, and given to the annihilated, so that Freud is having his revenge on Brücke himself. At a single stroke of the dissecting knife, Freud has laid bare the polarity of the dream: annihilating reproach // annihilated guilt :: the murderous will // and the helpless receptivity.

Freud's second dissection, of the phrase "Non vixit," is much more difficult, because it relies on verbal bridges that are ingenious. Incidentally, bridge in German is Brücke, so it may be said that Freud is out-Brücke-ing Brücke in his own laboratory in which the dream is set. My students are vexed by this side of Freud. They either feel he is stretching too far or implausibly, or that he is asking too much of them to follow him. My opinion is that Freud has a marvelous gift for language, which is hardly ever expected of a doctor. Already, we are getting past the original metaphor of composite biological structures, dissection and histology. If dreams could be confined to such a linear laboratory, they would be dissectable, in straight lines.

Fortunately, or unfortunately, depending upon your standpoint, dreams may start in Brücke's laboratory, but they go everywhere. As Shields (1990) discovers for us in his remarkable essay on The Interpretation of Dreams as itself a dream, the book is a condensation of the forms of scientific essay, Jewish mystical aphorisms, autobiography, confession, charter document for psychoanalysis, holy writ, memoirs of a world-conqueror, travelogue, pilgrimage, political manifesto against bourgeois civility, and gripping detective story. Shields is a professor of religion who has written only this one essay on Freud in an obscure journal of psychoanalysis.

So let us play the part of Dr. Watson and go with this Holmes over about five ingenious verbal bridges (Brücken). The first clue is one that eluded the master himself, until ". . . at last it occurred to me that these two words possessed their high degree of clarity in the dream, not as words heard or spoken, but as words seen. I knew then at once where they came from. On the pedestal of the Kaiser Josef Memorial in the Hofburg (Imperial Palace) in Vienna the following impressive words are inscribed:

Saluti patriae vixit
non diu sed totus.

For the well-being of his country he lived not long but wholly" (p. 458). This reminds him of another day residue, of the unveiling a few days previous of a memorial to Fleischl in the cloisters of the University. He infers that he must have regretted that P. had died so young in so brilliant a career in science that he was robbed of his memorial. Thus, Freud's dream gives him his memorial, after all, while also wiping him out.

Freud's mind is truly a maze of verbalism. Now he has doubled back to two more disturbing events, from which the dream discovers reflections. The disturbance isn't just Fliess's post-operative condition, but it is also the reproach from the relative that Freud ought not to talk about it (as if he would be indiscreet), and it is also the unveiling of the memorial to Fleischl.

Now, Freud constructs a second verbal bridge from the actual cadence or prose rhythm of a latent dream thought summarizing his disturbing feelings about P., namely: "As he had deserved well of science I built him a memorial; but as he was guilty of an evil wish (which was expressed at the end of the dream) I annihilated him" (p. 459). (The evil wish is explained on p. 522, that P. had been impatient for Fleischl to move on so that P. could take his place. Since Fleischl was seriously ill, this would be a euphemism for a death wish).

Now, as Freud writes, ". . only one passage in literature" (p. 459) has this cadence and this sense for opposite feelings about another man that Freud has about P.: namely, when Brutus justifies himself over killing Julius Caesar,

As Caesar loved me, I weep for him; as he was fortunate, I rejoice at it; as he was valiant, I honour him; but, as he was ambitious, I slew him." (iii, 2)

"Were not the formal structure of these sentences and their antithetical meaning precisely the same as in the dream-thoughts I had uncovered? Thus I had been playing the part of Brutus in the dream." (p. 459)

Surely, this is subtle detective work. No one would have suspected that Freud was playing the part of Brutus from the surface of the dream in which he is merely going to Brücke's lab and then sitting at a table between two old friends. This distance between surface presentation and lurking depths is why Freud lays so much stress upon the distinction between manifest contest and latent content. No other writer on dreams sees such intrigue in them as Freud. I will come back in my conclusion of this chapter to why Freud sees this way, and what is the domain of dreams that require such subtlety.

The third bridge is very simple, but of profound importance to Freud. Once he knows he is Brutus in the dream, he jumps in a flash to his childhood part of actually playing Brutus in a play with his loved and hated older cousin John playing Caesar (p. 460). This occurred when Freud was fourteen, but even at age two he had struck John because John had struck him! To hit in the language of later childhood is "wichsen" so this is why "Non vivit" had been turned into

"Non vixit" and why Freud's' hostility to P. actually belongs not with P. but with John. The emotional current from childhood which charges up from below has now met the current coming down from the day's troubles. The confluence of these currents is what agitates the dream.

Freud believes that these confluent currents do make it through to the surface of the dream, while the thoughts that go with them remain in deep disguise: ". . . hostile and distressing feelings -- overcome by strange emotions were the words used in the dream itself -- were piled up at the point at which I annihilated my opponent and friend with two words ("non vixit"). And again, at the end of the dream, I was highly delighted, and I went on to approve the possibility, which in waking life I knew was absurd, of there being revenants who could be eliminated by a mere wish." (p. 518) (my italics and parenthetical inclusion) These two confluences do crash on the beach, if senselessly for the mind that cannot read their portent. Is that not the common experience of mankind?

The fourth bridge comes readily from the disturbing cause of the dream, in which Freud feels a reproach in the remark of the relative not to discuss Fliess's condition. Why, Freud asks, should he be so touchy about the implication that Freud needed to be cautioned. It leads him quickly to being between Fleischl and P., where he is actually sitting in the dream. Freud had quite unnecessarily betrayed a confidence from one to the other, and been taken to task for it, and felt ashamed of himself. In Freud, these things really stick.

The fifth bridge is from Freud's delight in his own ability to annihilate: he is highly delighted in the dream to make P. disappear, as he was at age two to get his cousin John punished, as he was to punish P. in his mind at the memorial service for Fleischl. This in turn leads him to his thoughts at P's funeral:

. . How many people I've followed to the grave already! But I'm still alive. I've survived them all; I'm left in possession of the field! A thought of this kind, occurring to me at a moment at which I was afraid I might not find my friend (Fl.) alive if I made the journey to him, could only be construed as meaning that I was delighted because I had once more survived someone, because it was he and not I who had died, because I was left in possession of the field, as I had been in the phantasied scene from my childhood. (p. 523)

Now Freud is ready for step three which is the summation of the dream. For him, it is always the convergence upon a wish-fulfillment which is the great law of dreams: to-wit,

It cannot be denied that to interpret and report one's dreams demands a high degree of self-discipline. One is bound to emerge as the only villain among the crowd of noble characters who share one's life. Thus it seemed to me quite natural that the revenants could only exist for just so long as one likes and should be removable at a wish. We have seen what my friend Josef (P.) was punished for. But the revenants were a series of reincarnations of the friend of my childhood. It was therefore also a source of satisfaction to me that I had always been able to find successful substitutes for that figure; and I felt I should be able to find a substitute for the friend whom I was now on the point of losing; no one was irreplaceable. (p. 523)

Finally, Freud relishes his satisfaction in getting back a girl from his childhood named Pauline in the form of Fliess's daughter; and he notes that he gets Fleischl of the first part of the dream back in the form of Fliess in the second part (both Fl.); and he names his own children "in memory of people I have been fond of":

Their names made the children into revenants. And after all, I reflected, was not having children our only path to immortality? (p. 524)

Well, immortality is the last word on this dream for Freud and for his great wish come true. Supposedly, demonstratively, this is where we conclude the analysis of a dream. Before I come around to a different perspective on this dream of "Non Vixit" and on Freud's method of dissection, I want to show some of the difficulties caused by this convergence upon wish-fulfillment.

Hidden Self-Centeredness

For Freud, the convergence upon wish-fulfillment is what allows us to sleep. If we are disturbed by reproaches, we sleep because we can dissolve them in the wish-fulfillment. Thus, he says,

Dreams are the GUARDIANS of sleep and not its disturbers. (p. 267)

And in a letter to Fliess (June 9, 1899),

Invariably the dream seeks to fulfill one wish that has assumed various forms. It is the wish to sleep! We dream in order not to have to wake up, because we want to sleep. (p. 354)

According to Freud, we wish away (overcome, banish, annihilate) whatever would wake us up in our relation to the world. Thus, we sleep on. However, we cannot do it so baldly as children do when we have become adults. We censor the text of what we are doing, so that much of it is disguised, and thus appears senseless in its manifest form. This work of censorship is a huge subject for Freud that occupies two hundred and thirty-five pages in Section VI or over a third of The Interpretation of Dreams.

Thus, we have to be ruthlessly self-centered as princes to sleep by banishing all disturbing subjects, but we have to pretend that we are not doing this by censoring the text of our own activities.

Evidently, sleep requires two operations. Ruthless self-centeredness, and disguise. As Shields (1990) has argued, this leads to a kind of complacency about dreams themselves. For they are merely wishes, disguised.

Shields argues from the form of the book in which Freud presents this thesis that Freud is burying his own subject even as he brings it forward. Thus, dreams like "Non Vixit" are full of mad activities, yet they resolve into Freud's wish to sleep in immortality. Shields says that the scientific unity of the theory of wish-fulfillment is what brings about this monumental quality to the book. It is the manifest form of the book, literally a scientific monument to Freud's most profound wish.

Shields is posing a very serious epistemological problem about reading the maps of dreams, starting with Freud. If Freud is right, he himself can only sleep if the chaos of his mind is reduced to the simple order of a single wish. In terms of chaos theory, this consists of a reduction of dimensionality from about ten dimensions to two, as I will discuss in part II of this book. But as Shields is pointing out, Freud is writing his book on dreams as if mankind itself has to keep sleeping in a waking dream of coherence by some kind of forced unity. The unity is itself a lie, or wishful lie. Science then becomes one kind of false unity by which mankind sleeps. The science of dreams is then a falsehood, by which we sleep when we are supposedly awake.

Yet this leaves us with the question of why we can't do this openly in our dreams? Can we not tolerate our very self-centeredness? No, Freud replies, we cannot. For that would be too risky in a society that pretends that we put others first.

Society sleeps, by a censorship of its savage forces. This, Freud argues, is in deference to power or social hierarchy:

> Where can we find a similar distortion (to dream censorship) of a psychical act in social life? Only where two persons are concerned, one of whom possesses a certain degree of power which the second is obliged to take into account. In such a case the second person will distort his psychical acts or, as we might put it, will dissimulate. The politeness which I practice every day is to large extent dissimulation of this kind; and when I interpret my dreams for my readers I am obliged to adopt similar distortions. (p. 175)

The individual sleeps by dissimulating with himself. One system (called the unconscious at this point in Freud's theory) dissolves the world's interference by wish. A second system (called the preconscious at this point in Freud's theory) hides anything in this solipsistic activity that would offend the world. This is the paradox of sleep. You have to be utterly narcissistic to sleep, but you also have to be utterly right with the world.

This would seem to be a contradiction, but we will see that earlier writers in the 19th century like Tolstoy and Lewis Carroll were fascinated by the same finding, and found that so-called waking life consisted mostly of the same mix of utter narcissism and fitting in to society. After all, it is routine to pursue savage self-interest in Anna Scherer's soiree that opens War and Peace (1869) or in The Queen's Croquet Game of Alice (1865), while bowing in all the right places.

In any event, Freud figures out how to mix these two things in a palatable way for himself and for the world. In his personal life, his dreams are a rampage of his own narcissism, while his domestic arrangements are perfectly correct and sleepy as Shields points out from his letters to his fiancee, Martha:

"And when you are my dear wife before all the world and bear my name we will pass our life in calm happiness for ourselves and earnest work for mankind until we have to close our eyes in eternal sleep" (quoted by Jones, 1953, p. 139). Furthermore, it is as though the "eternal sleep" would include this life as well: "All we need is two or three little rooms where we can live and eat and receive a guest and a hearth where the fire for cooking does not go out. And what things there will have to be: tables and chairs, beds, a mirror, a clock to remind the happy ones of the passage of time, an armchair for an hour of agreeable daydreaming (etc.) . . . All of it a little world of happiness, of silent friends and emblems of honorable humanity" (quoted by Jones, 1953, pp. 139-140)

His dream book serves up the same mix, by showing the wild conglomeration of the actual text (of the book and of individual dreams), which is dissolved into his monumental theory of the science of wish-fulfillment in dreams. He gets in his findings, and passes by allowing humanity to go back to sleep.

In precisely this way, Freud is a typical Puritan driven to work with huge simplicity on the outside (super-ego), while being obsessed with licentiousness on the inside (id). He belongs as a character in a play like Measure for Measure (Shakespeare, 1604). I will discuss this religious context in which Freud fits as one in a series in Chapter 12. His is a Puritan theory of dreams and is very useful for dreamers in that domain.

Unfortunately, there is a great price to be paid for his successful distortion. He got dreams back into the conversation of humanity, but the theory of their convergence in wish-fulfillment often bludgeons them and misleads patients in dangerous ways.

Essentially, wish-fulfillment is narcissistic or egoistic in the extreme. Sexuality is one form of this egoism, which Freud puts in the dreams of his patients, while reserving the egoism of power for himself. Both forms of solipsism are amply present in The Interpretation of Dreams (1900). In that very year, Freud was analyzing Dora, strictly in terms of sexual and revengeful solipsism, the analysis published in 1905. Freud did the same with the Wolf Man in 1914, the analysis published in 1918. Both cases went miserably (Deutsch, 1957; Gardner, M., 1971). I will have to be very succinct with the voluminous material and confine myself to the first of the two dreams reported in the book-length report on Dora (Freud, 1905).

Dora

The dream was a recurrent one of an 18 year old girl, sent to Freud by her father. Freud says that:

24

in the year 1900 I gave precedence to a laborious and thorough study of dreams over the publications upon the psychology of neuroses which I had in view (p. 25)

Now he intends to

show the way in which the interpretation of dreams plays a part in the work of analysis (p. 30)

So here is the first dream:

A house was on fire. My father was standing beside my bed and woke me up. I dressed myself quickly. Mother wanted to stop and save her jewel-case: but Father said: "I refuse to let myself and my two children be burnt for the sake of your jewel-case." We hurried downstairs, and as soon as I was outside I woke up. (p. 81)

I will not trouble the reader with the labyrinthine connections of this dream, elicited or suggested. Suffice to say, Freud is sure that the girl was and is addicted to bed-wetting in its double-meaning. That is, he takes it as a mixture of infantile gratification in bed-wetting itself and as sexual orgasm. He expresses his conviction as follows:

I was further anxious to show that sexuality does not simply intervene, like a deus ex machina, on one single occasion, at some point in the workings of the processes which characterize hysteria, but that it provides the motive power for every single symptom, and for every single manifestation of the symptom. The symptoms of the disease are nothing else but the patient's sexual activity. . . . No one who disdains the key will ever be able to unlock the door. (p. 136)

The reader can go over Freud's proof that is certainly brilliant. The trouble is that such a convergent mind overlooks what will not fit into the proof.

If we just stand back twenty paces from this mad household, we can get an opposite view. The father is having an affair with his nurse, Frau K., and has pressed his daughter upon Herr K. The mother is a hausfrau bent upon cleaning. The girl has been propositioned by Herr K., and is disturbed. She rightly discerns that she is a pawn in her father's affair, and vows revenge. Freud tries to convince her that she is excited by Herr K., which would be very convenient for the father who sent her to Freud, but she'll have none of it and fires Freud. Fifty-seven years later, Deutsch reports that Dora died recently in New York City as a horrid neurotic mess (Deutch, 1957).

All the ingenuity in the world about Dora's secret sexuality misses the gross injustice of her situation. Her house is on fire. Her mother is saving herself, and her own property. Her father promises to get her out of it. She'd obviously like to believe in him, for, of the two parents, he is at least alive. Yet he is a complete manipulator. By the second dream she has given up on him too, as literally dead; she is too late for his funeral. As the ally of the father, Freud is also dead for her.

In retrospect, Freud says he wished he'd analyzed her love for Frau K. (p. 142f), saying that the girl was trying to hold on magnanimously to this lady who was also treacherous to her but had shown her the books of sexual knowledge. Yes, the girl was trying to get some adult on her side. Her hellish situation is that none can think beyond his or her own self-interest to the predicament of the girl. Freud is no exception, allied with the father to prove sexual excitement in the girl.

I am not arguing that much can be done for a young woman in this predicament who is betrayed all around. Certainly, the number one problem would be her certainty of betrayal by the doctor himself. One way to stay clear of letting her down would be to face the dangers with her, of going along with this Herr K. proposal, or opposing it -- for there is much to lose either way. She can become a sexual pawn, or she can be cut out of the intrigue. I am simply arguing that the reduction of the dream to sexual activity has left the girl further in the lurch about her awful choices. As if one of the two were particularly to be desired. It is a strange and distorted mapping that would overlook such a tragic dilemma (Gustafson, 1995a; 1995b).

Freud's Sonata from Hell

In Dora's world, everyone is grossly narcissistic (self-centered). Some are blatantly so, like Herr K., some in a specialized way over details, like Frau K., and some are buried by these purposes of others like Dora (only to explode in revenge). The odd thing about these three stories of mankind (Gustafson, 1992, 1995a, 1995b) is that the self-centeredness fits into social purpose, namely, the capitalist Director role of the father, the household manager role of the mother, and the sexual object role of Dora herself. Thus, humans tend to be utterly self-centered, while they play a part in the dance of humanity.

The three repetitive stories simply play out the slightly varying fates of these three characters: the Directors who have their way in everything, and dread showing any weakness; the Detail People who control counting something and get very tight trying to make it come out right; the Doormats who are compressed so much, that they finally burst into explosion. Herr K., Frau K. and Dora are humanity, in its three sterile forms, of the shaky Director, the tight Specialist, and the exploding Doormat (Gustafson, 1992, 1995a, 1995b).

Perhaps, it would take us too far afield to survey the three characters and their stories in Tolstoy's War and Peace (1869) and in Lewis Carroll's Alice in Wonderland (1865). One has only to call up the Queen of Hearts, and the White Rabbit, and little Bill the Lizard to have a rough idea of the terrain. The reader may refer to my previous chapters on these two books (Chapter 17 on the Queen's Croquet Game in Gustafson, 1986, 1997; Chapter 15 on Tolstoy's Fate in Gustafson, 1995a) for further elaboration.

My concern here is Freud and his map of dreams. There is something hugely accurate about his translations from manifest to latent dream content. All the translations are from proper appearances, to complete narcissism. This fits the world of Dora, as well as the worlds of Lewis Carroll and Tolstoy. The trouble is that it describes Hell, but gives no way out.

If everyone is but a playing card in 2-dimensions, with his suit on the back to fit into his Club, and with his face to the ground hiding his complete self-absorption, then we have a growing nightmare for someone like Alice trying to have some company and find her way around.

In these two dimensions, hell is necessary. Either she is assimilated to the narcissistic purposes of the others such as the Queen of Hearts or the Duchess, or they to hers. In a completely narcissistic world, your purposes use me, or mine you. We are completely perverse (Gustafson, 1992) for each other, which is what happens in every scene in Alice and most scenes of War and Peace.

So I am quite in agreement with Freud, Carroll and Tolstoy about the hazards of hell. It is no accident that the wall behind my chair in my office has Bosch's Haywain and that the wall behind my couch in my office has Bosch's Temptation of St. Anthony. The first is a vast canvas of the perverse use of others in the secular world, while the second is the same in the corrupted sacred world. My patients and I sit between these possibilities, which are posed for us.

Schorske (1980) is a well-known historian of fin-de-siecle Vienna who calls to our attention that the metaphor of Hell stands at the very beginning of The Interpretation of Dreams as the Latin legend of the title page:

Flectere si nequeo superos, Acheronta movebo.

In English, If I cannot bend the higher powers, I shall stir up Hell (the river Acheron).

These words from Virgil's Aeneid are spoken by Juno, divine defender of Semitic Dido against Aeneas, founder of Rome. Having failed to persuade Jupiter to let Aeneas marry Dido ("to bend the higher powers"), Juno summons from Hell a Fury, Allecto, who unleashes seething passions of sex and military aggression in the camp of Aeneas's allies. (Schorske, 1980, p. 200)

Now this little phrase of revenge from Juno turns out to be a pretty accurate summary of Freud's own dreams as analyzed by Schorske. Essentially, they turn upon Freud's historical fate as an outsider Jew in Vienna. He refuses to ask favors, but will "take vengeance on the Romans."

Freud-Hannibal as "Semitic general" would avenge his feeble father against Rome, a Rome that symbolized the "organization of the Catholic church," and the Habsburg regime that supported it. (p. 191)

Essentially, Schorske's argument concerns the musical development of this idea. At the start of his series of 47 dreams, Freud is quite pinned down. He is being denied his professorship by prejudice and he literally can't let himself go and enjoy what he admires most in ancient Rome. His revolution is to dissolve this frustrating politics quite as he dissolves P. in "Non Vixit":

By reducing his own political past and present to an epiphenomenal status in relation to the primal conflict between father and son, Freud gave his fellow liberals an a-historical theory of man and society that could make bearable a political world spun out of orbit and beyond control. (p. 203)

Eventually, Freud reduces society to the super-ego, the unconscious to the id, and the ego mediates this intrapsychic world. History, as Schorske notes, has quite disappeared. Such a map is unfortunate for a patient like Dora who is being taken to pieces by patriarchal arrangements which are entirely historical.

Despite Freud's monumental conclusions, in his dream book and his later structural theory, the music of a struggle with history is still there in the dreams themselves, as in "Non Vixit." The single word, "reproach," reverberates with Freud to the very depths of his history. It is what Freire (1970) would call a "generative word," which conveys the secret center of a political history of oppression. It "reverberates" as Minkowski (1933) (Bachelard, 1987, pp. 71-72) would say:

> . . . we discover a new dynamic and vital category, a new property of the universe: reverberation (retentir) . . . we should see the world come alive and, independent of any instrument, of any physical properties, fill up with penetrating deep waves . . . it is the dynamism of the sonorous life itself which by engulfing and appropriating everything it finds in its path, fills the slice of space, or better, the slice of the world that it assigns itself by its movement, making it reverberate, breathing into its own life. (Bachelard quoting Minkowski, 1987, p. 72f)

Now, the single word, "revenge" enters as a second generative theme, or counterpoint. It too reverberates equally with "reproach" in Freud. The two generative themes make up his sonata of hell, in "Non Vixit," as follows:

> the so-called first dream simply has Fleischl (Fl.) enter Brücke's laboratory where Freud is working: this is the entrance of the theme of "reproach."

> the so-called second dream (actually, just a developmental section, after the opening theme) begins with Fliess (also Fl.) reproaching Freud. Freud replies with the counter-theme of revenge, by piercing P. In its recapitulation, Freud alternates between the triumph of piercing mere revenants (ghosts) and the consolation of bringing them back again.

In other words, the dream conserves the objective world of history in its generative theme of "reproach" and it conserves the subjective world in its generative theme of "revenge" -- and the music consists of the counterpoint of these two polarities. In chaos theory, these are called strange attractors. In Levi-Strauss's structural theory, they are called the vertical elements, which resonate like harmonic centers through the horizontal lines of the orchestral score of the melodic lines of particular stories or variations. We will come back to chaos theory and structural theory in Chapters 10-12. We will see how Jung develops the objective pole and the subjective pole in Chapter 2.

In conclusion about Freud's map of the dream world, I would like to indicate the domain in which it is an accurate guide. In general, patients like Freud who are aspiring outsiders to the social hierarchy need a great deal of guile, with the world and with themselves. You can see this, for example, in Stendhal's hero, Julien Sorel, in The Red and the Black (originally published 1830; 1961). In such patients, the manifest dream will be greatly censored. I will finish with a simple case.

A Case of Being Dismissed for Eternity by a Norwegian Butcher

My patient was in the crisis of his life, because his wife had rejected him for his secret affairs which had come to light. Could he really be honest with her? He found it quite fearful. Guile had been his power, but had gotten him arraigned. Honesty just felt frightening. It was hard to say why.

Rather than a dream, he brought me a visualization. It was of himself and his wife talking comfortably at supper with four other friends. I asked him for his associations to this scene. Chiefly, this amounted to fear of being in the scene itself. He would be humiliated if they brought up the topic of his surfaced affairs.

Curiously, when I mentioned to him that Freud also dreaded reproach, he took courage. He told me of working in a grocery in high school. One day, a butcher told him he'd never amount to anything. He didn't know what he had done to earn this Final Judgment, but it devastated him. I remarked that Freud had been censured as a child for having to urinate in his parents' bedroom in quite the same Final Terms. My patient noted sadly that that was his childhood history as well.

But, he said, I have spent my life willing my way out of this vulnerability, and I have gotten very far. Yes, I said, but you are terrified that a specific fault will be given back to you as a Final and Universal Judgment. Hence, your secrecy, and your distance. You fear to go up the stairs like Prufrock (Eliot, originally, 1915; published 1958).

Now, his fear had taken a distinct shape, and he came closer to me. I remarked that his will was like a locomotive, to take him out of the primal ooze. This made him laugh. He remembered a fellow in the army driving a tank back into the ooze, magnificently. This is Freud's Puritan music from hell, which alternates between tremendous willfulness and solipsistic abandon. As Max Weber demonstrates in The Protestant Ethic and the Spirit of Capitalism (originally published 1904-1905; 1958) it is the very dynamic that fuels the hot engine of modern, bureaucratic man. I will return to this vast subject in Chapters 11 and 12.

Chapter 2. Jung.

In Jung's middle period of the 1930's he is most accessible as a map-maker for journeys into the unconscious. He is not so raw and terrifying as he was between 1912 and 1928, and he is not so mysteriously alchemical as he was after 1938. Therefore, I will first present him in the form in which he is most appealing, and, shall I say, reasonable.

Privately he is entirely absorbed by alchemy as early as 1928, but it is kept relatively apart from his public writing until the late thirties, and culminates in The Conjunctio (1955-1956 originally published; 1963). I will come back to this sequence in the middle section of this chapter summarized in the next sentence.

Having secured Jung's algorithm for searching the unconscious, we can face the terrors of his own individual development. Finally, we will see what his map has to show about the difficulties that lie in the way of individuation in America in the very late twentieth century.

Jung's Algorithm

For me, the single best statement of a practical method for delving into the dream is in Jung's aptly named essay, "Dream Analysis in Its Practical Application" (in Dreams, 1974)), which was given as a lecture first in 1931 and appeared in print in 1934. It is the essay I give to (almost) all new patients after the first sessions they have with me, to invite them into using their unconscious in dreams. (Some have too much of the unconscious already and need less of it to keep from bursting. See Gustafson, 1995a, Chapter 1.)

The Dream as Compensation to a One-Sided View

The leading idea of this essay is that the conscious mind is one-sided in its picturing of one's relations with the world. It is like a bright, focused light which sees only a focal area which it is intent upon. It is driven by willfulness. It is like a man bent upon finding a jewel, and directing a searchlight according to instructions received from headquarters. So directed, it will locate even fine needles in its path, but it will miss everything peripheral to its focus. Such a deliberate and conscious procedure may be necessary to the business of locating lost diamond rings, or picking up cancer cells on slides, or mowing one's lawn at midnight. However, it sets up its protagonist to be a perfect fool if he is trying to find his way in the hierarchy of careers or in romance. In these great realms of power and love, the surface is misleading.

The great way to see behind surface presentations is to dim the (conscious) light, and let in the periphery of shadows (Franz, 1975, pp. 94-95). This shadow perspective will compensate the one-sided conscious view with the shadow view, the two together giving a balanced picture. Thus, Jung denies that the shadow view is censored as for Freud. It is simply obscured by too much conscious light. He also denies that the shadow alone is a veridical picture as for the existentialists (Chapter 3 of this book). It is a compensatory picture, which, taken alone, would be absurd. He insists on the polarity of picture #1 of the #1 self, versus picture #2 of the #2 self, and on the vital necessity of putting the two pictures together (von Franz, 1975, p. 95f; "The

Transcendent Function," originally 1916, published 1953; Campbell, 1971). Without both poles, you get pictures which are caricatures.

Figure 2.1

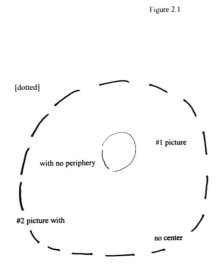

The Dream of the Overflowing Bathtub

For example, a woman thought very little of herself and very highly of her husband. Consciously, she didn't deserve him and was depressed. She was always worn out by her work and offered little to him at home, while he was full of energy and puzzled by her continually going to bed. In her dream, he left the water running in the bathtub on the third floor and flooded the entire house. Water gushed from every orifice.

This dream baffled my patient, until I simply said that her husband had made a terrible blunder. Then, she burst out laughing. The perfect man had finally done something wrong. This put him more on her level, and she could enjoy herself again.

From the perspective of her conscious mind and #1 self, it really could appear that she was useless to him, and he perfect. A great deal of evidence could be marshaled to this effect. It all seemed reasonable. Yet when we dimmed this light, to let in this shadowy picture, her husband was the great fool of carelessness. This is not to say the view of #2 self is true. It simply compensates for the excessive height of the husband for the patient, by bringing him down.

The Dream of the Spiral into the Pit

For another example, a woman was starting to break away from her mother's example of being a doormat. She was just beginning to privilege her own space and time and pleasures. However, she visited her mother on mother's birthday and was disgusted by mother kowtowing to her stepfather in the usual manner. She couldn't wait to drive away.

Or at least, so she consciously thought. In her dream, she was driving down a country road which turned into a spiral downward. She kept trying to turn away from the descent, but she was pulled back into the same path. It was a very dark mud, in which she became more and more mired.

The thing about this landscape was that she had no traction. Three times she tried to turn away, but three times she could not. It was terrifying. I took the dream in Jung's way as a compensation for her conscious view, which was that she wanted to save her mother from the hell she had lived in all her life with brutal men. I took it as a picture of hell in which the deeper you got in to rescue your mother, the less chance you had of getting out yourself. The brown mud swallowed you up, with her.

Literally, Jung's double perspective gave her a purchase on her situation. The view from her conscious mind #1 kept getting her drawn into hopeless rescues. The view from her unconscious mind #2 was too frightening to face by herself. Only when I was there to put the two pictures together could she face her dilemma, which was that saving herself and saving her mother diverged. This was the landscape or terrain in which she was fated to live. Interestingly, the nearness to mother was represented as a spiral drawing her down into a black hole.

I did not say to this patient that she was in the spell of the Virgin (Mary) trying to rescue the soul of her mother. I did not say that the spiral was the telltale of the lines of force of the circulatio which always surrounds the cult of the Virgin Mother. I did not say that the black mud is the stuff of Hell itself. If you think of the actual architecture of Dante's Inferno, where the Virgin remains atop the mountain of Paradiso, and where Hell is no place for her to venture, then you will realize what a grandiose thing it is that she is attempting. Only Christ could harrow Hell and release sinners (Turner, 1993).

Figure 2.2

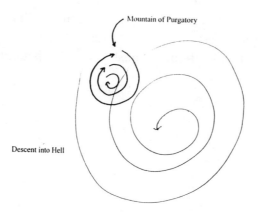

Mountain of Purgatory

Descent into Hell

32

I simply separated the two spaces, and noted the gulf between them: namely, the space of saving herself up the mountain of Purgatory, and the space of not being able to save her mother in the pit of Hell. The dilemma is that the two problems diverge.

In rendering the two previous dreams, I wrote about them as if I could interpret them simply from the contrast between the perspective of the conscious mind, and the compensatory perspective of the unconscious mind. I just combine the two pictures as a double description (Bateson, 1979). The conscious mind is the right eye, and the unconscious mind is the left eye, and two together yield binocular or depth perception: as in Figure 2.3.

Figure 2.3

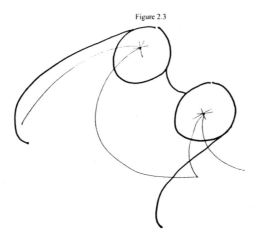

It is quite true that it is often possible to penetrate the patient's dilemma like this, without any of the translation of individual elements in the dream. In other words, a patient or a friend can write me a letter about a dream, and I can give him back an interpretation. I do not have to ask him to tell me more about various puzzling elements. All I need is the conscious standpoint of being troubled before the dream, and the dream text.

The Dream of the Brother Corpse

For example, a friend wrote me complaining that his dreams kept pounding the same difficulty. He didn't remember many of them, because they came "at too vengeful a pace." In any event, his conscious standpoint was that he was in an "inter-regnum period" between his last book, and his next book, in which he re-evaluated his work. Were the critics right about his erudition, that it was excessive for his thesis? He felt they were right, and he needed to state the case for his scientific hypothesis much more directly. Then he dreamt:

I was in a building stacked high with corpses and realized that the body of _____, _____'s husband, _____, was sitting up at the edge of a stack, not yet buried. I felt it was my moral obligation to see to his internment, even though his bowels were leaking out below his splayed legs, whether or not you looked at him straight on or turned him over on his stomach. It was then that I realized that his body was metamorphosizing, and his head was my brother _____'s and his body mine -- especially his middle-aged chest and slight paunch.

In very broad strokes, my friend cannot stay up high in his erudition, but must come down to own a body like his brother's. He has a head like _____'s husband who was overly pure, and he has a body like his brother's which is overly rotten. The extremes are savage. His difficulty is as old as Abel, slain by Cain, or as modern as Jekyll, overrun by Hyde. Balance is very hard, because the conscious mind (head) is too dry, but the unconscious mind is too fluid (body). Actually my friend is already on his way, when he tells me he is going to be more direct with his next book. But this brings with it great pain, taking in the Cain and Hyde in oneself.

Translation

Not all dreams are so evident in their broad outline. Their facade can be hard to read. This is not to say that the facade is completely misleading:

> . . . we must remember that the fronts of most houses by no means trick or deceive us, but, on the contrary, follow the plan of the building and often betray its inner arrangement (Jung, 1933, p. 12)

Thus, Jung differs with Freud about the facade or surface of dreams. Freud contends that the manifest content is often a complete deception, because of the dream work of censorship which hides the solipsism of the self and its latent content. Jung specifically sets himself against Freud's view as follows:

> We say that the dream has a false front only because we fail to see into it. We would do better to say that we are dealing with something like a text that is unintelligible, not because it has a facade, but simply because we cannot read it. We do not have to get behind such a text in the first place, but must learn to read it (Jung, 1933, p. 13)

How do we learn to read it? Jung actually has two quite different answers. The first is as follows:

> When we take up an obscure dream, our first task is not to understand and interpret it, but to establish the context with minute care (my italics, Jung, 1933, p. 12)

> When we have done this for all the images in the dream, we are ready for the venture of interpretation (my italics, Jung, 1933, p. 14)

Jung could not be more emphatic, that this work of "establishing the context" for "all the images" is opposite to Freud's work of translation by "free association" (Jung, 1968). The difference is that "free association" leads away from the image, and "establishing the context" leads away only so far as to find the patient's <u>particular history</u> with this specific image and returns strictly to this specific image as one of the set of images in the dream text. I will illustrate this work, by the particular dream that Jung translated in 1916 in his chapter called "The Synthetic or Constructive Method" (Jung, 1917, 1943). This translation will also allow me to demonstrate Jung's second method of reading the dream, which depends upon his extraordinary vocabulary of archaic learning. It turns out that you can only get so far with his first method of modern historical context, before you have to borrow from his second method of translating the primitive mind. It is as if, finally, you have to know ancient Greek. This is what he calls his "method of <u>amplification</u>" (1917, 1943). To amplify is to bring in the ancient history in the symbol itself as in the symbol of the crab in the following dream. The etymology of the collective history gives a second axis of meaning to go with the personal history with the symbol which is the first axis of meaning.

The Dream of the Crab in the Ford.

This dream has the virtue for our purposes of being brief but highly condensed with meaning. Jung introduces it as follows:

> A woman patient, who had just reached the critical borderline between the analysis of the personal unconscious and the emergence of contents from the collective unconscious, had the following dream: <u>She is about to cross a wide river. There is no bridge, she finds a ford where she can cross. She is on the point of doing so, when a large crab that lay hidden in the water seizes her by the foot and will not let her go.</u> She wakes up in terror. (Jung's italics, 1917, 1943)

Jung begins by asking her to establish the context of these several images. The river is the obstacle that slows her analysis, the ford the analysis as an opportunity, and the crab the cancer that killed her acquaintance, Mrs. X., and somehow threatens to drag herself into the river, also.

This reminds her of just having had another terrible row with her closest friend. Every scene "tired her to death," trying to straighten out their misunderstandings. Jung believes they are trying to be too close by always unbosoming to each other like the patient had done with her own mother before she died. The arguments are "trying to put a distance between them, but they refused to listen" (p. 82).

Both the patient and Jung already know perfectly well that she is stuck to her mother, and the mother substitute, of this friend. But this is useless. "It only reiterates what I have known for a long time," the patient would have rightly said. "The interpretation, in fact, tells the patient nothing new; it is therefore uninteresting and ineffective" (p. 83).

Here is where Jung departs from Freud. He refuses to believe that the unconscious would paint a picture like this one, unless it were trying to get across something missed. Of course, this

octrine of the compensation of the conscious mind, by the unconscious mind. To repeat
e conscious mind already knows, in a Freudian parallel between love of mother and love
riend, is to be no compensation and help at all.

Therefore, he comes at the crab image, from a different angle. He asks, "Why should the
er-friend appear as a crab. A prettier and more graphic representation would have been a
-nymph ('Half drew she him, half sank he under, etc.'). An octopus, a dragon, a snake, or a
would have served as well" (p. 84).

Now, when the analytical or causal-reductive interpretation ceases to bring to light
anything new, but only the same thing in different variations, the moment has
come to look out for possible archetypal motifs" (p. 84).

ng is going to change his procedure, from establishing the context of the images, which he
lls "interpretation on the objective level" by equating "the dream images with real objects."

In contrast to this is the interpretation which refers every part of the dream and all
the actors in it back to the dreamer himself. This is what I call interpretation on
the subjective level (p. 84).

To condense several pages of argument (see pages 85 to 89): The crab is a lower animal that is a
part of her, which draws her towards the fate of Mrs. X. The dream plainly says so. Why is she
identified with Mrs. X.? Because she is fascinated by her career in an immoral life with an
artistic man. Therefore, she clings to the endless quarrels with her girlfriend-mother, to avoid
being drawn into the depths of her fascination with this animal element in her nature.

In my own language, she is pictured at a crossing in a dire dilemma, as shown in Figure
2.4. If she clings to her mother-friend, she is "tired to death" of quarrels, but if she descends into
her fascination with the artistic life, she is destroyed like Mrs. X.

Figure 2.4

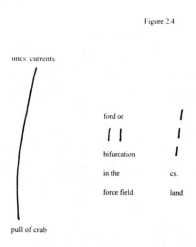

36

The forces on the land of consciousness are linear and vexing, while the forces in the water of the unconscious are non-linear and too much for her. However, the map of the dream is a kind of transitional object to take with her into these turbulent waters. The map gets her ready as a swimmer for the rip tide that would pull her under if it caught her unawares and unprepared.

Jung has slyly introduced an archaic concept here, with little attention being called to it. It is the idea of a totem animal, in this case, a crab. The idea is that the totem animal is a kind of primitive instinct. It has both vitality, and terror. It can organize a group, in a common fascination, which can prove a livelihood. But it is a great danger for modern man, who is entirely unfamiliar with its huge pull.

There is a huge archaic vocabulary to learn from Jung, starting from something slightly familiar like the totem animal. It is indispensable, I believe, for reaching into the most primitive and most overwhelming forces within us. His term for this region was "the collective unconscious." It has both a heavenly aspect, when the instincts of collective man are clothed in gods, and it has a hellish or chthonic aspect, when the instincts of collective man are clothed in animals. Rather than lay out this vocabulary in the abstract, I will demonstrate Jung's own struggle with it in the next and middle section of this chapter, after I have introduced one more term of Jung's Algorithm.

Sequences of Dreams

The third dimension of Jung's reasonable method or algorithm for the search of dreams, following the idea of dream as compensation to the one-sided conscious mind, and following the idea of translation by establishing the context for all images, and their primitive resonance, is the idea of dream sequence. The idea is that the sequence of dreams over weeks and months and years, even over a lifetime, can be a kind of pilgrim's progress in what Jung called the "assimilation of the unconscious." By this, he meant that an individual could enjoy its vitality, without being swept away by it. In the example of the patient at the ford, the fascination with the descent into the artistic life of Mrs. X. could be afforded, without being wrecked by its power. But this assimilation of the primitive instinct of the crab would be followed by the next image from the primitive unconscious, which would offer new vitality and new danger at the same time. The sequence that will come forward is a sequence of primitivisms, which are the province of archaic man. There are three possible decisions, for coping with this tremendous in-pouring of primitive energy.

The first and the most common is to run away from it, and attempt to dissociate it. Jung called this "the regressive restoration of the persona" (1916, 1935). That is, one flees from the archaic power, and puts on a persona, or mask, to play a stock role. This is essentially the wasteland of modern life, of masses playing these little segmented parts in one assembly line or another. It is the utilitarian life.

The second way is to identify with the first archaic image that comes up, and to worship under its aegis. This is essentially what Freud did with sexuality, which became his religion, and that of highly numerous followers. Jung calls it "identification with the collective psyche" or being taken over by the power of a "primordial image" (pp. 169-171, 1916, 1935).

The third way is neither to run from the primitive nor become its mouthpiece. It is to assimilate its power, successively, in a very long sequence of dreams which usually takes years. This is what Jung called "individuation," and it is the very aim of his mapping of the unconscious (1916, 1935, pp. 173-241).

Jung has provided a number of extended works, which illustrate the sequence of dreams in the assimilation of the unconscious which supposedly brings about a particular individual being, filled with the vitality of the unconscious, without being driven by it. The reader may refer to the analysis of the dreams of the famous physicist, Wolfgang Pauli, which appear in The Portable Jung (1971) under the title of "Individual Dream Symbolism in Relation to Alchemy" (originally 1939, pp. 323-455). Another of this length is "A Study in the Process of Individuation" (1950, pp. 290-354) in The Archetypes and the Collective Unconscious (1968). Yet another is "The Psychology of the Transference" (1946) in The Practice of Psychotherapy (1966). The earliest and most monumental of these recorded journeys is his Dream Analysis, Notes of a Seminar, 1928-1930 (1984).

I do not think they actually illustrate what Jung purports to show in them. While they certainly show huge struggles with archaic forces and symbols, they do not end up in individuation. They end up with maps of collective and primitive man. They end up the same. As in primitive being.

Jung's Personal Individuation

This is precisely what I think happened to Jung himself in his attempt at individuation between 1912 and 1928. He struggled mightily and several times near madness (p. 189, 1963, 1989) for these sixteen years to assimilate the primitive mind in himself after he broke with Freud. Certainly, he showed extraordinary courage as an individual explorer, and he made marvelous discoveries, which I will try to illustrate. Yet, he concluded by hiding out in the primitive mind, in a kind of refuge like a Chinese sage in his tower, from the barbarism of the modern world (p. 197, 1989). This was established by 1928, and little changed thereafter.

I want to go swiftly over the ground covered by Jung himself in his autobiography, Memories, Dreams and Reflections (1963, 1989) by taking three dreams from the outset, the middle and the conclusion of his voyage into the unconscious. I do not think Jung himself would have any objection to my taking his personal voyage for the sum of his science, for he wrote exactly that himself:

My life is what I have done, my scientific work; the one is inseparable from the other. The work is the expression of my inner development; for commitment to the contents of the unconscious forms the man and produces his transformations. My works can be regarded as stations along my life's way. . . . All my writings may be considered tasks imposed from within; their source was a fateful compulsion. What I wrote were things that assailed me from within . . . They represent a compensation for our times. (1963, p. 222)

As Jung said in his Dream Seminar of 1928-1930 (p. 241, 1984) individual dreams tend to have an exposition, a development, and a catastrophe or solution. Here he follows Aristotle in his Poetics, or the classical sequence of the sonata allegro form in the symphony. At another (fractal) level, the entire sequence of dreams in the voyage of a lifetime will also have this form. Campbell (1949), to some extent following Jung, called it the monomyth of the hero, who breaks with the sterile regime; descends into the depths to make his great discovery, risking his life to do battle for it with the demons who hold it below; and returns to insert it and re-invigorate the world which is fertile again with his insemination.

In precisely this sequence, Jung follows the ancient path which is the only individuation man has ever known. If he ends up swallowed up in a collective image he has certainly lived as a particular individual along the way. A close parallel is Stravinsky bursting out with "The Rite of Spring," also between 1910 and 1912.

I hope my terse account will inspire the reader to fill in what I have had to leave out from Memories, Dreams, and Reflections (1963, 1989) as I note only a beginning, middle and concluding dream, from the great voyage of his life.

The Departure

Sometime in the year or two leading up to his publication of The Psychology of the Unconscious (1911, 1949), Jung dreamt of his forthcoming break with Freud as follows: Jung's Dream of the Knight of the Red Cross.

It was toward evening, and I saw an elderly man in the uniform of an Imperial Austrian customs official. He walked past, somewhat stooped, without paying any attention to me. His expression was peevish, rather melancholic and vexed. There were other persona present, and someone informed me that the old man was not really there, but was the ghost of a customs official who had died years ago. "He is one of those who still couldn't die properly." (1963, 1989, p. 163)

...after a hiatus came a second and far more remarkable part. I was in an Italian city, and it was around noon, between twelve and one o'clock. A fierce sun was beating down upon the narrow streets. The city was built on hills and reminded me of a particular part of Basel, The Kohlenberg. The little streets which lead down into the valley, the Birsigtal, that runs through the city, are partly flights of steps. In the dream, one such stairway descended to Barfüsserplatz. The city was Basel, and yet it was also an Italian city, something like Bergamo. It was summertime; the blazing sun stood at the zenith, and everything was bathed in an intense light. A crowd came streaming toward me, and I knew that the shops were closing and people were on their way home to dinner. In the midst of this stream of people walked a knight in full armour. He mounted the steps toward me. He wore a helmet of the kind that is called a basinet, with eye slits, and chain armour. Over this was a white tunic into which was woven, front and back, a large red cross.

One can easily imagine how I felt: suddenly to see in a modern city, during the noonday rush hour, a crusader coming toward me. What struck me as particularly odd was that none of the many persons walking about seemed to notice him. No one turned his head or gazed after him. It was as though he were invisible to everyone but me. I asked myself what this apparition meant, and then it was as if someone answered me -- but there was no one to speak: "Yes, this is a regular apparition. The knight always passes by here between twelve and one o'clock, and has been doing so for a very long time (for centuries, I gathered) and everyone knows about it." (pp. 164-165, 1989).

Now there is a great deal to say about this dream, but I have to leave out all of Jung's commentary in the interests of brevity, to simply note that it is a calling to take up the neglected quest of the crusader.

The Descent into the Abyss

Little did Jung know, little does any young man know, what the descent would cost him, offered as it was in such a luminous light of the sun at its zenith. If this was 1910, it cost him 18 years between the age of 35 and 53 to 1928, of terror, and complete loneliness and despair, for his remarkable visions. Once underway, he decided that his only salvation was "to let myself plummet down into them . . . for I realized that if I did not do so, I ran the risk of their gaining power over me" (p. 178). "It was during Advent of the year 1913 -- December 12, to be exact -- that I resolved upon the decisive step."

Jung's (Dreamlike) Vision of the Dead Youth:

I was sitting at my desk once more, thinking over my fears. Then I let myself drop. Suddenly it was as though the ground literally gave way beneath my feet, and I plunged down into the dark depths. I could not fend off a feeling of panic. But then, abruptly, at not too great a depth, I landed on my feet in a soft sticky mass. I felt great relief, although I was apparently in complete darkness. After a while my eyes grew accustomed to the gloom, which was rather like deep twilight. Before me was the entrance to a dark cave, in which stood a dwarf with leathery skin, as if he were mummified (recall the customs official in the previous dream quoted). I squeezed past him through the narrow entrance and waded knee deep through icy water to the other end of the cave where, on a projecting rock, I saw a glowing red crystal. I grasped the stone, lifted it, and discovered a hollow underneath. At first I could make out nothing, but then I saw there was running water. In it a corpse floated by, a youth with blond hair and a wound in the head. He was followed by a giant black scarab (Egyptian dung beetle), and then by a red, newborn sun, rising out of the depths of the stone (recall the Knight of the

Red Cross in the previous dream quoted). Dazzled by the light, I wanted to replace the stone upon the opening, but then a fluid welled out. It was blood. A thick jet of it leaped up, and I felt nauseated. It seemed to me that the blood continued to spurt for an endurably long time. At last it ceased, and the vision came to an end. (1963, 1989, p. 179) (my parenthetical remarks)

Jung realized that "it was a hero and solar myth, a drama of death and renewal, the rebirth symbolized by the Egyptian scarab. At the end, the dawn of the new day should have followed, but instead came that intolerable outpouring of blood" (p. 179). He had at least several visions of these rivers of blood, and at least several of floods of ice (pp. 175-176). Of course, he was full of the world war that was to break out, August 1, 1914.

Now my task was clear: I had to try to understand what had happened and to what extent my own experience coincided with that of mankind in general . . . I stood helpless before an alien world; everything in it seemed difficult and incomprehensible. I was living in a constant state of tension; often I felt as if gigantic blocks of stone were tumbling down upon me. My enduring these storms was a question of brute strength. Others have been shattered by them -- Nietzsche, Holderlin and many others. But there was a demonic strength in me, and from the beginning there was no doubt in mind that I must find the meaning of what I was experiencing in these fantasies. (pp. 176-177)

All of this whirling and shattering and so forth went on and on in what Jung called "a diabolical mixture of the sublime and the ridiculous" (p. 178).

Resolution

Jung only began to emerge from this chaotic darkness as the world war came to an end (p. 195). This also coincided with breaking with a certain lady, and beginning to draw and understand mandalas (p. 195). These became his chief symbol of himself, and he got some peace, as illustrated so clearly in the following dream.

Jung's "Liverpool" Dream.

I found myself in a dirty, sooty city. It was night, and winter, and dark, and raining. I was in Liverpool. With a number of Swiss -- say, half a dozen -- I walked through the dark streets. I have the feeling we were coming up from the harbor, and that the real city was actually above, on the cliffs. We climbed up there. It reminded me of Basel, where the market is down below and then you go up through the Totengässchen ("Alley of the Dead") which leads to a plateau above and so the Petersplatz and the Peterskirche. When we reached the plateau, we found a broad square dimly illuminated by street lights, into which many streets converged. The various quarters of the city were arranged radially around the square. In the center was a round pool, and in the middle of it a small island. While everything round about was obscured by rain, fog, smoke and dimly lit darkness, the little island blazed with sunlight. On it stood a single tree, a magnolia, in a shower of reddish blossoms (recall the Red Cross and red sun in the two previous dreams quoted). It was as though the tree stood in the sunlight and was at the same time the source of light . . ." (p. 198) (my parenthetical remarks)

Notice the distance traveled between 1910 and 1928 in terms of the changing of the map (dream). At first darkness is all at the Austrian border, while eternal light calls up the crusader. Then Jung descends into the darkness as the crusader and wrestles all the daimonic forces of Europe for nearly 18 years. Gradually, he emerges with his discovery of peacefulness in himself in a little island of light, surrounded by grim darkness:

> This dream represented my situation at the time. I can still see the grayish-yellow raincoats, glistening with the wetness of the rain. Everything was extremely unpleasant, black and opaque -- just as I felt then. But I had had a vision of unearthly beauty and that was why I was able to live at all. Liverpool is the "pool of life." The "liver," according to an old view, is the seat of life -- that which "makes us live." (p. 198)

His journey departed from Basel/Bergamo in 1910, and ends here in Basel/Liverpool in 1928. He began feeling that Freud had made everything prosaic and base . . . "like the black lees that spoiled the taste of life by showing me only too plainly the ugliness and meaninglessness of human existence" (p. 166). His crusade was to bring the transcendant heavens back to earth, but, of course, their insertion into the dross of modern industrial Europe had to be confined, at last, to a little temple of the self.

Individuation in America

While there is a very great deal to learn from Jung's crusade into the unconscious, its terminus is not individuation but retreat into a private world of ancient symbolism. This second half of his life (after 1928), as he calls it (p. 200) was his attempt to

> find evidence for the historical prefiguration of my inner experience. That is to say, I had to ask myself, "Where have my particular premises already occurred in history?" If I had not succeeded in finding such evidence, I would never have been able to substantiate my ideas. Therefore, my encounter with alchemy was decisive for me, as it provided me with the historical basis which I had hitherto lacked (p. 200)

Jung was also very relieved to find precedent in Goethe, especially in his <u>Faust</u> (1832):

> He called it "his main business," and his whole life was enacted within the framework of this drama. (p. 206)

So, this became Jung's "main business" as well, and occupied him the rest of his life. He lived in his tower at Bollingen on Lake Zurich as an archaic man. Interestingly, World War II gets not a single reference in his autobiography. He had gotten free of modern man.

I would like to go back to where Jung got off the track of individuation, and show how it is possible to get back in its path. Let me review his findings which are valid about this aim. First of all, he rightly argued that nearly everything that we feel, think or do is ancient in its pattern. There are two overwhelming tendencies which capture us in their lines of force. The outer pull (Gustafson, 1995a, 1995b) is to play a stock role in the group life, which Jung called a persona or mask. Nowadays, the parts that are available are instrumental and increasingly bureaucratic. That is, one performs repeated procedures by formula, whether in business, academics, or science. The procedures are heavily focused in the conscious mind, like the psychopharmacology and cognitive behavior therapy which govern psychiatry.

The inner pull that gets us (Gustafson, 1995a, 1995b) is to dive into the unconscious and come under the sway of primordial images, like Jung with the crusader of the red cross. Ordinarily, this becomes a kind of fixed romanticism, which defies logic. Nowadays, young people go through a certain period of such intensity, mostly in romantic love which crashes against modern realities, and then they retire back to playing a stock part as grown-ups. This is what Jung called regressive restoration of the persona.

2.5

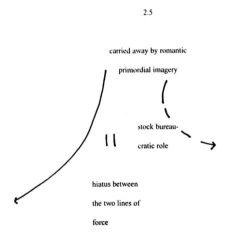

Secondly, Jung was highly accurate about the lines of force on the romantic or inner side. He became an expert in living with dreams, visions and daily practices like an ancient man. I will try to illustrate some of this vocabulary in the following examples.

However, he retreated entirely from the right side of the force field. Whatever he saw of modern man, he feared and hated, and he had plenty of reason in the two world wars that surrounded him in Switzerland. Even without the catastrophic violence of modern man, Jung profoundly disliked this narrowness in the conscious mind. Jung called this "compartmentalized man" (Jung, 1928-1930, 1984), and described its malfunction beautifully in one sentence.

> ...the psyche of man is no longer a self-regulating system but could rather be compared to a machine whose speed-regulation is so insensitive that it can continue to function to the point of self-injury, while on the other hand it is subject to the arbitrary manipulations of the one-sided will. (Jung, p. 285 in Campbell, 1971; originally written, 1916).

The trouble with Jung's map of individuation is that it is wrong in prescribing immersion in the archaic mind for "compartmentalized man" as a path of individuation. It is a map of relief from modern sterility. But it leads into the most repetitive archaic symbols. All cases become more or less alike, and thus collective.

In his own terms, he becomes subject to being lived by the primordial images. He even gets highly comfortable with them. He has steered clear of the emptiness of modern man, to fall into the fullness of archaic man.

Compare him with Stravinsky again. Both are full of the extreme tension between archaic instincts, and modern machinery in the years 1910-1914. Listen to the Rite of Spring (1912) for its explosive alternations between ancient melodies and staccato machinery. There is nothing, I believe, as powerful in Western music.

Jung was full of the same tension as we saw him with World War I coming on. Ancient melodies and staccato machinery. He was full of the crisis of his times, between the old world and the new, quite like Stravinsky. We can hardly blame Jung for opting out of the tension. Especially considering his gifts to us borne of enduring it. Jung shone individually, before subsiding into the collective.

Now, the difficulty of individuation is to remain between primitive instinct and modern machinery and bear the tension, without sacrificing one to the other. For we all have to make the circuit between them diurnally, or every day and night. We sleep as primitives, and we work like moderns. But most of us will just cut off the messages from the night, in order to bear the tedium of the day.

So what is involved in balancing primitive instinct against modern group life? And how are dreams indispensable to this balance? And how is individual expression the result?

The American Force Field

Henry Adams (1907) outlined the problem for individuation in America in our most famous autobiography, but especially in his chapter about the turn of the century called "The Dynamo and the Virgin." Essentially, he was interested in these lines of force I illustrated in

Figure 2.5 which pull into the collective life like magnetic fields. We cannot resist them, out of a mixture of reverence and fear which is called being in awe. We dare not be left out of them. Thus, we surrender our individuality.

For us, a hundred years later, there is little surprise in the dynamos that arrested Adams at the Gallery of Machines at the Great Exposition of 1900:

> His historical neck broken by the sudden irruption of forces totally new (p. 382)

For us, the previous lines of force are much stranger, if we know them at all:

> Symbol, or energy, the Virgin had acted as the greatest force the Western world ever felt, and had drawn man's activities to herself more strongly than any other power (p. 388)

Adams knew this very well at Chartres (Adams, 1904) and a few other places where it could still be tracked, but his countrymen did not know what he was talking about, concerning his education:

> The knife-edge along which he must crawl, like Sir Lancelot in the twelfth century, divided two kingdoms of force which had nothing in common but attraction. They were as different as a magnet is from gravitation, supposing one knew what a magnet was, or gravitation, or love. The force of the Virgin was still felt at Lourdes, and seemed to be as potent as X-rays; but in America neither Venus nor Virgin ever had value as force -- at most as sentiment. No American had ever been truly afraid of either. (p. 383)

Actually, Adams is only right about public man in America, who only worships the machinery. Privately he may have known the huge force of love which seized him from the unconscious. In any event, Adams has precisely stated the mechanics of individuation:

> Yet in mechanics, whatever the mechanicians might think, both energies acted as interchangeable forces on man, and by action on man all known force may be measured (p. 388) . . . the historian's business was to follow the track of the energy; to find where it came from and where it went to; its complex source and shifting channels; its values, equivalences, conversions. (My italics, p. 389)

The business of individuation is to track these forces as well, to keep from being utterly seized by them. I think only dreams map them well, or well enough to give this reckoning. In part, this is because dreams are about the only place to feel this fearful Virgin or Venus, which has been driven out of the modern world of the Dynamo. That is, the only place to feel this primitive seat of power with one's motor system safely turned off. You can feel it in a romance with a woman, but the results are apt to be drastically out of control.

Three Dreams of the Author Concerning the Power of the Virgin

Part of my debt to Jung is that he showed me what to watch for, concerning the force field of the female goddess. These three dreams were literally stunning, so I came to know what he meant by enduring the experience. I am also indebted to him for showing me the clarity of sequence. Three dreams about a half year apart which return to the same terrain show the progress or retrogression in coping with this force field. Compare Jung's three dreams of the red force 18 years apart: red crusader; red sun; red magnolia. I will try to indicate that the progress in this series is the very thing that puts us back on the track of individuation that Jung got off.

The Dream of the Queen of Heaven Selling Her Palace.

This dream was heavily influenced by a trip my wife and I took to Mont Saint Michel and Chartres, following Henry Adams's path outlined in his book of this title (Adams, 1904). I was about to go to Door County, Wisconsin to give a workshop on psychotherapy.

In the dream, I am in a hotel which is a superimposition of one at Mont Saint Michel and one at Door County. I decide that this Norman fortress (from which England was attacked in 1066) is too confining and I make my way down three sets of chutes with two men friends. We came out upon a highway and I am stunned by a cloudlike vision high up to the left. It is the palace of the Queen of Heaven (Mary of Chartres) which is being sold. It is whirling in such a way that its magnetic field is creating huge tidal waves along the coast, and in such a way that bulldozers are madly driving downhill making chutes along its lines of force -- as illustrated in Figure 2.6.

Figure 2.6

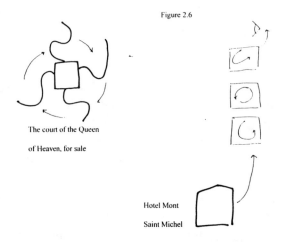

The court of the Queen

of Heaven, for sale

Hotel Mont

Saint Michel

46

Here I am getting acquainted with the force field Adams was talking about, but at a distance in the clouds, while I remain with my feet on the ground. Cloud is the right metaphor, for the circulation of this force was quite like the vortex of a cumulus cloud. Jung had point out to me as the circulatio (Jung, 1944, 1952, "Dream Symbolism in Relation to circulation around the center of a square or sacred alarming, as Adams had predicted.

The Dream of Being a Hostage to the French Counter-Revolution.

About a half a year later, in the first days of January, I dreamt of being a pr. Queen who seemed to be French who was galloping in a carriage in a circuit around with her court. I had been made to swallow shit, to prove my guilt. I literally could to sit, and it did taste awful. At one point, the circuit/square turned into a concert theater, and a young woman whom I had heard in college giving the Emperor Concerto of Beethoven (in Sanders Theater at Harvard, to be exact) was playing. The Queen shouted "Bravo" in my ear, as we continued to rocket around the circuit/square. At this point, I knew we were at the lower left corner, and the Queen was quite like the Queen of Hearts in Alice shouting, "Off with their heads!"

In any event, I was feeling a mixture of great importance and dread, for I could see this Queen was wild in her enthusiasms for praising and for executing. As we came around the right upper corner of the circuit/square, I felt I had to get off this mad roller coaster, so I began separating my legs, which by now were over my head in self-defense. As I did this, the roller coaster machinery gradually slowed down, and I could literally hear it clinking to a stop. All of this passage is shown in Figure 2.7.

Figure 2.7

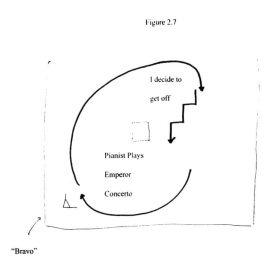

"Bravo"

The beauty of this dream was that I could be in the grip of extreme circulation, and bring it to a halt myself. I could get off the equivocal madness of the concert tour. It was like giving birth to myself. I went from being a hostage man to being a woman giving myself a rebirth. I experienced all the sensory modalities, from wild kinesthesia, to gustatory shit, to dazzling concert hall, to dark birthing. Thus, I had the full vigor of primitive vitality, while I also had a way to limit its grip on me. All I had to do was separate my knees, which were pressed together in terror, for the entire circus to slow down. Oddly, pressing my knees more tightly started it up again!

The Dream of the Mango Salt Lick, of the Detour into Saginaw, Michigan, and of the Mad Rotating Square.

The third dream, which was a trio, took place about a year after the first, and a half year after the second. In its first part, our chairman was giving out money to his followers, while I was putting out a huge orange fruit the color of a mango, but the size of a huge desk. The idea was that the students could come and take from it as they liked, like the deer at a salt lick I knew as a child. Obviously, I was contrasting the rewards of the machine or Dynamo, versus the rewards of the fertility of the Virgin.

In its second part, I was driving with my wife near my home town to go on vacation in Michigan with my extended family. I felt pulled into a right turn, which would drag me into this industrial wasteland, which I swerved away from to get to where we wanted to go. Here, I am tempted to get near the industrial machinery, symbolized in the first part by the power of my chairman.

In its third part, I am coming up to one of these rotating squares for the third time in a year. This time it is not at a distance, nor am I in it, but I am coming up to it from a distance. A huge crowd sweeps by me going up to the left out of control. A young man is swept up to the right on a bicycle towards another continent. Animals and children are pulled off to the lower right to a barren place in the American West. I find a papoose in the lower left, which has been neglected, and which I decide it is up to me to take care of. Then the cyclist returns from another continent and nearly falls into the square which is all water. He teeters on a knife's edge (like the Lancelot of Henry Adams, between the two lines of force) along the lower edge of the square, but manages not to fall in (to the unconscious). I then make a little soap box for myself at the left lower corner of the square, quite like those of the mad speakers in Hyde Park, London, and give an oration on this entire subject to two listeners. The topography of this dream is shown here in Figure 2.8.

Figure 2.8

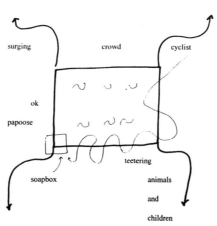

If I am getting too self-congratulatory about sharing the beautiful fruit of my studies with the students at the deer lick, I immediately feel the pull to the right of the Dynamo industrial power. I have to swerve to avoid its lines of force. Then I am being pulled into the power of the Virgin of the Rotating Square to the left. Its chaotic effects are flying north, east, south, and west. The mad crowd (I knew they were going to Yale! East!). The mad cyclist (South). The lost children and animals (West). The neglected papoose (North). Essentially, these four directions were allusions to friends of mind caught in the four winds, from the force field of the Virgin. That is, the mighty non-linear force field that is no longer supposed to exist!

This sequence of three readings over a year's duration of my relation to the lines of force of the Virgin has for me a progression, which is typical of individuation. I get to know the force at a distance, in which it is still awesome. I undergo its primitive vitality, but get my grip. I meet it again and reckon its huge effects, without being drawn into them myself.

Notice the oscillation in the third (trio) dream, between the Virgin and the Dynamo. First, the contrast of their fruits, the Mango versus cash. Second, the near swerve towards the cash to the right. Third, the tremendous pull towards the vitality of the Virgin to the left, which has such devastating effects for those drawn into her rotation willy-nilly.

The Government of the Tongue

In other words, individual expression only occurs in this space between the collective lines of force which will force dictation. While the forces in my three dreams are hugely collective, of the Virgin, and of the Dynamo, respectively, I believe the expression is particular to me, in such things as the cumulus cloud of the Queen of Heaven, or the mango of the salt lick.

For these metaphors draw together things far apart in nature, to show their beautiful similarity. This is the mark of individual expression, for few but me would have imagined such connections.

You will only have such leaps of original expression if you are not caught by one of the two lines of force, and denied access to the other. Conversely, individual expression leaps across the gap, between the two lines of force, like lightning, to illuminate a comparison, and a connection.

For us, in America, the lines of force are those of the Dynamo and the Virgin, as Adams showed us, and as I hope I have illustrated. You are lost if you are the mouthpiece of either. You have a chance if you can get back and forth between the two, and this is the way of individuation. This is where I believe I have improved Jung's map on the subject.

This path will not get you a place in academia, certainly. Nor in any other of the stock places which govern us with their formulas. This path will not get you a place in the various religions, by which compartmentalized man desperately seeks relief in meaning. But it could allow you a certain vitality, coupled with adaptability, and a certain delight in yourself as a particular being. Seamus Heaney called this region a place governed by the tongue, in its transitory glory:

> Faced with the brutality of the historical onslaught, they (the arts of the imagination, including poetry) are practically useless. Yet they verify our singularity and stake out the ore of the self which lies at the base of every individuated life (p. 107, 1988)

Earlier, he put the secret of this gift, quite in terms of access to the opposite poles of the lines of force. For him, as an Irishman, the right is England and its force of literature, and the left is Ireland and its force of his ancient people.

> Certainly the secret of being a poet, Irish or otherwise, lies in the summoning of the energies of words. But my quest for definition, while it may lead backward, is conducted in the living speech of the landscape I was born into. If you like, I began as a poet when my roots were crossed with my reading. I think of the personal and Irish pieties as vowels, and the literary awareness nourished on English as consonants. My hope is that the poems will be vocables adequate to my whole experience (P. 36-37) (my italics)

So I end my statement on individuation, equating the secret of being an individual with the secret of being a poet. It's hard. It's wrenching being pulled between these extremes of ancient instinct and modern machinery. It's tempting to get off and out of the tension, as Jung did. But we needn't be misled by him, and we can have his gifts, if we know exactly where he went off the track.

Chapter 3. The Existentialists.

Existentialism has been a minor movement in psychotherapy, and in the analysis of dreams, which seems to have passed by already. Yet its relatively simple treatment of dream as metaphor is extremely useful, as a correction on Freud and Jung. In some ways, it is the most accessible map, like an x-ray of the soul's relationship to its world.

On the other hand, existential psychotherapy needs to be rescued from itself. It lacks the capacity to carry its own burden, which is the plight of modern man. The objective world of factories, bureaucracies and science rubs out interest in the individual subject; but the two Swiss writers of existential psychotherapy, Binswanger and Boss, are barely equipped to map an opposition. I will try to give them help with their project, by indicating what is solidly useful, and what more is absolutely necessary to the full use of metaphor in dreams.

I will map dreams as metaphor in my usual way of three stages. First, I will address the plight of modern man as posed by the existentialists, which essentially is the problem of the subject/object split. This diagnosis means that the individual subject is split-off and disappears (is alienated) from the objective public world in which the machines of business, government, school and so forth dictate the parts to be played. Recall that Jung wrote essentially the same diagnosis in 1916 in "The Transcendent Function;" Campbell, 1971. Secondly, I will show how individual metaphor refinds the individual subject, especially in terms of how he constructs his own time and space as a particular being-in-the-world. This is the gist of the map from Binswanger and Boss. Thirdly, I will try to augment their account by showing what they leave out of their pictures of the force-field of modern man. Their countryman, Durrenmatt (1956, 1962) gave much better pictures. They underestimate the force of distortion from the objective world, and so underprepare their patients for its collisions; and they underestimate the huge, non-linear forces from the primitiveness of instinct which will seize their patients by the neck. Metaphor is much too great a vehicle of knowledge to be left to play a minor part in our defense.

The Existential Diagnosis of Modern Man

The diagnosis of the alienated subject certainly would not be understood in my hometown of Saginaw, Michigan. There the admired characters are the salesmen who sell the most, and the athletes who win the most, and the doctors, lawyers and merchants who own the rich area of Golfside near the country club. Alienation from such a positivist world would be a sign of being a misfit, and requiring correction as soon as possible. This indeed is the role of American psychiatry, since its inception (Deutsch, 1949; K. Gustafson, unpublished). The psychiatrist or alienist is to bring the alienated into line with the march of progress.

The notion that something might be wrong with modern progress is a European idea, which sprang from many sources. Criticism of progress got to America through the back door of literature, where it remains to this day. Hawthorne and Melville, Twain and Henry James, have hardly altered the main thrust of American culture, and hardly anyone I have ever met could tell me their objections. Criticism of progress got briefly into American psychiatry in the sixties, in a few books like Existence, A New Dimension in Psychiatry and Psychology (May, 1958), but the dimension has disappeared with hardly a trace. In Chapter 6, I will show the brave attempt to keep it going on the very periphery of psychoanalysis, as well as its shallow bowdlerization in the popular culture of Gestalt Therapy and Encounter Groups and other forms of Group Therapy. Existential ideas get watered down so badly in popular culture, that they become just one more cliché of the popular salesman.

In any event, the European reaction against modern progress has many sources, from the Romanticism of poetry as in Blake, to the novel as in Dickens, and to philosophy as in Marx. Existentialism arises like Marxism, within philosophy, as a reaction to Hegel. It lasts about a hundred years, from Kierkegaard in the mid-nineteenth century to Nietzsche in the late nineteenth century, to Heidegger in the early twentieth century, and coming to its conclusion in the mid-twentieth century with Sartre.

To make a long story short, with some violence to its nuances, I will summarize what these highly individual writers have in common concerning this word "existence." Essentially, it is an individual's construction of his own way of being in the world. It begins with Kierkegaard (1813-1855) exclaiming that he did not want to add a paragraph to Hegel's system.

Interestingly, this outcry is close to Thoreau's (1817-1862) objection at about the same time. So is Thoreau an existentialist? Yes, I think there is no essential difference. He has the cardinal characteristics, of finding modern conformity a disaster, and in its stead living in line with a transcendent belief. The subsequent existentialists, Nietzsche, Heidegger, and Sartre, to name the principal ones, combine this very pair of virtues. It would be beyond the scope of my subject of dreams to delineate the criticism of conformity, and the transcendent alternative, in each of these writers.

I do need to say a little about Heidegger, however, because his analysis is taken over quite literally by the Swiss clinicians, Binswanger and Boss, who do address mapping dreams as metaphor. Heidegger's principal work, Being and Time (1927), is a huge throwback to pre-Socratic Greek philosophy, tragedy, and epic. Perhaps, his lecture from 1935 called An Introduction to Metaphysics (1959) is the least difficult introduction to his concerns. The gist of them seems to be that the ancient spirit of vitality so evident in the Greek poets and earliest philosophers like Heraclitus and Parmenides has been gradually lost by a point of view which is fastened on things already being settled: "permanence . . the always identical . . the already-there . . . and already-realized " (p. 202). In other words, being is reduced to "ousia, meaning permanent presence" (p. 205). By contrast, the earlier senses of being that Heidegger wants to retrieve culminate in his presentation of the first chorus from the Antigone of Sophocles:

> There is much that is strange, but nothing /
> that surpasses man in strangeness. /
> He sets sail on the frothing waters /
> amid the south winds of winter /
> tacking through the mountains and furious chasms of the waves...

The reader may refer to Heidegger's eloquent penetration (pp. 146-165) of the entire first chorus, for a glimpse into his feeling for this kind of man which is denoted by the word, "deinotaton, the strangest."

In this contrast between the ancient Greek of strange daring at sea and the modern European of fixed things like furniture lies Heidegger's diagnosis of the disaster of modern man:

> The spiritual decline of the earth is so far advanced that the nations are in danger of losing the last bit of spiritual energy that makes it possible to see the decline (p. 38) . . . Our questioning brings us into the landscape we must inhabit as a basic prerequisite, if we are to win back our roots in history (p. 39). The lives of men began to slide into a world which lacked that depth from out of which the essential always comes to man . . . All things sank to the same level, a surface resembling a blind mirror that no longer reflects, that casts back nothing . . . In America and Russia, this development grew into a boundless etcetera of indifference and always-the-sameness -- so much so that the quantity took on a quality of its own. Since then the domination in those countries of a cross section of the indifferent mass has become something more than a dreary accident. It has become an active onslaught that destroys all rank and every world-creating impulse of the spirit, and calls it a lie (p. 46).

American Literature

Heidegger's dread of this progress is quite familiar in American literature. Listen to Tom Sawyer (Twain, 1876) forced to go to church on Sunday morning:

> After the hymn had been sung, the Reverend Mr. Sprague turned himself into a bulletin board, and read off "notices" of meetings and societies and things till it seemed that the list would stretch out to the crack of doom. (1985, p. 306)

Heidegger's return to the sea of archaic man is the very theme of Melville in Moby-Dick (1851):

> Circumambulate the city of a dreamy Sabbath afternoon . . . Posted like silent sentinels all around the town, stand thousands upon thousands of mortal men fixed in ocean reveries. (p. 23)

Heidegger's determination to divest himself of the "already-is" for what could pulsate into a strange being is the very direction taken by Faulkner in "The Bear" (1942) which he called "relinquishment:"

> later it describes how the boy surrenders to the wilderness and the bear by setting aside the instruments of industrial power -- gun, compass and watch -- so that he "then relinquished completely to it" (Poirier, 1966, p. 78)

Given that American writers have been deeply familiar with the trap of the "already is," and the need to depart for stranger water for a hundred years before Heidegger, what is then to be learned from him? Is there really anything to gain? I think so, particularly when I look at how Binswanger and Boss borrow from him.

Mapping the Dream as a Metaphor of Space and Time

Of the two Swiss writers, Binswanger is by far the better educated and subtle to read, while Boss is almost unbearably pedantic. Yet each carries his own useful emphasis from studying Heidegger.

Binswanger

Very little of Binswanger's writing in German is available in English, chiefly a collection of his essays published under the title of Being-in-the World (1963) and several more in Existence (May, 1958). The only one specifically devoted to dreams is in the first collection and is called "Dream and Existence" (pp. 222-248).

Here Binswanger strives to correct both Freud and Jung in their emphasis upon the dream as a subjective event. Like Shakespeare, he believes that dreaming is often a misguided fiction about one's own specialness:

> there come moments when a man must decide, whether in pride or defiance, to cling to his private opinion -- his private theater, as one patient put it -- or whether to place himself in the hands of a physician, viewed as the wise mediator between the private and the communal world (p. 244).

This doctrine goes back to Heraclitus:

> Those, he says, "who are awake have one and the same world in common; in sleep each (Hekastos, Singularis) returns to his own (world) (p. 242)

In this regard, Midsummer Night's Dream (1595) is typical:

> Bottom: (wakes): . . . I have had a dream, past the wit of man to say what dream it was. Man is but an ass if he go about to expound this dream . . . The eye of man hath not heard, the ear of man hath not seen, man's hand is not able to taste, his tongue to conceive, nor his heart to report what my dream was . . It shall be called "Bottom's Dream," because it hath no bottom . . . IV, I, 199-216

Of course, Bottom is not wanting to wake up from his delusion of his own mixed-up profundity, which has all the senses tuned to the wrong kind of sensations (eyes hear, ears see, etc.)

A Mephisto Dream from Binswanger. Such a difficulty built into the longing to be special that runs so deep in humanity is to be found in the only dream that Binswanger provides for analysis from a patient in this essay:

> Tired and tormented by a powerful inner unrest and uneasiness, I finally dropped off to sleep. In my dream I was walking along an endless beach where the constantly pounding surf and its never-ending restlessness brought me to despair. I longed to be able to bring the ocean to a standstill and enforce a calm upon it. Then I saw a tall man wearing a slouch hat coming toward me on the dunes. He wore a broad cape and carried a stick and a large net in his hand. One eye was hidden behind a large curl of hair which hung upon his forehead. As the man came before me, he spread out the net, captured the sea in it, and laid it before me. Startled, I looked through the meshing and discovered that the sea was slowly dying. An uneasy calm came over me and the seaweed, the animals, and the fish which were caught in the net slowly turned a ghastly brown. In tears, I threw myself at the man's feet and begged to let the sea go free again -- I knew now that unrest meant life and calm was death. Then the man tore open the net and freed the sea and within me there arose a jubilant happiness as I again heard the pounding and breaking of the waves. Then I awoke! (pp. 244-245)

Binswanger takes the dream as a metaphor of that very German aim of Faust (Goethe, 1832) to call in the Devil, Mephistopheles, to subdue the entire world for his vanity. The dilemma pictured in Figure 3.1 is a painful and even tragic one: If he is just another man, he is lost in the endless surf; if he is so special that he can control it altogether, he kills it.

Figure 3.1

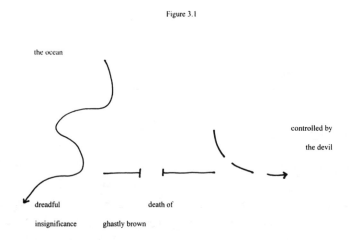

This is the simplest of readings, and yet it is very telling. Occasionally, Jung would consent to such a reading, as when he says:

It (the dream) simply creates an image (in reply to a problem) that answers to the conscious situation. (originally 1928-1930; 1984, p. 133)

In other words, the image directly pictures how things stand with this particular existence. Interestingly, this comes forward in the structure of a dilemma (Gustafson, 1995a, 1995b).

Of course, Binswanger is able to read the image or night painting as a dilemma, because he has already thought out the dilemma of modern man with the help of Heidegger, and his view into the history of philosophy from Heraclitus to Hegel. He already knows that complete objectivity is unbearable for dissolving the subject as in the sea, and he already knows that complete subjectivity is pure illusion, as for Faust. So, he is on the alert for metaphors which picture this dilemma.

The other big idea about dreams in Binswanger is that the metaphor of the patient's dilemma will picture it in terms of the distortions of space and of time. Concerning spatial distortion, Binswanger writes in his greatest essay, "Extravagance" (Verstiegenheit) (1963, pp. 342-349):

In mountain climbing, one goes too far only if the overall structure of the precipice is hidden from view or unknown . . . What we call psychotherapy is basically no more than an attempt to bring the patient to a point where he can "see" the manner in which the totality of human existence or "being-in-the-world" is structured and to see at which of its junctures he has overreached himself. (p. 348)

In the dream essay, he writes:

The nature of poetic simile lies in the deepest roots of our existence where the vital forms and contents of our minds are still bound together. When, in a bitter disappointment, "we fall from the clouds," then we fall -- we actually fall (p. 223). . . . our outlook is said to be "clouded" by passionate hopes, wishes and expectations, or we say, when we are happy, that it is like "being in heaven." But falling itself and, of course, its opposite, rising, are not themselves derivable from anything else. Here we strike bottom ontologically. (p. 225)

A Dream of Mörike's Painter Nolten. A very simple example of what Binswanger means by this "pulse of existence, its systole and diastole, its expansion and depression, its ascension and sinking" (p. 230) is in the following dream from Mörike's novel:

Right before my eyes a bird of prey attacked a white pigeon, wounded it in the head and carried it off into the air. I pursued the creature with shouts and clapping of the hands. After a long chase I succeeded in chasing the bird of prey from the pigeon. I lifted it from the ground and to my great sorrow found it was already dead. (Binswanger, 1963, p. 229)

Binswanger takes the dream quite as Homer would take it in The Odyssey:

Even as he (Telemachus) spoke, a bird flew by on the right, an eagle, bearing in his talons a great white goose, a tame fowl from the yard, and men and women followed shouting. But the eagle drew near to them and darted off to the right in front of the horses; and they were glad as they saw it, and the hearts in the breasts of all were cheered. (Binswanger, 1963, p. 237)

Binswanger poses the universal drama as the dilemma of rising and falling:

What we have here, on the other hand, is a struggle between two creatures in which one represents the aspect of victorious soaring and the other of defeated falling (p. 229).

For Binswanger, we can do more than rise and fall as the forces inside us and outside us wax and wane. We delude ourselves in a false separateness, if we think we are apart from these huge dynamics. We have a chance, however, to be more than objects of these forces, if we can see them coming, and gracefully take ourselves down when the time has come for that descent, and pick ourselves up to allow for the time of ascent:

An individual turns from mere self-identity to selfhood when he decides not only to seek to know "what hit him," but seeks also to strike into and take hold of the dynamics (my italics) in these events, "himself" -- the moment, that is, when he resolves to bring continuity or consistency (my italics) into a life that rises and falls, falls and rises. Only then does he make something. (p. 247)

If we do not "strike into and take hold of the dynamics . . that rises and falls, falls and rises," we will get stuck up too high in the heavens, and crash, or stuck down too low in the swamp, and be polluted. It is necessary to see the map of the space and timing of our existence, if we are to be prepared to "take hold of the dynamics." So, the dreams help us see the space and time which is ours, and avoid the "selective inattention" (Gustafson, 1995a, 1995b) which is completely unprepared for the next rising or falling force which is coming. We are either helpless objects, or subjects who can ride with the way in which we are moved.

Boss

Boss is very hard to take, because he has a modest addition to offer us, while fancying himself superior to Freud and Jung. It is tempting to leave him out altogether, visiting violence upon him as his just desert for that power which he has wielded so unfairly. I will forego this, because his one idea which he has borrowed from Heidegger is as practical as a hammer.

First, let us demolish his claims. He proposes to dispense with Freud, because dreams are directly read. He has no need to work up each element of the dream for its latent content. He takes the surface of the dream in its "metaphorical" sense (p. 132, 1977). Thus, a tooth is just the "behavioral potential for seizing, grasping, and comprehending the things of your world" (p. 132). While, it is useful to consider such direct statement, his fiat canceling out the possibility of latent associations to "tooth," that have been censored, simply shows how dogmatic Boss is (p. 261, 1963). Similarly, he purports to have bypassed Jung (p. 262, 1963) because Jung is merely adding the "subjective" reading of the dream to Freud's "objective" reading. He, Boss, reads the subject-in-the-objective-world directly from the dream pictures. Actually, Boss's readings are mostly about the patient's subjective experience of his relation to the world, with very little grasp of the objective machinery at work on the patient and very little grasp of the subjective machinery of the overwhelming instincts. Boss becomes ideal for the American and especially California stages, in which the patient is exhorted to live his full potential of humanity which is nicely kept apart from the actual world. In this way, he is very like Gestalt Therapy (Perls, Hefferline and Goodman, 1951; Craig and Walsh, 1993). The formula is:

> You are limiting your potential to x, while resisting full contact with yourself and others in y and z.

The technique follows Reich (1933; Sharaf, 1983) in hammering on the resistance of the patient, until he lets in y and z and his "full humanity" (Boss, pp. 76 and 77, 1977).

In Boss's long catalog (pp. 59-127, 1977) of dreams subjected to this method, there are some very nice examples of its benefit. I especially like his concept of the patient's own distance from his own metaphors of his own space and time. This concept allows the doctor to limit his hounding of the patient, because the patient somehow needs the distance from his own self-portrait.

The Dream of the Patient as a Noun of Feminine Gender Disguised with a Masculine Ending. This patient was a thirty-year old married woman with a chief complaint of frigidity.

> I dreamed I was supposed to decline a Latin noun, one of the ones whose masculine ending disguises its feminine gender. I was supposed to decline it with an adjective, so that the feminine endings of the adjective would betray the true gender of the noun, despite its masculine forms. But I had a hard time performing this task; in fact, I never managed to finish it. Even while I was dreaming, I wasn't sure just which word was involved. (p. 59, 1977)

Here, Boss is reasonably respectful of this woman's need for hiding in masculine ending, which makes her frigid (and muddled as in the end of the dream), because the revelation of her feminine gender must be quite harrowing. Otherwise, why such pedantic distance from herself as a part of speech, in Latin?

Dream of the Patient as Santa Claus. While most of the metaphors are spatial to show the patient's distance from herself, this one shows as well the patient's utilization of time. She was a forty-three year old woman with no children and many psychosomatic gastrointestinal complaints.

Last night I dreamed that my husband and I were visiting families dressed up as Santa Clauses. What I mean is that I was Santa Claus, and my husband was Santa's manservant, whom we Germans call "Schmutzli." I made a great effort to praise or scold children the way I was supposed to. It surprised me that another year had passed so soon. The previous winter had just ended, it seemed, and nothing had happened between last December 6th and the present one; there had been no spring, summer, or autumn in between. Yet here it was, December 6th again. (p. 116, 1977)

Again, Boss takes ample notice of the patient's distance from herself in all the levels of disguise (man, boss, duty, once a year visits), and in the complete suspension of time as development.

He also can sometimes reckon that the distance of space and the suspension of time can be absolutely necessary to the patient staying out of total despair and suicide, or overwhelming tension, pain and psychosis. The patient lives on the outer surface of a world that is unbearable if lived on the inside surface. Jung called attention to this occasionally (pp. 135-136, 1963, 1989), and Laing (1959) shows many telling examples.

But Boss simply cannot refrain from pushing against a patient's resistance when he is out to outdo Freud and Jung. Such a patient presented himself after a "Freudian analysis" from 25 to 28, and a "Jungian analysis" from 28 to 30. The man was dull, but dogged by guilt. The so-called Freudian analysis is reported as a parody of discovering the Oedipus complex with no change in the patient, and the so-called Jungian analysis is reported as another parody of intellectualization of archetypes, instead of the Oedipus archetype, again with no change in the patient. Perhaps, he is even worse, since he spends a great deal of time polishing glass crystal. With Boss, he keeps dreaming of locked toilets. Boss is determined to confront this resistance:

The analyst was prepared to precipitate a stormy resistance to the therapy in this painfully well-bred aesthete, this hyper-clean crystal collector, by rattling at the doors of his locked toilets with his questions. But perhaps he overestimated the capacity of his patient, whose relation to the obtruding fecal sphere and to all "lowly" bodiliness rapidly took on a severely psychotic form once he could no longer ward off these realms of his world by the compulsive collecting and cleaning of "pure" crystal glass. (p. 276, 1963)

Perhaps he overestimated the capacity of the patient? The dream is an extraordinary testimony against the folly of rattling the doors of locked toilets (even if Boss tided him through the psychosis with a claim of final success).

The Dream of Suspension Between Fecal Hell and the Heavenly Bell. Certainly this is an unforgettable night-portrait of a predicament which is simply an unbearable torture:

Once again, the patient found himself standing outside the locked door of a toilet. But this time his urge to defecate was so overpowering that he flung himself against the door with all his might and burst it open. But instead of getting through to the toilet, as he had expected, he discovered he was standing in the middle of a large church, directly in front of the baptismal font. A thick rope hung from the vault of the ceiling over the font. It was the rope with which the sexton tolled the largest bell in the tower. Now at his wit's end, he had no choice but to hoist himself, on the bell rope, high up to the baptismal font where, still clutching the rope, he relieved himself. His bowel movement would not stop; soon he was standing knee-deep in his own stool. He tried to escape the rising mass of excrement by scrambling up the rope to the church tower, but his feet stuck fast in the feces. And somehow, with all this frantic scrambling, the bell rope had twisted itself inextricably around his neck. Besides this, his frenzied efforts to climb up the rope had meanwhile set the bell in motion in the tower. Worst of all, with each resounding peal of the bell, the rope, in some inexplicable way, wound itself around the revolving axis of the bell, so that between the tug of the bell rope dragging him upward and the binding mass of feces tightening its hold on his feet, he was rapidly being torn in two. In the agony of this bodily torture he startled out of the dream. (pp. 276-277, 1963)

Metaphor As Vehicle of Knowledge

This last dream from Boss is as dramatic as a great painting. I am reminded of the one of a man being pulled apart by four ropes tied to horses. So it is quite possible that dreams can be simply night-paintings that picture the patient's predicament. Yet they are often cryptic, and cloudy, and censored, as Freud and Jung rightly demonstrated.

Even if we stay with the possibility that the dream can be a metaphor with a relatively direct comparison of the patient's dilemma to something like feces in a Gothic church, yet there is a remarkable constriction of metaphor in these existential writers. If I just open at random some pages from Kierkegaard, I get:

He understands that letting the self go is, after all, a conversion of property

Or Nietzsche:

I longed to go under when I aspired to the height, and you are the lightning for which I waited. (p. 155, 1954)

Or Heidegger:

But to lay bare the horizon within which something like Being in general becomes intelligible, is tantamount to clarifying the possibility of having any understanding of Being at all (p. 231, 1962)

Or, finally, Sartre:

Since the Other is the foundation of my being, he could not be dissolved in me without my being-for-others disappearing. (p. 476, 1966)

In sum, the metaphors are self as property, other as lightning, being having a horizon, and other as foundation. In my experience of these authors, this random culling is entirely typical. Indeed, it could not be otherwise, for they pound the reader with the same metaphors over and over again. The metaphors have become theoretical structures. A theory is a privileging of a metaphor, or set of related metaphors.

Existentialism is readily recognizable by these metaphors of foundations, horizons, and heights, which are its spatial preoccupations, as well as by metaphors of lightning and dissolving and property, which are its preoccupations with spirit in a material and propertied world. Probably, one should add despair and loneliness, anguish and boredom, as its typical coloration. They readily become cliché by sheer repetition, and parody would be not difficult. As Kundera (1990) argues, philosophy is a watered down art, and psychotherapy is further watering down of philosophy. The play of possibilities is reduced from ten dimensions to two to one.

Metaphor in Further Dimensions

I wrote earlier in this chapter that Thoreau could be taken as an existentialist, for these metaphors are commonly used by him. Yet he is much more of a writer than his overlap with Kierkegaard, Nietzsche, Heidegger and Sartre would reveal. Take any page of Thoreau, again, at random, and you will see how many more dimensions there are to him:

> After a night's sleep the news is as indispensable as the breakfast. "Pray tell me anything new that has happened to a man anywhere on this globe" -- and he reads it over his coffee and rolls, that a man has had his eyes gouged out this morning on the Wachito River; never dreaming that he lives in the dark unfathomed mammoth cave of this world, and has but the rudiment of an eye himself (originally 1854, p 346, 1947)

For one thing, he is humorous, which hardly ever happens to an existentialist. The grotesque is something he can laugh over, like the man reading of a gouged out eye, while being ignorant that it is his own condition.

Metaphors Missing in the Existential Repertory

Metaphor may be the chief vehicle of our understanding of the world, and of ourselves. Let us consider, precisely, how it works. The definition gives a good working idea:

> metaphor (F. metaphore, fr. L., fr. Gr. metaphora, fr. metapherein to carry over, transfer, fr. meta beyond, over + pherein to bring, bear). Rhet. Use of a word or phrase literally denoting one kind of object or idea in place of another by way of suggesting a likeness or analogy between them (the ship plows the sea; a volley of oaths). Syn. See COMPARISON. (Webster's Collegiate, 1943)

Theories are metaphors. If they are scientific theories, the invention of the hypothesis is the poetry of the science (Maturana and Varela, 1980; Gustafson, 1986, 1997), while the testing of the hypothesis is the empirical aspect of the science. For example, Freud's theory of neurotic misery is that it is a compromise-formation concerning sexual aims. For example, current psychiatry's theory of neurotic misery is that it is a result of too little or too much of the neurotransmitters. For example, existential psychotherapy's theory of neurotic misery is that it is an existence stuck up too high or down too low.

By inspection, it becomes rather obvious that these are one-sided theories. In all probability, sexuality is a sufficient force to make patients miserable, as is a collapse of the neurochemicals, or an existence that is stuck up too high. Of course, empirical testing ought to decide between them. In practice, the world of psychiatry is a set of one-sided advocates of one one-sided theory or another, who specialize in counting results within their favorite one-sided theory. The science is more like the product-testing of salesmen, to find out which antidepressant gives the best results or which interpersonal protocol. In this precise sense, we have become a nation of salesmen (Shorris, 1995), who are determined to deal with what already-is, or is only slightly different, as from Prozac to Zoloft. Heidegger turns out to be right about the general drift of Western culture.

Thus, science is going to be no help in the foreseeable future with our problem of one-dimensional man, the salesman, of the already-is. It is itself part of the problem. Oddly, existential psychotherapy is also part of the problem, by posing a single metaphor, or perhaps two, of what is wrong. It becomes another kind of salesman, especially in the hands of someone as pedantic as Boss.

Walker Percy's Use of Metaphor

I am inclined to think that only the poets and novelists and dramatists are going to save us from the low-dimensionality of the philosophers and the applied philosophers which we call psychotherapists. For example, the novelist, Walker Percy, writes of "Metaphor as Mistake" (1975, Chapter 3), by which he means that the strangeness of the comparison makes it seem at first like a mistake. If the terms compared are from very far apart in the world, the beauty is greater. For example, a few days ago, I was about to get on my bicycle at the hospital, when I looked back at the entrance to see a strange conjunction. A red maple tree was giving off its last leaves in the sunlight, while directly behind were flapping huge and dark canvases from the construction on the hospital. It was as if nature was going down, while techno-man was building up. But the beauty was not in the paraphrase, but the strangeness of the conjunction of the terms.

Percy has some striking things to say about such an experience as this:

. . . something very big happens in a very small place. (p. 66)

Literary men, on the other hand, once having caught sight of the beauty of
    metaphor, once having experienced what Barfield called "that old authentic thrill
    which binds a man to his library for life," . . (p. 67)

We can only conceive being, sidle up to it by laying something else
    alongside. (p. 72)

. . . as men, who must know one thing through the mirror of another.
(p 82)

Finally, Percy borrows from I. A. Richards the concept of the metaphor as a reaching across by bow and arrow. Here is a metaphor of the definition of metaphor, in the Greek sense, metapherein, to carry over, to transfer, meta beyond, over + pherein to bring, bear:

If we deviate in either direction, toward a more univocal or accustomed likeness or toward a more mysterious unlikeness, we feel at once the effect of what Richards calls the tension of the bow, both the slackening and the tightening of it. (p. 80)

The trouble with repeated metaphors which have become theories is that they become accustomed, and the bow goes slack at the lack of distance to be covered.

Shakespeare's Metaphors

Shakespeare grasped the problem of the existentialists long before they came to it, that is, the disjunction between high and low, heaven and earth. But he could retain the strangeness of the terms. Let us consider how he did it. Perhaps, he could help us from becoming slack in our work.

First of all, as Kott (1974) argues so movingly, Shakespeare was himself of the last Renaissance generation, like Leonardo and Galileo, which literally lost the connection to divinity, and fell into the dark globe where only power will be the judge. The tragedy of Shakespeare, Leonardo and Galileo, discussed by Kott in his essay, "Prospero's Staff," is about surrender of the divine powers (the staff), to the march of history which is only about power.

Nevertheless, Shakespeare is not a Samuel Beckett of limited means (and often called an existentialist -- See Kott's comparison in his chapter, "King Lear or Endgame"). This is because the separation of heaven and earth leaves him with more than a grotesque being-in-the-world of the now empty wasteland between. Shakespeare gets a full development of his account of the grand staircase of history (Kott, 1974), and he gets full development of the imagination cut loose from its moorings (Bayley, 1981).

I will leave to the reader much of the great wonder of these books and return myself to Shakespeare in Chapter 12, but I will indicate their argument. Kott introduces his or Shakespeare's vast subject in his first essay, "The Kings," concerning Richard the II (1593-1596) and Richard the III (1591-1594) with the quite schematic idea of the grand staircase mechanism of history: to-wit,

> The flattering index of a direful pageant,
> One heaved a-high to be hurl'd down below, . . Richard II, IV, 4

A simple diagram of this image of history would look like Figure 3.2

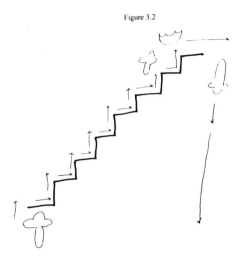
Figure 3.2

Yet the world misses it altogether, and so arise the multiplicity of plots:

> In this great Council scene (Richard III, Act III, 4), Shakespeare maintains a tremendous tension and does not let the audience relax for a moment. It is so still one hears people breathing. This is indeed the essence of history. (p. 26)

Kott's argument about the tension concerns who catches on and who is caught unprepared:

> Only two people in this tragedy reflect on the order of the world: King Richard III, and a hired assassin. The one who is at the top of the feudal ladder, and one placed at the very bottom . . . Neither of them has any illusions: they are the only ones who can afford not to have them.

Notice how the assassin catches the king's brother off guard:

> Clarence: In God's name, what art thou?
> First Murderer: A man, as you are.
> Clarence: But not as I am, royal.
> First Murderer: Nor you as we are, loyal. (I, iv, 158-161)

If this is the world, and its variation, then the opposite development is the letting loose of the imagination. Bayley captures this for us as follows:

Shakespeare is so accustomed to going out of himself in order to write in the tragic manner that his attitude toward it is ultimately insouciant. His obligations to the form mean a lack of obligation to what he himself makes of it. All is avowedly pretense, all is unconcerned. And this, more than anything else, divides his genius from the modern era. (Bayley, 1981, p. 14)

Just to give a single example among thousands, there is the famous one in King Lear (1611), in which Edgar leads Gloucester, blind, to the cliffs of Dover, and breaks out into a description for the unseeing man of what he sees:

> The crows and choughs that wing the mid-way air
> Show scarce so gross as beetles. Halfway down
> Hangs one that gathers samphire, dreadful trade.
> Me thinks he seems no bigger than his head . . . IV, vi, 11-15

Edgar goes on some while like this with the sights off the cliffs, and Bayley remarks:

> But there is no purpose, only the sudden sense of freedom and exhilaration. The crows and choughs, the mice-like fishermen, the samphire gatherer, are beheld by spectators as if they had abruptly floated off into a world outside the play. (p. 8)

Coming back to Walker Percy and I. A. Richards and the bow of metaphor, we never do quite know what Lear or MacBeth or Hamlet will fly into next, but the reach is tremendous. Such things as Hamlet saying, to Rosencrantz, in their famous discussion of Denmark as a prison:

> Rosencrantz: . . . Tis too narrow for your mind.
> Hamlet: Oh God, I could be bounded in a nutshell and count myself a king of infinite space, were it not I have bad dreams. II, ii, 251-254.

In other words, Shakespeare has all the extremes that he chooses to take, once he has accepted the Renaissance tragedy that the world is raw Machiavellian power, and the imagination is free to have "angelic perceptions" (Bayley, p. 13). As Bertrand Russell said over three hundred years later,

> Once you have accepted that the world is a terrible place, you may begin to enjoy it (Gustafson, 1986, p. 341)

When you have not accepted this, you get cramped agonizing over it, which uses up a tremendous amount of otherwise available energy, and becomes highly repetitious.

Dreams of the Author Concerning the Existential Problem

As I write these chapters, I dream their theoretical problems, quite as Freud did with his Irma Dream in 1895 (Kuper and Stone, 1982). After all, the existentialists are quite right that dreaming <u>can be</u> simply metaphorical, or a reach into relevant and perhaps far-flung analogies. I will close with a little metaphorical extension to the existentialists.

<u>Dream of the Bishop of Lichfield, and the Bishop of Pittsfield</u>. All this dream consisted of was these two phrases, so close to the ear, "The Bishop of Lichfield," and "The Bishop of Pittsfield." The first phrase alludes to Samuel Johnson, one of my college heroes because of the great lectures of Walter Jackson Bate. Johnson was born in Lichfield, England, and I had not thought of the place for most of the last 35 years. Johnson was one of those men like Thomas More for all seasons. The second phrase alludes to a colleague, whose criticism I was being subjected to, who could not be counted on to be interested in more than the accession of the great staircase of history. With such economy of wit, my dream was saying: Lich- and Pitts- are both fields, and both places of bishops, but they are worlds apart, like heaven and earth.

<u>Dream of the Rent in the Veil</u>: In the next night, I dreamt there was a rent in the veil of heaven, which looked like Figure 3.3.

Figure 3.3

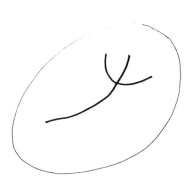

This is a similar vein of humor to the first dream, because the rent is in the shape of a cross, which curves like a smiling mouth. It alludes to Joseph Campbell's idea about the hero needing to go through a strange passage in his way out of the world, and cope with the turmoil of the forces in this liminal region.

<u>Dream of the Lock of the Psyche</u>: In the third and final night of this series, I had been thinking, because of a penetrating question from a patient, why she had been able to depart into her imagination, and why her husband had stayed put. The reply of my dream was a lock, with a very peculiar structure: as in Figure 3.4.

Figure 3.4

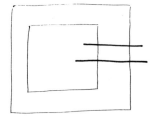

Essentially, the logic of the lock was that the burr-hole on the inside surface emptied the unconscious and left it null, while the burrs fixed it, so you couldn't rock it, and loosen the outside surface. It fixed you on the staircase of the world, where you agonized endlessly. This is the situation of my ambitious colleagues who have no use of dreams.

Several nights later, as I prepared to finish this chapter, the little punch dreams (Gustafson, Chapter 13, 1995b) gave way to an epic dream (Gustafson, Chapter 13, 1995b), putting the pieces together.

Dream of the Redress of Psychiatry: I dreamt that I was riding in a bus to a college tennis meet, where I was eager to show my stuff. To my chagrin, the bus driver announced he was sick, and that we had to go back. I decided I had to go on myself, and set off on roller blades, solo. I got lost off to the right, near what looked like a department store in Chicago, by the Chicago River. Everyone in the store was a number (#). Several of us broke out, and began to move along a wall to the left of grey, unbroken stone, or brick, like the wall around Harvard Yard. We were outsiders, and considered how to break in. Suddenly, we came to a wide gate, which I somehow knew was the Gdansk shipyards in Poland. A beautiful young woman of about 21 came out, and I began dancing with her. At first, she pushed me away, and then changed her mind. The lot of us went into the Shipyards, and the translucent shield over us sent the military missiles straight back at our assailants. Next I knew I continued along the grey or brick wall to the left, and came to a rubber flap about three feet by three feet at the street level, like an entry for a house cat at night only big enough for me. As a person slipped out, I could slip in, and found myself in a Harvard library that I knew belonged to Seamus Heaney. Regular students came in the other end freely, while I slipped in through the rubber flap, and began to pour through a black book that gave away the secrets of the best courses. All of this space is indicated in Figure 3.5.

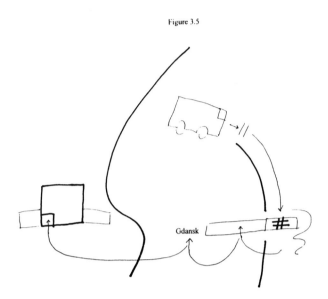

Figure 3.5

The metaphors are relatively straightforward. The bus is a kind of magical mystery tour bus of the 1960s (like the Beatles had) and the driver is a composite of my teachers who have reached their limit. The department store of #s refers to a conference I gave in Chicago for clinical social workers which was pitched at too high a level for these hard-pressed professionals hoping to survive at all. The movement to the left, on the outside, shows my outsider position with a few friends. The gate of the Gdansk shipyards refers to my romance about 1990 of the Solidarity Movement in the writings of Adam Michnik (1986) -- as if there could be solidarity outside of history, like the innocence of Ferdinand and Miranda in The Tempest (1611). It is a parody of this romanticism. Actually, solidarity is only for those at the bottom of the staircase of history such that they are equally excluded. Once they get on it, they shove each other off, as the subsequent history of Poland has shown once more.

Finally, the dream gives a modest re-entry, or redress, for me, like my neighbor's cat. It alludes to my delight in Heaney's new book, The Redress of Poetry (1995), which I had put down at bedtime. I can have all the wealth I want reading him, for he is a very treasury of reading. It turns out that literature is my spiritual home. As Heaney writes,

> The nobility of poetry, says Wallace Stevens, "is a violence from within that protects us from a violence without." It is the imagination pressing back against the pressure of reality. (Heaney, 1995, p. 1)

Chapter 4. Developments From Freud.

The misfortune of Freud was his success. Like Marx, he had a mind in many dimensions, but he was also a great simplifier. His followers seized on the latter. Kundera (1990) calls this reduction from many dimensions to one or two, "imagology." By this, he means that modern politics works like advertising or any other kind of salesmanship. The public buys images, with labels, like "Kennedy," or "Chevrolet," or "Psychoanalysis." Any given image-with-label has a certain amount of symbolic capital (Bourdieu, 1977). Groups own the symbolic capital, like a trademark.

Marcuse (1964) in One-Dimensional Man argued that the one-dimension which was subsuming the entire world, of science, of business, of government, of everything, was quantification (#). Its purpose was anticipating and projecting:

> The technic, the art of anticipation extended
> in infinity (p. 164)

Its result is that every other dimension becomes trivial, or fungible.

Fungible:

> Law. Such that one specimen or part may be used in the place of another in the satisfaction of an obligation, as money, food, etc. (Webster's Collegiate Dictionary)

Thus, an idea from medieval law that allows an exchange of many dimensions as value becomes an idea that empties out all dimensions but for their exchange-value:

> Only in the medium of technology, man and nature become fungible objects of organization. . . . The social position of the individual and his relation to others appear not only to be determined by objective qualities and laws, but these qualities and laws seem to lose their mysterious and uncontrollable character; they appear as calculable manifestations of (scientific) rationality. The world tends to become the stuff of total administration, which absorbs even the administrators. (Marcuse, pp. 168-169, my italics)

Freud's ideas about dreams circulated principally through the vehicle he created, psychoanalysis. The organization of psychoanalysis, like any other modern organization, operates by the control of an exchange-value which is its business and very survival. Always, this requires a gross simplification of the product to about 1-dimension or sometimes 2-dimensions. In 1902, Freud began to share his ideas in a semi-public form of discussion, which he called the Wednesday Psychological Society.

The History of Simplification in Psychoanalysis
With Particular Respect to Dreams

I am quite aware that the metapsychology of psychoanalysis could become quite complicated, with certain thinkers like David Rapoport (Rapoport & Gill, 1959) and others (see Gedo, 1979), who emphasized the different points of view inherent in their scientific theory of the psyche: the topographical, the dynamic, the economic, the structural, and so forth. Nevertheless, this theorizing had very little practical effect on the clinical mapping of dreams. It did have effects, which we shall follow. But the general tendency of the analysis of dreams became highly reductive.

This is not to say that the main line of analysis on dreams is useless. Indeed, it has very definite uses. I will distinguish two phases. I will leave out several analytic writers from this discussion, because they are outlyers with little effect on the main line of technique and because I want to take them up separately for their value towards a new interpretation of dreams. I am referring to Lewin (1973), Winnicott (1971b), Margulies (1989), and French (1970).

First Phase: The Solipsism of the Id and the Censorship in Deference to the Super-Ego

Early psychoanalysis was delighted with Freud's idea of hidden sexuality. In terms of dreams, this meant utilizing the dream as a compromise-formation. Its text was to be taken as a more or less censored document, hiding the great self-absorption of the dreamer in his wishes. A clever writer in this phase is Alexander (1925), who is quite instructive.

Alexander's Dreams in Pairs: Alexander plays a pretty variation on the balance between super-ego and id, by showing a dream under the influence of the super-ego, a punishment dream, which is followed in the same night by a dream under the influence of the id, a wish-fulfillment dream.

Dream I. I am on the sea-shore. My brother comes up in a rowing boat. He gets out but immediately jumps back into the water by the boat. The boatman is very angry at him for jumping back into the water and begins to abuse him, but my brother pays no attention to him. Now my brother is out of the water again and we go off together. The boatman behind us continues to shout and I say to him that he has no right to abuse me, for I have done nothing. We run towards town and the boatman pelts us with stones from behind. Curiously enough, it is only I who am in danger and not my brother, for he has suddenly vanished.

Dream II. I am with a little girl of about eleven or twelve years old. She says that I may kiss her arm on a certain place at her elbow (as if it were difficult to do). But I am able to do it and kiss her all over the upper part of her body. (p. 450)

Like Freud, Alexander obtains associations to the elements of the two dreams. He mentions in particular two of them:

An experience from the day before suggested the little girl whom he kissed. He had met on the previous day at the analyst's house a little girl of five or six, accompanied by her mother. He had been struck by the precocious, boastful manner and speech of the little girl. His association to kissing the arm at the elbow was that it was there that he and his brother loved to kiss their mother when they were little children. He even thinks that he copied his brother in kissing his mother in this way. (p. 450)

Now, the dream fits beautifully into Freud's classical map. The punishment in the first dream of the brother, and then himself, refers back to the forbidden pleasures of his childhood. The fulfillment in the second dream substitutes the little girl for his mother, so that he can have the ancient pleasure displaced onto a different object.

> . . . the punishment dream serves as a sop to conscience, so that it may not disturb the gratification in the second dream. We can see at once that this mechanism corresponds to that of the obsessional neurosis, in which activities displaying a masochistic tendency to self-punishment serve to liberate other, sadistic tendencies. The account must balance. (p. 451, my italics)

So here is a pretty little application of Freud. Compared to some of Freud's own dreams such as "Non Vixit," it has very little complexity of censorship. But it has the essential thing, of childhood sexual solipsism, having to be disguised to keep from being punished.

Ella Sharpe's Dream of the Dog Man. Twenty-five years later, very little has changed (between 1925 and 1950) in the way of mapping dreams. Sharpe is well named, however, for she has a very sharp use of her senses. For example, she is attuned by ear to her stairway:

> One patient comes up two stairs at a time and I hear just the extra thud; another hurries and I detect the hustle; another is sure to knock a suitcase or umbrella or fist on the banisters. One patient two out of three times blows his nose like a trumpet. (p. 129, 1951)

She listens for the (kinesthetic) movements of the body, but she also watches for them once the patient gets in the room:

> One brings in hat, umbrella and suit-case. They have to be disposed of somewhere. One patient bangs them down on the first piece of furniture available. One carefully selects a place and puts his things down. One patient flings himself on the couch. One walks round to the farther side of the couch before lying down. One patient hesitates and looks round at the room before trusting himself to the couch at all. One lies still on the couch and then moves about when tired of one position. Another will roll about from the first moment and become comfortable and still as the hour proceeds. (p. 129)

Sharpe is not caught up so much in words as in the body, because she wants to bring it forth from its censorship. You have to attend to its music very carefully, to catch the first incipient movements. Enter the case in question:

> But I never hear this patient on the stairs. He never brings his hat or coat or umbrella with him. He never varies. He always gets on the couch one way. He always gives a conventional greeting with the same smile . . . He puts one hand over the other across his chest. He lies like that until the hour is over. (pp. 129-130)

Now the beauty of her tuning:

> I have said I never hear him on the stairs, but for a few days prior to this hour just before he came into the room I had been aware of the smallest and discreetest of coughs. You will judge of the dearth of unconscious manifestations in bodily ways when I say that my ear caught that tiny discreet cough with great joy.

Sharpe just waits, not wanting to scare if off, and is rewarded by the patient noticing it himself. He is annoyed he cannot control it (of course), and suggests it is the kind of thing he did to warn his brother and his girlfriend that he was coming into the room where they might be intimate.

Now he drops deeper, for this little cough reminds him of a louder sound he might make, if he were in a room he ought not to be and did not want to be discovered. He would bark like a dog! Now a third drop:

> That reminds me of a dog rubbing himself against my leg, really masturbating himself. I'm ashamed to tell you because I did not stop him. I let him go on and someone might have come in. (The patient then coughed). I do not know why I should now think of my dream last night. (p. 132)

I will not go into the dream and her analysis of it, which is of a considerable sexual vitality, in which the patient discovers his own bodily strength. It has been held back by fear of its violence. I simply want to call attention to Sharpe's lovely sensory attention. Even the <u>moment</u> where the patient drops into the dream itself becomes of precise importance:

> The first thing of importance is to find <u>the cardinal clue</u> to the significance of the dream. We can do that <u>by noting just the moment</u> when it came to the patient's mind. He had been speaking of the incident of a dog masturbating on his leg. The moment before he had been speaking of imitating a dog himself, that is, he identified himself with a dog. Then he gave a cough. Then he remembered the dream, a long and exciting dream from which he awoke hot and perspiring. The deduction concerning the significance of the whole dream is that it is a masturbation phantasy. That is of first importance. (p. 138)

<u>Greenson's Dream of the Vomiting Man</u>. Another twenty years later and we get a similar attunement in Greenson (1951 to 1970). Yet Greenson (1970) fears it is dying out, and hopes to put it back in its "exceptional position" as the cardinal reading of the depth of the unconscious.

74

Here is his first example, from a man fearing free association, which might prove him empty or loathsome:

> I was making a phone call to some guy in a men's clothing store. I had ordered some clothes made to order and they didn't fit. I asked the guy to take them back but he said I had to come in myself. I told him I was not going to pay for the clothes until they fit. I said it seems like you just took them off the rack. I repeated, I won't pay for the clothes until they fit. As I said that I began to vomit, so I dropped the phone and ran into the bathroom to wash out my mouth. I left the receiver dangling and I could hear the guy saying, "What did you say, what? What?"

The patient freely associates to the dream that Greenson is the phony salesman of stock interpretations, roars with laughter so tears stream down his face, and realizes he has made Greenson into the father he feared as a child. Free of this transference fear, he remembers vomiting as a child in his mother's arms, and how kind she was.

It's all very nice and relieving, like a two-room schoolhouse. One room is the transference, as it were in the horizontal, and the other room is the childhood vitality asking to be let out, as it were in the vertical -- as illustrated in Figure 4.1.

Figure 4.1

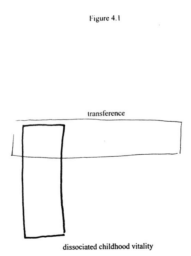

As a map, it is either very neat, or very confining. When it fits a patient, it is very neat.

<u>The Dream of Saving the Family from Chicago</u>. My patient came for help with compulsive masturbation. He was a very agreeable fellow, who was working very hard to help support his little family. His wife was not very interested in sex. After she'd go to bed, he

would masturbate often for hours, with porno videos. He felt he ought to give up his disgusting habit. An early dream was this little fragment:

> He is back in Chicago with his infant son and wife anxious to protect them from the violence of the city, and to move them to Wisconsin.

Chicago for him is the exciting place, where he was involved in the theater. He'd be up at all hours, with his pals, and his wife would be miserable and pulling him to leave. He'd be angry. Obviously, it was a perverse situation, where his pleasure was her unhappiness. The violence refers to the nasty neighborhood they lived in, which he actually didn't mind.

So he did protect his family by moving to Wisconsin. This is what his wife wanted. Now it is her way, which is perverse for him. They work all the time, and have too little excitement.

I tell him that the dream shows his determination to protect his family, by being understanding of his wife's needs. He replies that he has always been that way. Even in first grade, he could not complain of another little boy, without his mother telling him: "Oh, but Harry is so unhappy." So, his character is to be understanding.

Yet, I note, that behind the surface of the dream in the word, Chicago, we came upon all his pent-up excitement in the theater. Even then, he did not know what to do with his anger at his wife. Either, it is his way, and she is miserable, or it is her way (his mother's way, also) and he is very frustrated. So, the masturbation is indeed a classic perversion as compromise-formation. He submits to his wife's (mother's) way, and secretly gratifies himself. There are patients like this, for whom Freud's simplified map is quite right. They bow to their parents, secretly gratify themselves, and censor the dream text to comply with their consciences. The manifest text is for the super-ego, and the latent text is for the id.

Second Phase: The Dream as Simple Metaphor of the Self, or Parent, or Doctor

Freud (1900) allowed that there could be a certain degree of self-perception in dreams, especially in the process of waking up:

> The representation may be in terms of such images as crossing a threshold ("threshold symbolism"), leaving one room and entering another, departure, home-coming, parting with a companion, diving into water, etc. (pp. 542-543)

Technically, this is called endopsychic perception (p. 544). Freud admitted it, but didn't come across it much himself (p. 543).

From about 1950, there is increasingly more of simple self-reflections. It is as if the patients stopped being so devious as Freud argued, and just gave simple pictures of themselves, or their parents, or their situation in treatment. These are just the simplest of metaphors, such as we discussed in the existential tradition of Binswanger and Boss.

This shift occurs as theory is shifting towards object-relations and self-psychology. Now that the doctor is less interested in devious sexuality, he will get less devious dreams. Now, he will get the pictures of the self-structure and object-relations that interest him. Could it be that patients are so selectively attentive to their night wanderings as to report what the doctor will credit?

Even in Sharpe (1951), there is a great deal of interest in metaphor. For example: Synecdoche is a figure of speech in which a part does duty for the whole. (p. 24) The poetic device of metonymy means literally a "change of name." (p. 22) In the dream, "I take a piece of silk from a cupboard and destroy it," I found that silk as silk per se stimulated no important associations, While the phrase "take silk" is the device of metonymy and means "to be called to the bar," i.e. to become a barrister.

So the dream is simply a metaphor of his urge to destroy the lawyer in himself and in his father.

This becomes the typical report of a dream. A list of simple examples will show the idea:

Guntrip's Pictures of the Stalemate:

"I got on a tramcar and walked straight through to the driver's platform, turned the driver off and drove the car myself." I put it to her that the tram was the treatment and I was the driver and she felt the situation to be one in which she was in my power, as she had once been in her father's; and this she could not tolerate. Only if she could take complete charge of the analysis and run it herself, could she go on with it: but in that case it would not be treatment, it would merely be turning the tables on her father in my person, and nothing would really be changed. (Guntrip, 1968, p. 295)

Kohut's Pictures of the Patient's Predicament:

". . . a starkly outlined image of the mother, standing with her back turned toward him" -- it was filled with the deepest anxiety he had ever experienced. . . . On the most accessible level there was this simple meaning: the mother was turning her back to him - she would now abandon him because he was moving closer to his father . . . The deeper meaning of the dream was contained in its invisible part: it concerned the unseen, the unseeable frontal view of the mother. . . . her distorted personality and her pathological outlook on the world and on him -- of features, in other words, that he was not only forbidden to see but whose recognition would in fact endanger the structure of his self as he knew it. (Kohut, 1979, pp. 19-20)

More examples are hardly necessary (Lacan, p. 158, 1991; Gedo, 1979, pp. 128-129; Weiss and Sampson, 1986, Chapter 7; Oremlund, 1987, Chapters 8 and 10, etc.) to illustrate the trend. A more sophisticated version comes from Anna Ornstein (1974).

<u>Ornstein's Dream of the Transference Dilemma</u>. Essentially, a gloomy patient stayed gloomy to be close to her mother, because getting free of this would be to lose her altogether. With the doctor, it was the same. At first, she was in a gloomy silence. Then, she began to feel better and felt panic. So, she was in trouble either way. Then she dreamt:

> . . . there was an area with water, it was muddy, there were some coins at the bottom, some flowers growing in it too . . . The coins were only partially visible, like my thoughts, I was digging for them giving them to someone. (p. 245)

Here she was doing something new, being close to her mother-doctor with something valuable:

> I then recalled a dream she had had several weeks before, about a pool of water where half the water was crystal clear and the other half muddy; nothing visible was dividing the two bodies of water, but they remained strangely separated . . . (p. 245)

The dream shows the patient's own awareness "of the dissolution of the vertical split" in her own being, as illustrated in Figure 4.2 (p. 245). The **angry mud** had stood in the way before, keeping away the patient's love.

Figure 4.2

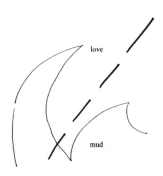

<u>The Dream of "The Wall Feeling."</u> As Weiss and Sampson (1986, Chapter 7) point out, a patient often stays shallow, because the depths are overwhelming. This is particularly true of any patient with a terrible childhood. The only way to face it is a little bit at a time. Even this may strain the patient's capacity. A sequence of dreams will allow it to be comprehended, like a collection of photographs from different angles. For example, a patient that spent several years

on such a terrible series of revisits to incest with her father began to turn to the aspect of her mother's hatred of her. She dreamt:

> My mother is bending over me. It's the wall feeling. (What is that like?) Like a coffee cup that is getting ever larger, and I can't get away.

When I say to her that she must have been very small, she feels comforted and cries and feels very grateful. This panics her, for she sees a picture of herself as an adoring little girl looking up at her father, only to be taken advantage of, sexually. Since we have been through such scenes hundreds of times, in hundreds of dreams, she comes through this particular scene with slightly less crying than before, and the childhood is a little more integrated. This means that she can risk connection and comfort (see Chapter 8 on the approach of dream screens), which previously she had to keep at a great distance by giving it to others.

Erik Erikson's (1954) Essay on "The Dream Specimen of Psychoanalysis:" The Force That Through the Green Fuse Drives the Flower

The trouble with Freud's two-dimensional map is just the history I have traced. There is almost no development. Its analytic product is like someone in one of Max Weber's (1904-1905) iron cages of asceticism, which drive the capitalist energy. The super-ego asks for work. The id asks for relief. The work week builds up tension, and the weekend discharges tension, as illustrated in Figure 4.3.

Figure 4.3

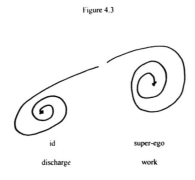

id   super-ego

discharge   work

Thus, the characters that appear in Alexander, Sharpe, and Greenson, Guntrip, Kohut and Ornstein, have hardly any individuality at all. The same is true of the two cases I illustrated, of the man saving his family from Chicago, and of the woman with "the wall feeling." They are either doing the required thing, or gratifying themselves. Dickens (1981, 1850 originally) was the great portrait painter of this industrial character, in its high-flying mode of Mr. Dick, its twisting around like Uriah Heep, or its servility in Mrs. Crupp. You can feel the tension build in the part played in society:

> Mrs. Crupp, who had been incessantly smiling to express sweet temper, and incessantly holding her head on one side, to express a general feebleness of constitution, and incessantly rubbing her hands, to express a desire to be of service to all deserving objects, gradually smiled herself, one-sided herself, and rubbed herself, out of the room. (p. 406)

It is very hard to be a playing card, in society. It makes a person sick, Freud argued in Civilization and Its Discontents, (1930) unless the circuitous path of censored instinct can find its way out. Thus, all of these cases are relieved, when the dissociated child is let out. But just as one playing card is like another, so is one child like another. We remain, essentially, in the two-dimensional schoolhouse of psychoanalysis.

As Bion (1959) argued, there is no development when work is in one compartment, and instinct in another compartment. And this is precisely what modern society is set up to allow for. Spare time is for a great deal of discharge, so the worker can get back in harness.

The Author's Dream of Dead Flies in the Tomato Juice. I remember when my wife and I took a train from Athens, Greece up through Yugoslavia into Austria on our way to a pilgrimage to Berggasse 19 in Vienna, Freud's home and office. The train was something of a riot of eating and drinking, smells, sights and shouting. When we came to the Austrian border, a little corps of cleaning ladies in neat costumes got on and swept the train clean. When we got to Vienna itself, we could see it was a city of old monuments. The young people complained to us that all the life had gone out of it as in a huge bank.

When I was contemplating this psychoanalytic world earlier this year, I had a simple and startling dream:

> I dreamt that "my mother" was showing me how to clean out a place, but then she poured dead flies into the open pitchers of tomato juice.

Figure 4.4

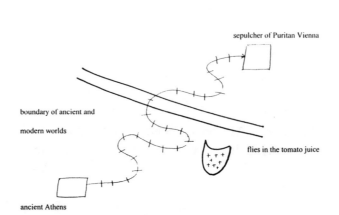

sepulcher of Puritan Vienna

boundary of ancient and

modern worlds

flies in the tomato juice

80

ancient Athens

This is illustrated in Figure 4.4, wherein "my mother" is actually like some lady out of Greek tragedy, putting the ancient "flies" back into the blood. The dream reverses the train from the ancient to the modern world. I get the dimensionality of the Greek world back again. Yet, this "mother" also is cleaning up, in the modern way of the Austrian sweeping ladies. So, the dream retains the modern world, as well. When you put modern man and his work together with the instinctual vitality of the ancient man, then you get a third thing which is startling. As in this dream, you get metaphors with a long reach to them.

This is not my actual mother. Cleaning up is not just for the super-ego. Pouring flies into the tomato juice is not just a discharge of hostility. It is actually a gift of symbolic dimensions, which gets us out of the two dimensions of psychoanalysis. A certain amount of audacity is needed to break a dead system. "My mother" of this dream shows another way, like the Virgin Mary at Chartres shows the way out of Norman militarism. The floor may belong to these men of power, but the rose windows are all hers. (Adams, originally 1904, 1986)

Erikson's Audacity

Now, I left one other writer out of my history of the development from Freud, and that was Erikson (1954) in his single essay on dreams. Erikson dares to reanalyze Freud's own Irma Dream, which was his showcase "Dream Specimen of Psychoanalysis" (Chapter II of The Interpretation of Dreams, 1900 originally, 1965). Now many have put their hand to this reinterpretation of the master, by adding a point or two, an angle. That was not what Erikson was up to. I count thirty dimensions to his musical score, many of them from counterpoint, inversion, and even reversing the dream. It is an extremely startling piece of musical composition. Like Brahm's "Variations on a Theme by Haydn," it takes the old music and discovers immense possibilities. Then, it disappears with hardly a trace in the literature, or in Erikson's subsequent work.

The S(E)INE Dream. While he is getting underway on "the Dream Specimen," Erikson throws in a little piece of virtuosity to alert us to what is coming. It is like a second theme, to the Irma theme itself.

> I pause here for an illustration, the shortest illustration, from my practice. A young woman patient of German descent once reported a dream which consisted of nothing but the image of the word S(E)INE (with the E in brackets), seen light against a dark background. (pp. 18-19)

The verbal play in it turns out to be astounding, a cadenza for the tongue, which becomes an instrumental dimension all its own (see Freud's Rat Man (1909) for the only comparable passage, of the cadenza of Rat language (Gustafson, 1995a, 1995b)): to-wit, SEINE, the river in Paris where the patient had been overcome by agoraphobia; SEHN, German, "to see," which is what the patient was doing at the Louvre, when she became immobilized; E for Erikson, the "anchorage" (p. 119) for the dream; SINE, Latin for "without."

All of this combined makes for the riddle "To see (E) without his . . . in Paris."
Once this riddle had come to light, it was not many steps to visual recovery of the picture at the Louvre itself, a "Circumcision of Christ," without his loin cloth, a SIN to behold.

But Erikson has hardly begun to play. Now, he shows the dimensions that are <u>absent</u> in the theme, but drive its figure, from the ground:

> The dimension of movement, which is absent, but "muscles" its way in, namely, the urge to tear off the clothes of the Saviour (Doctor); hence, the literal stock stillness of the dream and of the immobilized patient herself.
> The dimension of light/dark, so that the milling crowds in the Louvre go unnoticed in the dangerous freedom, which has disappeared into a dark lacuna for the painting itself.
> The dimension of time, come to a stop, like the patient's sexual life.
> In other words, only verbality has free run, while the others are canceled:
> Thus, all the omitted dimensions of the manifest dream, with the help of associations, could be made to converge on the same issues on which the one over-clear dimension (the visual one) was focused. (p. 20)

Erikson has made the missing dimensions sing as well as the manifest dimension. In this little performance itself, he has already developed Freud's work beautifully. I certainly have never heard anyone analyze a dream for the dimensions which are <u>not</u> in it.

<u>Back to the Irma Dream</u>. In the interests of relative brevity, I am going to take the risk of omitting Freud's dream text itself, and his own associations (the reader may refer to my previous analysis of this dream, and its holes, or selective inattention, something like Erikson's missing dimensions (Gustafson, 1995b, Chapter 13, "Dream as an Individual Map of Dilemma")). I am not so much interested in the themes of the dream itself, but of the dimensions that Erikson can derive from it.

First, there are the dimensions taken singly: time, space, movement, the interpersonal crowd, affects, words, history, conflict-free regions, color, shading, trigger, transference, holes, and social status. I will let the reader see for himself what Erikson brings out in these single dimensions, because I want to show the musical power even more virtuosic of combining them.

<u>Synesthesia</u>: The dreamer is all "eyes" until he feels the same as Irma in his own body.

<u>Spatial zoom</u>: From spacious hall to a tight scene by the light in a window to constriction to body parts.

<u>The crowd of characters</u>: ". . . make their determined entrance like a host of unsorted strangers, until they gradually become a chorus echoing a few central themes." (p. 11) This is quite like the dimension of opera.

The actions of the dreamer: I take, I look, I think, I take, I look, I think, I find, I quickly call, etc. Collectively, these reveal a highly vigorous character.

The religious dimensions: This dream is a ritual of scapegoating for uncleanliness, very deeply important to Freud as a Jew.

The group psychology: This is a group vindicating one man, driving out another (in group, and out group).

Awakening, sleeping: Freud is charged with alarm at the outset, as his sleepy reception for guests, but sleeps in the bosom of his in-group by the end.

Stages of life: This is a man in his generative period, of giving birth, or contributing-in (Winnicott, 1971a). He needs desperately to have his conception well-received.

Reverberation of old weak points: Mistrust, shame, guilt, inferiority, diffusion of identity, isolation, stagnation, disgust all smell their way in.

Nakedness, and clothing. All these men are fully clothed in their insignia of status, while this woman is their object. Freud dares to become the woman himself, to lay himself bare, in order to discover.

The central point, or navel: Speaking of nakedness, Irma turns out to be three women (as well as Freud himself). This is his navel, or, more precisely, the navel of the dream: "If I had pursued my comparison between the three women, it would have taken me far afield." (Freud, p. 143n)

The muse of the dream. It is played toward a heavenly queen, who is a rival to the analyst. This is like a vanishing perspective.

The pulling apart of the self. The tension between the male investigatory Freud, and the female investigated Freud, is almost unbearable, a horrible dissonance.

The dream played backwards: If it ends in vindication, it is played backwards to a reception in his own hall. (p. 49)

The range between the point of fixation and the point of arrest: There is musical tension, in yet another way, between his point of greatest gratification where he secretly wishes to return, and his point of arrest, where he got so hurt he stopped growing. (p. 51)

Evil, and moral mission. Speaking of Freud's point of arrest, he was determined not to be a "dirty squirter," as his father had denounced him. His moral mission is "the ambition of uniqueness . . . almost an obligation to his people." (p. 54) Erikson has demonstrated, fulfilled it for us.

So there's thirty dimensions for you. I haven't even come close to exhausting them, either. The close reader will find many more.

The Force That Through the Green Fuse Drives the Flower

So why should such an astounding performance disappear with hardly a trace. A trace there is, such as one passing reference in Margulies (1989, p. 33), which is typical. This work of musical genius is leveled out with all the other bits in the lore of the Irma dream.

First, Erikson did himself in. At the same time he was writing this essay, he was writing Childhood and Society (1963, first edition, 1950). It is all right, but a greatly inferior work to his dream essay. He is developing his formula of the eight stages of life, which he would apply to Hitler, Luther, Gandhi, and so forth. It is really a very simple formula: the endocosm of the body is parallel to the microcosm of the soul which is parallel to the macrocosm of the society as envelope. This took him over. This is what the great staircase of history (Kott, 1974) will do with a talented man, which is to show him how to rise in the world. The two dimensions are number, and suit, as for a playing card. The Jack, Erikson, rose to Ace. He largely gave up his other twenty-eight dimensions, to show how power works. It works quite well in two.

Secondly, psychoanalysis had no more use for him if he got out of two dimensions. The group is powerful, much more than Erikson knew. He saw its action on Freud, not on himself. It is especially powerful, when you fail to see its interference. If you see the required cards to play in two dimensions, you can proceed to the music of the other twenty-eight. This is essentially what Lewis Carroll demonstrated in his topology of Alice (1865). I will be coming back to this huge theme in Chapter 11, "A Search for Survival on the Frontier."

Erikson reminds me of Dylan Thomas, that other fertile genius of thirty dimensions, who made himself into a playing card of the drunken Welsh poet (not before a great many marvelous performances, see Heaney (1995)). Look at the Prologue to his Collected Poems for such music. Then, read his "Lament" of the stages of man (much truer than Erikson's) and see what drove it in "The Force That Through the Green Fuse Drives the Flower." It is ancient, and it is the instincts in service of the group. Samuel Johnson put it in laconic and mild English form:

Every person has a native wish to feel considerable in his native place.
If you cannot subdue this to its minor place it belongs, it will eat you up.

Chapter 5. Developments from Jung

Jung's system for handling dreams is quite stable in the hands of many Jungians. Perhaps, it is even eternal. It turns up the same in nearly any exegesis or summary of Jung. For example, in Joseph Henderson's "Dream in Jungian Analysis" (1993), the analysis relies on Jung's ideas of compensation, archetypes and amplification.

Dream of Depressed Air Force Pilot Returning to Civilization After 65 Missions. "I had to get somewhere by a certain time. On a diagram I saw how to get there. First I was to go along a narrow street called 65½ Street which cut obliquely into a broad boulevard paved with many-colored, bright, glazed bricks. I was to go into a house numbered 654, a sort of roadside residence or restaurant. I was there received by a fat, semi-Oriental maid of no particular age, in a black silk dress, named Todida. She handed me a glass of orange juice. She was big and jolly, and there was a sense of rightness about her. I saw I had arrived ahead of time, 9:00 AM. I was not due until 1:00 PM. I asked her to have ham and eggs with me. Instead of answering, she put her face into her hands and went into a trance" (p. 370).

As a compensation, it is an encouragement to a demoralized man about going past his 65th mission, to 65½ or 654. As an archetype, it is a handmaiden between death (Tod is the German word for death, Dido the Carthaginian princess who died when Aeneas left her) and rebirth (orange juice of sunlight, like many-colored, bright bricks near Reims Cathedral). As an amplification, it is a "semi-Oriental" goddess who invites him into an Eastern trance, a needed improvement on his ambivalent tie with his mother.

The images of the dream are interesting: 65 missions; a narrow street called 65½ Street cutting obliquely into the broad boulevard; 654, the house; Todida the fat, semi-Oriental maid of no particular age in a black silk dress, handing out orange juice to him; an urgency of time, arrival at 9:00, instead of 1:00 PM. The dreamer has a precise mathematical sense of sequence, topography and time, and a startling contrast of color between orange and black.

Unfortunately, the analyst hardly enters the dream space in his report. Jungian concepts, almost always traveling in long and big nouns, like compensation, archetype and amplification, tend to float higher and higher into the heavens. If this is transcendence, it is not what Jung meant. Any set of concepts has this tendency to ascend into empty space. This vantage point gets high enough above the grounding of the dream that it can see what it wants to point out. It has become the conscious mind, barely in touch with the strangeness of the unconscious. It has become didactic.

The Bottle Can Dream of the Gay Man Dying of AIDS. Fortunately, there have been a number of Jungians well aware of the hazards of Jung's intellectual system. They are willing to descend with the patient into his particular dream space, and bear its grief and rage, without fleeing into the skies (see Genova, 1995a; 1995b). The following dream reported by Beebe (1993), "A Jungian Interpretation of Dreams," was from a subservient gay man, long bullied by other gay men. Being high-minded, he had great trouble in feeling the actual violation (p. 89) which was his history. He typed out the following dream for Beebe as follows:

I looked down at the top of my right thigh. There were round formations about the size of buttons on the surface. It almost looked as if soft-drink bottle caps had been pressed into the skin and released, producing the button effect. I thought of Kaposi's. (p. 90)

Interestingly, his dream begins "looking down" -- from his high-minded perspective. Yet Beebe is willing to go down there with him. Essentially, the trail leads back to the 1950s of his boyhood with bottle caps, stamped with the faces of baseball heroes. He had engaged in a circle jerk-off with a group of boys, who had gotten him to be the gay goat. This destroyed him in the school, and he was branded forever. "The lid had come off their bottles," as Beebe puts it, and he, the patient, was stamped on.

The transcript shows Beebe more moved than the patient. Interviewer: "I'm having feelings of outrage. I mean, I'm impressed by what we've done." Subject: "Well, it fits in so beautifully with what I've been learning from the Simonton books . ." (p. 95). Still, it is a triumph. Beebe marks it as a "decisive engagement with affect that had eluded us earlier in the treatment" (thirteen years!). "It saved the quality, if not the fact of his life" (p. 99).

My relief reading Beebe's report is that here is a doctor like Virgil in The Inferno (Dante, 1300) who is willing to descend to be alongside the patient in hell:

> As the session suggests, the mystery of dream interpretation ought to reside in the dream itself, not the language or idiom with which we approach it. . . . The point was to connect him with his own imagery. (p. 98)

The mystery of dream interpretation is not to interpret. Rather, it is to connect the beleaguered conscious mind, here in its "high-mindedness" with its unconscious imagery, there of "violation." Beebe likes to call this shift the work of Hermes, the trickster:

> . . . usually, the trickster is the dream's great healer. It reflects the part of the self that can shift the ground on familiar sets of thought to introduce a really new perspective on a seemingly open-and-shut situation. To this patient fearing the development of Kaposi's sarcoma, the dream brought alarming news of another malignancy blighting his persona -- the psychosocial malignancy of the internalized prejudice against homosexuality. The dream's sick visual pun released his resentment (p. 99). . . . There is an art, which lies in catching hold of the paradoxical, outrageous level of the dream. It is the trickster level which shifts the emphasis of one's concern as one dreams -- a grasp of it takes the dreamer beyond appreciation of the compensatory effort of the unconscious to the threshold of genuine personality change. (p. 100)

Beebe's phrases are exact, for "appreciation of the compensatory effort of the unconscious" is like watching from afar in the appreciation of a force, and energy, and imagery, that has little to do with oneself. One is safe in the dark theater, of anonymity. But the image has the potential to draw the patient out of his seat, and over the threshold, into being an actor himself in his own tragedy. Hermes is needed to usher the patient slyly along and downward into his own denied history of hell. This gives the catharsis.

Hillman's Perspective from the Underworld, or from Downside Up

Part of what Hillman (1979b, originally 1973) has to say is entirely parallel to Beebe's argument for descent:

> Hence my stress upon two things: the dark eye that makes our brightness unsure; and careful precision in regard to what is actually there, a method that Lopes-Pedrazza felicitously calls "sticking to the image" (p. 194)

Hillman means that bright minds see what they want to see in their own theoretical light, and are worse than useless in the dark.

Hence, Hillman undergoes the experiment of doing away with the world as we know it, consciously. The dream is not our wish (Freud), nor our help (Jung), nor anything for our daylight world (existence) at all. It is the underworld of the dead of night, taking us over for its purposes.

When I first read this at the urging of one of my friends (Peter Miller, personal communication), I thought Hillman was crazy or, perhaps, just metaphorical. In other words, if Erikson could turn the dream every which way like a composer doing thirty variations on a theme, then Hillman could certainly add one more that Erikson had not thought of. Downside-up could be another kind of musical development, in the classical sonata form.

When I returned to reread Hillman months later to write this chapter, I saw I was wrong about Hillman. That alarming sentence that I wrote,

> It is the underworld of the dead of night, taking us over
> for its purposes,

is more than a new angle. It turns out to be a view into a process in which human beings are actually destroyed, routinely, and stolen away to Hell forever. It is something clouded over, for the daylight mind. In these clouds, or holes, however, is the action of the underworld. It is stealing souls, in a kind of huge suction. Solzhenitsyn meant something like this, when he described the Gulag Archipelago (1973) as a lost continent within the U.S.S.R. of prison camps of ghouls, robbed of their lives:

> We have been happily borne -- or perhaps have unhappily dragged our weary way -- down the long and crooked streets of our lives, past all kinds of walls and fences made of rotting wood, rammed earth, brick, concrete, iron railings. We have never given a thought to what lies behind them. (p. 4)

Thus far, just the daylight mind, missing the underworld two yards away:

But there is where the <u>Gulag</u> country begins, right next to us, two yards away from us. In addition, we have failed to notice an enormous number of closely fitted, well-disguised doors and gates in these fences. (p. 4)

Suddenly, it is too late:

And all of a sudden the fateful gate swings quickly open and four white male hands, unaccustomed to physical labor but nonetheless strong and tenacious, grab us by the leg, arm, collar, cap, ear, and drag us in like a sack, and the gate behind us, the gate to our past life, is slammed shut once and for all. (p. 4)

Hillman's perspective is more terrifying. While the <u>Gulag</u> is situated or was situated somewhere on earth, in particular, the kingdom of the dead is everywhere around us. There is no getting away from it. Oddly, modern man goes on not seeing it.

I imagine most of my readers have little idea, yet, of what I am talking about. You are in for a shock, once you do get it. Allow me to conduct you there, step by step. It will grow on you, once you get used to seeing in the dark.

Let's start from Freud (1920), writing <u>Beyond the Pleasure Principle</u> in the aftermath of World War I. He just could not keep arguing that human beings were chiefly motivated by pleasure. Not after the grotesque struggles of the war in the trenches. Those men were not there for pleasure. Nor did they dream back to these horrors to fulfill wishes. The war just canceled Freud's theories, at a stroke:

. . . there really does exist in the mind a compulsion to repeat which overrides the pleasure principle (p. 605, in Freud, 1989) . . something that seems more primitive, more elementary, more instinctual than the pleasure principle which it over-rides (p. 605) . . . when they act in opposition to the pleasure principle, give the appearance of some "daemonic" force at work (p. 611).

If it is in the war, and grown-up men, Freud reasons, it must be in children in advance. It happened that Freud happened to stay with a family, who had a boy of one and a half, playing a game of throwing away objects like toys:

As he did this he gave vent to a loud, long-drawn-out "o-o-o-o," accompanied by an expression of interest and satisfaction (the German word, "fort" (gone)) (p. 599)

When he pulled back one of these toys, a reel on a string by its string
    and hailed its reappearance with a joyful "da" (there). This, then, was the complete game
    -- disappearance and return. (p. 599)

Freud calls it a game of revenge (p. 600). If his mother leaves him, the passive object, he revenges himself by throwing her away. The same with his father:

A year later, the same boy whom I had observed at his first game used to take a toy, if he was angry with it, and throw it on the floor, exclaiming, "Go to the fwont!" He had heard at that time that his absent father was at the front . . . (p. 600)

From this child, Freud proceeds to the situation of not only humanity, but all living things. They combine, like germ-cells

to combine organic substances into ever larger unities (p. 616).

Or they destroy larger entities, and start over. Little boys do this, and all living things do this: two kinds of processes are constantly at work in living substance, one constructive or assimilatory and the other destructive or dissimilatory (p. 618)

Freud called these Eros and Thanatos, while we call them now in modern biology, the anabolic and the catabolic processes. At a cellular level, they do not alarm us. But what if we ourselves are set up to create families in our youth (Eros), and then promptly die (Thanatos)? What if we are determined, soon after our procreation has carried out its work for the species, to become ghosts?

I used to think that late Freud was off his rocker. Hillman took him very seriously. I will explain why I am mostly persuaded. In Hillman's Latin terms, we are more like ephemera, or moths, than what we think of as solid men. We are puer, or youth, and then we are senex, or ghosts. We are built up, and then we are taken apart, like the toys of the little boy. See if this is not true. Look around you, after I have taken you through the argument.

I will conduct you to Hillman's perspective proper in three steps. The first step is taken directly from Freud. Dreams can be looked at as necessary destruction. There is no rebirth without death. As the little boy knew, there is no "There!" (Da), without "Gone" (Fort), which clears the stage for the return.

Dreams as Images of Destruction

Repetition is death, once it is stuck in its cycle. Dante pictured exactly this in his Inferno (1300). It also dulls, so its victim is anesthetized against his own fate. How is he to be awakened? Only by seeing himself from below, turning in his death, like the fly in the web that he is. Consider the two dreams we have taken already. The fighter-pilot is caught in his sixty-fifth mission, and Todida (Death Dido) is his servant. The AIDS patient has been stamped for death with a bottle-cap.

Hillman does not put it this way, but I would say that people get caught in dead metaphors (clichés are dead metaphors). The hero from afar gets to be pretty deadly, when his only freshness is that he came from a long way away, to yet another woman. He can only have the illusion of freshness, by changing partners. If he kept the same one, she would recognize the trick. The salesman is of the same kind. He brings new products (youth), to replace old and outmoded products (ghosts). Yet, the change is relatively trivial. Market research (Shorris, 1995) has figured out that this trick of the slight change will sell. The great hero, or salesman, is a dead metaphor, hiding in the novelty of variations of phrase. Think of Willy Loman (Miller, 1949): the old man with his old woman, pretending to be a youth, is Everyman.

What is virtually dead has to die, but it can put off a long time. Going around in circles of slightly new to old to slightly new again, will disguise the circle, as if it is leading somewhere, in a progress. Dreams, according to Hillman, destroy these fixations:

> When a dream image is moistened, it is entering the <u>dissolutio</u> and is becoming, in Bachelard's sense, more psychisized, made into soul, for water is the special element of reverie . . . Moistening in dreams refers to the soul's delight in its death, its delight in sinking away from fixations in literalized concerns. (p. 152)

Like the little boy of Freud, we build up things in the day, and we destroy them at night. Dreams disassemble:

> Entering the waters relaxes one's hold on things and lets go of where one has been stuck . . . (p. 152). Literalizations that kill the flow and bury the soul always need dissolving . . . (p. 153)

<u>The Dream of Pablo the Destroyer</u>: My patient had been stuck for many years in a tie to a motherly woman for whom he had no sexual passion. He decided to move on, but needed my help to do so. He dreamt:

> A mass murderer named Pablo is coming. I am with my relatives trying to lock the house against him. It is my responsibility. I try to lock the doors and windows, but I cannot. I go outside, and find I am locked out myself. I find a little red square door, and discover I can kick it in easily. Someone telephones that Pablo is coming, but is killed before he can finish the call. (//)

> I go inside, and hear people calling out from the basement, as if they are being disemboweled. Then a woman comes up with a bucket of fish. I go down into the basement, and don't see anything, and then I go farther and look around a corner. Pablo is with my relatives. He has a small cannon, with a mouth like a fish, but nothing comes out of it. It is no big deal to subdue him. A small, white, fluffy, French poodle sniffs around me like it is going to bite me. Now, I realize that the screaming was just the gutting of fish, "eaaah . .!" as the guts come out. Pablo whacks me off.

When I entered this dream space with the patient, "moistening" the dream images as Hillman would say, one by one, I found that the patient was chiefly pleased with himself. I can abridge his commentary on the many elements of the dream without much damage to their sense, because it converged over and over on how much he enjoyed doing all of these things: kicking in red doors, referring to vaginas; cutting up blue gills, the common fish; subduing Pablo, himself a fish, and so forth.

Pablo, he realized at once, is his hero, Picasso, who can cut up the reality of women into pieces and reassemble them in different planes. He did not have to take them as they were, and be stuck with them. He was discovering the pleasures of freeing himself from his mother / motherly girlfriend, yet it is also true that he was anxious to protect them from himself. The dream essentially shifts from himself as defender // to himself as penetrating artist. I placed a paragraph in my text of the dream, where he shifts from the fear of the assaultive Pablo coming // to his own investigations of the basement. This shift of scene is what Grinnell (1970) calls a hiatus (// is my symbol for it). Grinnell is discussing Jung's dream, which I presented in Chapter 2, of the Knight of the Red Cross. First, it is located on the Austrian border, where Jung meets the ghost of the customs official who had died years ago . . . 'who still couldn't die properly.'" Then, there is an abrupt break of scene, or hiatus, to high, blazing noon in an Italian city like Bergamo fused with Basel, where Jung meets the ascending knight in the white tunic "into which was woven, front and back, a large red cross." Grinnell comments on the hiatus as follows:

> Psychologically the hiatus is analogous to those empty centers which Jung noted as characteristic of modern mandalas. And it is synonymous with ancient images like sea, depths, abyss, eternal death, draco, leviathan, or the nihil from which God drew creation . . . . It is at once the emptiness of death and dissolution and the seedbed of new developments . . . In our dream, the hiatus acts as the fulcrum and the turning point. It is the "night" intervening between the vesperal consciousness of the official (//) and the matutinal consciousness represented by the Crusader. (pp. 28-29) (my italics)

For Jung, the hiatus is the death of the customs official which is long overdue // and the birth of the Crusader. For my patient, the hiatus is between his old job as defender of the females // and his freedom as Pablo who disembowels the blue gills. The literal and dead defense of frontiers sinks into the abyss, and the symbolic attack rises out of its silence.

Dreams as Entirely Spatial

Another aspect of Hillman's underworld perspective, besides the uses of destruction, is the abrogation of time:

> We can stop time by not reading the dream as a story . . .A dream is stuck within itself, its actual imagery, and has to be read in terms of what is going on in it. It is stuck within the limits of its framework, like a painting in which nothing comes first and nothing comes later and which is read by articulating and deepening the internal relations of its image. (p. 158)

Of course, clocks and hurry and dread about punctuality appear in this space:

> Then we learn that the dream-ego is terrified of slowness, especially the slowness in its own lower body. We learn that images of punctuality are ideal adjustments to the time of others. Dream punctuality shows a dream-ego in accord with daylight-consciousness,

and retardation shows a dream-ego drifting into the disorientation of underworld timelessness, despite panicked efforts. (p. 156)

A Dream on the Staircase of History. My patient has been struggling mightily with the academic hierarchy of her department, for justice. She dreams:

I am walking outside in a perfect starry night, as in the country. I am lying on my back on a rubber raft looking at the starry night. The raft is on a staircase, which leads up to a ranch house.

Behind me, I then feel the eyes of the chairman and the vice-chairman of my department, which takes away my comfort altogether. I also feel I am in magnetic fields, which alternately expand me and contract me.

I am drawn by the magnetic field into a graveyard.

Notice that the dream is told as a story in time. First, comfort in the perfect starry night (I think of Van Gogh's "Starry Night" here, which is well known to the dreamer who is a painter herself). Second, the disturbing eyes of the authorities, and the magnetic field that seems to go with the eyes, expanding and contracting her. Third, being drawn into a graveyard.

Let's see what develops if we take the "time" in the dream as part of timeless space. Since the patient painted the dream as well as told it to me, we have the literal space of her painting to assist us, as in Figure 5.1.

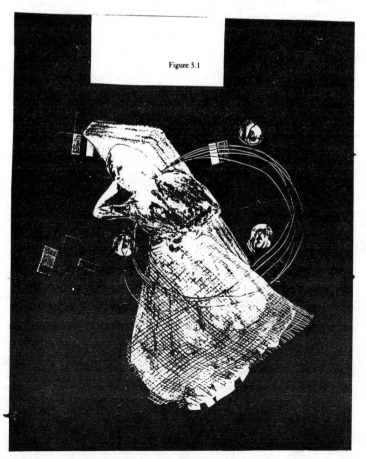

Figure 5.1

As Hillman would say, the patient and I began to moisten the dream images, as follows. Starry nights on the desert refer to the patient's childhood growing up in the country. She would comfort herself in high school, lying on her back in the swimming pool, looking at the stars, while talking out loud to her father, who sat silently in a chair by the edge of the pool. In this telling, the patient's eyes became tearful, pained. Her father never said a word. Perhaps, he wasn't listening at all.

I added that her chairmen might not be listening at all, either, for they were precisely in the space of her father. She replied, her tearfulness and pain more evident, that she had once believed in these men, when they were young challengers who seemed idealistic. Now, they cared only for themselves. I replied that this was very hard for her to bear. She wanted to bring the starry night to earth. Perhaps, she could bear her fall from the stars, if she understood that men can hardly help this terrible change in themselves. Prometheus challenges Zeus, but he too will become a new order. The young turn old, when they start defending their places on the top of the staircase (Kott, 1987; original, 1974).

Back in the dream images, her pain again worsened as we discussed the expanding and contracting of herself by the magnetic field. She felt sucked in, and pulled out in endless alternation in complete helplessness. Then, she is in the graveyard.

I suggest that this is a picture of an intolerable position, which will finally kill her. The alternation of inflation and deflation by the force field of the staircase of power // is interrupted by a hiatus, where she is thrown into the graveyard.

The following week she began by telling me she had located a new office at some distance from the chairmen, by which she hoped to keep some psychological distance on their maneuvering. It was as if she were now half-way between the stars and earth, and facing them. If she went along with their meetings, she would be invisible to their self-serving // but if she objected, she could be sure that she would be the messenger bearing bad news. If this registered a great deal of pain in her face, it was a little better than placing them behind her like listening fathers.

Healing by Dying

The third aspect of Hillman's underworld perspective that seems powerful to me, after the necessity of destruction and after the abrogation of time, is the idea of release from an eternal circling. This idea is exactly what Dante was picturing in 1300 in his Inferno. The damned are stuck in vicious circles, which are timeless, and which need to be seen to be destroyed.

In archaic Western symbolism, the circle is a place of death. We find it in the sepulchral ring or burial barrow later recapitulated in Christian circular churchyards. Both the wheel and the ring (especially as wreath) may be read as underworld symbols. To be put on the wheel in punishment (as Ixion) is to be put into an archetypal place, tied to the turns of fortune, the turns of the moon and fate, and the endless repetitions of coming eternally back to the same experiences without release. Everything moving and nothing changing, all life as deja vu. (pp. 16-161)

Every tie in our lives can become a circle of death:

> Rings are closed circles and the circle closes on us whether in the marriage band, the crowning laurel, or the wreath on the grave. . . . A wheel puts the closed circle in motion, and now we are in a cyclical, compulsive rolling, no end to it. (p. 161)

One of the very disturbing ideas I had in the early 90s as I began to take plot seriously in the lives of my patients was that there only seemed to be three of them, and that they were entirely circular in the form of what I called a "strange loop" (Gustafson, 1992). The most common, by far, I called subservience, by which I meant that the patient devoted herself to service, gradually swung into outrage, and felt guilty, and crept back to her post of service. The rage got her too far out, like a comet at apogee. A strange loop is a circle folded on itself, as it is in Figure 5.2.

Figure 5.2

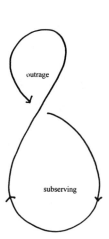

If you think of my previous patient, lying on the staircase of power in a magnetic field, you can imagine her eternal cycle. Contracted, deflated, at the perigee, as she is ignored in subserving the chairmen who do not see her // Expanded, inflated, at the apogee, as she is filled with rage which terrifies her.

If it helps to be able to bear the image of the cycle of hell in which one is stuck, it also helps to have the way out posed. If there is no Purgatorial Mountain to climb, then there is nowhere to go outside of the circle. Since 1992, I have learned to see the dilemma, and its two horns, which needs to be posed as the topography of hell (Gustafson, 1995a, 1995b). In other words, my patient will be terribly injured if she subserves chairmen who do not see her like her father did not see her // and she will be killed if she makes herself fully visible in her anger, like all messengers of bad news. She will be impaled on the inner horn, or the outer horn, of her harsh dilemma, as in Figure 5.3.

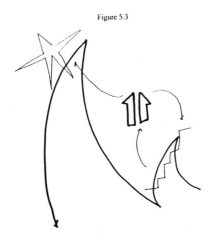

Figure 5.3

The way through the horns, which she is already grasping, is to keep herself from being less injured, facing them, instead of lying with them behind her while she gazes at the stars // while choosing her occasions to object carefully, and even slyly. She can still ascend to the heavens, but she also has to descend to the staircase of history. A second perpetual circle is what I called an overpowering story (Gustafson, 1992) or a story of entitlement (Gustafson, 1995a; 1995b). It is the reverse of subservience. The patient's constant attitude of self-admiration (Reich, 1933; Gustafson, 1986) creates a perigee of inflation // which is crushed and sends the patient into an apogee of deflation.

What is Wrong with Hillman's Underworld Perspective and the Jungian Religion of Greek Gods

If I feel quite indebted to Hillman for his perspective from below (and to Dennis Merritt for acquainting me with Lopes-Pedrazza and Paris), I certainly do not intend to be confined by it as the final world. As one of his fellow travelers puts it,

. . . each God and Goddess expresses an area of weakness as well as an area of strength (p. 114, Paris, 1990)

I would say the same for this entire perspective of the underworld. It is an area of strength, and it is an area of weakness. How so? I have demonstrated, I hope, its powers of delivery from death, by taking death's powers seriously.

Yet, there is something all too serious about Hillman in his cause. While he claims that the underworld perspective is humorous, I have yet even to smile faintly, reading him. I think this is because he is grinding an ax. This is most evident in his most historical essay, called "Peaks and Vales" (1979a). Here he argues that the disaster of Western civilization goes back to the Church Fathers at Nicaea (787 A.D.) and Byzantium (869), when they made a disastrous compromise. Up until this time, there was still room for image (soul), as can be seen in old Byzantium. The New Testament was an attack on image, dream and soul (psyche), in the name of spirit (pneuma), but human nature remained tri-partite spirit, soul and body:

> The Epistles, the presentation of doctrine, the teaching of the school, could expose its theology and psychology without too much need for the word soul. For Paul four times was enough.

> Much the same is true in regard to dreams and myths. The word to dream does not appear in the New Testament; dream (onar) occurs only in three chapters of Matthew (1, 2 and 27). (p. 55)

Seven centuries later, the decisive and final death of image takes place according to Hillman:

> At Nicaea a distinction was made between the image as such, its power, its full divine or archetypal reality, and what the image represents, points to, means. These images become allegories. When images become allegories, the iconoclasts have won. The image itself has become subtly depotentiated (p. 56).

This is why Hillman hates (p. 57) spirit (pneuma), because it makes soul (psyche) a captive to its doctrines or ascent to the heavens. His essay certainly makes a fierce brief against this destruction of imagination. It has largely taken place, in Western culture, which has become a staircase of winning and losing.

What makes Hillman so serious is that he is attacking a dead culture of spirit which is bad // by substituting an older religion of soul which is good. This is the ax he is always grinding. This becomes his allegory, or continuous sermon. It will save us, to allow the underworld to destroy the deadness of Western culture.

I am not so sure. I would rather the Marx brothers destroy the opera, than Hillman. It releases a great deal more vitality. When Hillman, Lopez-Pedrazza (1977), Paris (1990) and the lesser Jungians begin to run on about what Hermes is really up to, I want to run away. They seem all too familiar with him, which, itself is a contradiction of his supposed nature. It really is not possible, so the presumption is wrong from the start. Listen to Lopez-Pedrazza, beginning:

If we psychotherapists behave in too dignified a way in psychotherapy, then how can we contact the great percentage of patients who mostly come to the analyst in the first place to discuss the undignified episodes in their lives? Only the undignified Hermes in the analyst can constellate a communication with the undignified side of life . . . (p. 19)

Already, from a fine feeling for indignity, he is "constellate(ing) a communication" and soon he will be bowing to Jung's arcane obsessions with the hermaphrodite in alchemy. Still, he has beautiful things to say, briefly, like

Hermes has no need to fight for his center; he does not have one. (p. 23)

Yet to write a book and go on and on about Hermes is a contradiction to glimpsing him. Paris (1990) is worse, for her tone of familiarity with Hermes is like she is introducing one of her favorite uncles (contrast this with R. Otto (originally 1923; 1958) who retains the objective experience of being shaken by a god). Still, a sentence shines forth here and there:

The most eloquent representation of Hermes is probably the bust with two faces: one is turned toward humans, the other toward the Gods, thus symbolizing the dual meaning of all reality, the double meaning of all speech (p. 62).

Shakespeare understood this, in his doubling of adjectives, one for "the gods" and one for "the pit" (Hughes, 1992):

O spirit of love, how quick and fresh art thou,
That, notwithstanding thy capacity
Receiveth as the sea, nought enters there,
Of what validity and pitch soe'er
But falls into abatement and low price,
Even in a minute.
                              Twelfth Night, I, i, 9-14.

Hughes catches the trouble:

The three words here that might have given his groundlings pause are "capacity," "validity" and "abatement." . . . When he tosses the fine word to the Lords' box, he bends to the groundlings and quite shamelessly adds "that means a cutback to . . . low price." (Hughes, pp. 141-147)

I have skipped over Hughes on the similar translation of capacity to "receiveth as the sea" and validity to "pitch," but I am simply trying to illustrate that art has the quickness, which is labored in these Jungians.

The Problem of Deadness and Vitality

Vitality is not a substance which lasts very well in this world. Certainly, it lasts badly in its usual vessels. From the poet who lasts best, we get the tersest statement of the trouble:

Youth's a stuff will not endure. <u>Twelfth Night</u>, II, iii, 49

Shakespeare has the best maps, because he has more dimensions than whatever vessel is proposed. As Bateson argued about mapping,

> No, you see it's not possible to map beauty-and ugliness onto a flat piece of paper (p. 210, 1979)

Coming back to Hillman and the Jungians. They are helpful insofar as they show us what is already dead. Especially when it is hard for us to face it.

They are harmful, when they subsume everything to their underworld perspective -- for they just cut out other dimensions of vitality. For example, Hillman is simply dead wrong to argue that the Church destroyed image and imagination at Nicaea (787) and Byzantium (869) (Ruth Gustafson, personal communication). If it were not for the Church, we would never have had Gothic cathedrals and western painting and music. The soul did remain in the Church, with the spirit, and with the body, as Henry Adams has shown as well as anyone in <u>Mont Saint-Michel and Chartres</u> (1904 originally, 1986). It was the Dynamo that killed the Virgin, by about 1900. Hillman is just weak on history.

Still, I admire Hillman's contribution. He did pose the problem of deadness and vitality. Ever since I began contemplating this chapter in earnest, I have been dreaming from his perspective of things in my world that are dead which I could not admit. I have dreamt of:

> Being Jan Kott going to Germany as a dramaturge in
> a dead theatre of psychoanalysis,
> Fleeing downtown Saginaw, Michigan (where I grew up)
> over a dead (Saginaw) river into an underworld
> of murderous outsiders (even crossing a tram track
> where my great-grandfather and namesake, James
> MacMillan, was murdered in Pittsburgh)
> Being invited to "Henry Straub's Place by the Sea"
> which was a Buckminster Fuller polygon of
> compression, with the sea tumbling in harness,
> Visiting my dead father's garden, where the oars of
> the crew of Odysseus were bound in a circle of
> talking heads facing inward, a mound to the end
> of adventure.

This is just four in a row, in a much longer series. I mean to say that the underworld is <u>a kind of imagination</u>, which agitates my own.

I have also noticed that Lewis Carroll (1865) and Mark Twain (1885) were also agitated by the walking dead, so that Alice meets nothing else in her underworld, and Huck meets nothing else when he and Jim go ashore. Their journeys take them into very interesting topography. Alice goes down, sideways, tiny, HUGE, down, into the skies, flat, into the trees. She just has startling changes of direction whenever stuck. Huck and Jim just get back on that big and mysterious River, to fly from the assaultive men that are everywhere along the shores. In other words, they duck out of the horizontal axis of history, which flows east to west in the United States to the frontier (Frederick Jackson Turner, originally, 1920; 1994), into the vertical <u>axis mundi</u> of the Mississippi, as in Figure 5.4, flowing north to south.

Figure 5.4

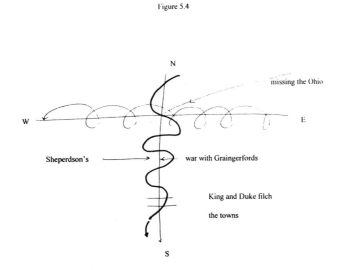

The vitality of Alice and of Huck and Jim, seems to me to come from their ability to change directions and to develop in their education. Change of direction alone could mean go around in circles, like the drifter in the American West who simply repeats himself in different places as if he were a tumble weed. A lot of people just went farther west, over and over, and did about the same thing (Turner, 1920, 1994) in each new location. Development in one's education means that one also integrates or puts together more dimensions in one's work.

Two Dreams of the Author

For example, I put together between 1970 and 1990 many experiences of the social world into a book with Lowell Cooper (1990) called <u>The Modern Contest</u>. One of its central ideas is that it is possible and desirable to distinguish a number of compartments between the inner world and the outer world: like, solitude, play, civility, the central compartment (of ambiguity), contest, and war (Chapter 11, Gathering Strength). I argued that many grave errors are made in reading which compartment the subject is located in: for example, imagining he is in civility when he is in contest. I suggested the free and clear passage between these compartments might be a blessing. Notice it is a free movement along the horizontal. It is even better if I can also move freely along the vertical. I can sight what is dead from the underworld, and I can laugh from above like the Olympians.

A Dream of the Kingdom of the Dead. After my long series of underworld dreams, I seemed to have one as a kind of summation of this entire kingdom of Hades:

> I was visiting an Irish clan, and, just as I came in the door, I saw a red-haired mother (of the IRA certainly) go out with a grim expression like she was on her way to killing someone. Her child caught my attention on the floor below me, mishandling a cat. He was all mouth, with huge lips, and huge teeth. I foolishly tried to set him straight about the poor cat.

> Some of my colleagues of narrative psychotherapy were about to drop me off on my street, but veered away, because they had urgent business to attend to first. I was told I could find my baggage in a department store. I went there and saw a kind of mass grave of baggage about a block long. I realized it was impossible to dig mine out of there.

> I was in Yankee Stadium, where the oddest baseball game I ever saw was going on. The pitcher stood up out of one deck, and threw the ball to a batter who stood up out of another deck, and knocked it into the stratosphere. Acrobats did flips down the decks, and right over their edges, into . . . certain death.

The first scene alludes to a patient of mine, who lives in a killing household, and also alludes to the mad Duchess and her child in Alice, as it were, superimposed. The comparison between the two families makes my helpfulness absurd: it is crazy to instruct a monster. The second scene alludes to the circuit of psychotherapy shows, and makes appearing there also absurd: it is crazy anonymous like airport baggage. The third alludes to the Beatles in Yankee Stadium, and makes the cult of youth absurd, and the pitcher and batter stand on the shoulders of the crowds in the two decks, while the other youths tumble into the void. The central images of these three scenes are illustrated in Figure 5.5.

Figure 5.5

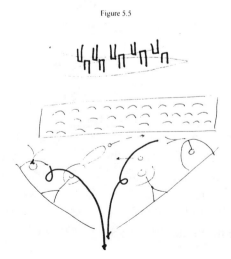

I enjoyed this dream very much, for its clarity on both the horizontal and vertical axes. Horizontally, I was clear, reading left to right from private to public, what is deadly about certain families, certain circuits of psychotherapy, and certain cults of the mass culture itself. Vertically, I was also clear, because I could see from above or from below.

From above, the monster mouth is silly, like the barren mountains of baggage, and the useless acrobatic plunges. Yet, there is also something beautiful in the heroics of the IRA lady, and the urgent colleagues, and the batter and pitcher rising literally out of the anonymous crowds in the decks. From below, it is just the dead circles of hell. I had rather have perspective from above and below. What if painters could only paint from below?

<u>Dreams of the River Coming Out of the Mountains of China</u>. About a week later, just as I was about to close this chapter, I dreamt nearly a final say for me on the limitations of the underworld perspective.

I was standing alongside a huge river coming out of mountains of China. I was deciding which way to go. A fisherman came along walking right up the river, and I declined to join him in such a huge current. A single file of monks in black rose up a long series of switchbacks leading to Tibet, and I declined this steep path. So far I had been unwilling to take either the low or the high road. Then I noticed a beautiful baroque Church beside the river, and went inside. I was dismayed at its emptiness which blinded me with a white sheen, and I went out promptly.

I decided to edit one of the videotapes of my interviews. An Irish nymph appeared from nowhere and waltzed with me alongside the river in a beautiful back and forth. All of this is pictured in Figure 5.6.

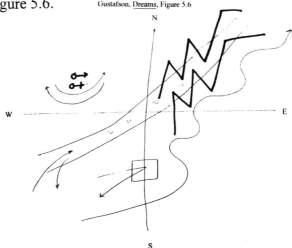

Gustafson, <u>Dreams</u>, Figure 5.6

The river coming out of China alludes to my grandfather, David, who was a missionary in China from 1919 to 1925, and took his family up into the mountains to get out of the summer heat, at Mokanshan. The fisherman is he of the poem of Yeats, "The Fisherman" (1919), a hero of mine since college. The single file of Buddhist monks alludes to a friend who has lived with them in Tibet. The low or high road is from the well-known song about getting to Scotland. The baroque church is a building on our campus, and the empty white sheen inside alludes to El

Greco. My mother is Scotch-Irish, and was once a great company for me in my youth. Oh yes, the waltzing alludes to a poem by Theodore Roethke, "My Papa's Waltz" (1948). Roethke was from my hometown, Saginaw, Michigan, and his sister, June, was my ninth-grade English teacher, and the best grammarian I have ever come across. The waltz is my papa's waltz. Finally, my son, Ian, loved to pen beautiful drawings as a child of the mountains of China.

My dream replies to Hillman. Yes, you are right about youth wading upriver against the torrent of the unconscious. Yes, you are right about the altitude of monks in flight from history. Yes, you are right that academic churches are dead. No, you are wrong that that is all, for look what my grandfather, and my spiritual father, and myself and my son have done. Look at what the company of my youthful mother did for me. History has its development, especially family history. And Heaven has its dances, as my friends, Roethke and Yeats, have long taught me.

In other words, I will move freely east to west along horizontal axes, and I will move north to south along vertical axes, and this is an improvement on five years ago. Mostly, then, I knew about getting into the mountains to flee the dead, like the Buddhists and like my grandfather of the Old Testament. I am learning better to waltz. I go more freely up and down, into heaven and hell.

A Dream of a Musical Score. My unconscious always has another reply, for it opposes everything I say, in the next night. Vitality comes, as Hillman said, about overturning every literal thing. I dreamt:

I was off to England to a conference on groups, where I was supposed to be an authority (I am). Deviously, I found the place, and put my chair near the first speaker in an oblong (not enough spirit up or soul down, as Jung would say) space. As the conversation (spirit) moved from one speaker to another, I moved my chair next to that next speaker, and quickly traversed the length of the room, as depicted in Figure 5.7.

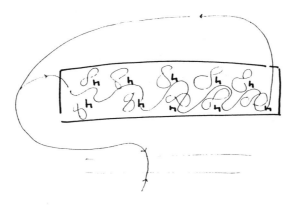

Figure 5.7

When I reached the far right end of the room, I fled the way I had come, looking over my shoulder like a fugitive (Orpheus) from hell (Hades). I feared I would be pursued, but I got home by the way I had come.

I was enjoying my quickness at their expense, and so Hillman has a very good point about a certain enduring instinct, from the underworld. It is as at home on earth or in heaven (Guthrie, 1950). Only when I drew its path did I see the beauty of its music, moving up and down, left to right, through the static of the strange loops.

Chapter 6. Developments from Existentialism

The later developments from existentialism, in Sullivan, Laing, and Margulies, occur on the margin of the school of psychoanalysis. Each opens up possibilities of perception in the dream which would otherwise be lost to us. Sullivan's view is concerned with oversights in the present external world. Sullivan and Laing both are concerned with situations which are so untenable, as to leave the patient no option but psychosis. This is the first third of this chapter.

Margulies' view is an extension from the work of Semrad, which was also a venture into the domain of untenable existence. Semrad's work was to make an existence in hell more bearable by sharing its <u>pain</u>. Margulies was steeped in this tradition with Semrad, and took it farther into sharing the patient's <u>perceptual</u> world, of sight, and hearing, and taste, and smell, and kinesthetic motion. Margulies borrows the term "inscape" from Gerard Manley Hopkins (1966) for his inner mapping of the world of the patient. The patient has an inscape, and the doctor builds his in parallel. This is the second third of this chapter.

This going-with the patient into a shared inscape is so persuasive that, at first, it seemed to me the only thing to do. I too began with Semrad, as my first teacher, so I share with both Semrad and Margulies the conviction that it is absolutely necessary to feel one's way into the patient's world (Margulies, p. 33, 1989). Anything less is too far away. It arouses the most hesitant of patients. It gives them company in the most unbearable things. It supplies a kind of missing parent.

Yet it stops quite short of full company, as I explain in the third third of this chapter. It lacks many of the dimensions we have been looking into in the previous five chapters. It is so highly familial. These inscapes are familial inscapes, with hardly any of the politics of Freud himself, the religious dimensions of Jung, the heaven of Hopkins, the underworld of Hillman, the musical variations of Erikson, or all of these dimensions in Dante. Margulies refers a great deal to Proust for precedence, but it is a Proust without the cruel sense of in-group and out-group in society that is the "Overture" to <u>Swann's Way</u> (Proust, 1913). So, it turns out to be one kind of inscape, in a much larger set of inscapes, which we have been collecting here in Part I of this book, and which we now bring to a close, completing the canon of the first hundred years of the use of the unconscious in dreams.

Sullivan and Laing on Dreams as Perspectives on the Life Situation

Sullivan makes a very odd existentialist. He is pragmatic like William James (1902 originally, 1958), but he lacks the interest in the transcendental. You will find hardly any reference to heaven and hell in Sullivan. If he is a contemporary of Binswanger and Boss, you will not find him trekking up Binswanger's mountain of extravagance, nor will you find him in Boss's hell of a latrine. Indeed, he hardly has written about dreams at all.

What he did write (Lowell Cooper, personal communication) is invaluable to me, as it pictures a kind of existence of oversights. In Sullivan's view, the dream is a metaphor of the patient's "life situation" which he cannot turn around and face up to by himself:

If one awakes from a terror dream, it is quite certain that one's life situation is treacherous. If one wakes with inexplicable anxiety, it is quite certain that one's life situation includes plenty of cause for anxiety. The fact that he knows nothing about what he dreamed is a suggestion, not an inevitable index, but a strong suggestion that the problem is in the field of something dissociated from the self system, or by the self system, if you will (p. 69, 1946).

In Sullivan's view, the self system is for security. It is a little performance, like the subservience of Walter Mitty with his wife (Thurber, 1942). However, the security-operation has to get rid of dimensions which would threaten the establishment in which the performer has a foothold. Thus, Walter Mitty dare not murmur against his wife's management of him. He has to go and get his galoshes, as directed:

"I don't need overshoes," said Mitty. She put her mirror back into her bag. "We've been through all that," she said, getting out of the car. "You're not a young man any longer." (p. 1405)

Mostly, his protest is stilled, until he gets out of her presence:

He raced the engine a little. "Why don't you wear your gloves? Have you lost your gloves?" Walter Mitty reached in a pocket and brought out the gloves. He put them on, but after she had turned and gone into the building and he had driven on to a red light, he took them off again. "Pick it up, brother!" snapped a cop as the light changed, and Mitty hastily pulled on his gloves and lurched ahead. (p. 1405)

So here in Thurber (1942) about the same time as Sullivan's first lectures (1940, published 1946), we have a portrait of an existence of a shaky self system for security, which is dissociating the dangerous rebellion. God seems to be dead, with his higher and lower worlds, and poor humans are left to scamper like Mitty in the flats of Connecticut.

Now, dream in this kind of existence is a chance to relax the performance, quite like Mitty getting away from the authorities (his wife and the cop):

It is the part of life in which we are almost by definition relieved from the necessity of maintaining security. (Sullivan, 1953, p. 329)

Not quite. The self system remains vigilant in sleep, if the dissociated material is too overwhelming to let loose:

Evidences of its actual state of functional activity are perhaps most vividly demonstrated in the relatively frequent occurrence of the onset of schizophrenia during sleep. Quite a number of people who are tense and extremely uncomfortable while awake, have a frightful nightmare, one night, which they cannot wake up from, even though they objectively "wake up," and not very long after that such people become unquestionably schizophrenic throughout their apparent waking life. (Sullivan, 1953, pp. 330-331)

To some extent, the vigilant self system can forestall the nightmare from which one cannot awake (psychosis) by waking the patient up. If the nightmare's content is also obliterated, it is a blank night terror (p. 334).

But if the dissociated material is not too great, the subject can let go of vigilance: Thus, the depth of sleep is in a certain sense really a simple function of the extent to which the activity of the self-system can be abandoned . . . (p. 331)

We go over into a realm, where we are not watching ourselves very closely:

But what we can recall of dreaming is never any too adequate, unless the dream is very brief and marked by tremendous emotion. My point is that there is an impassable barrier between covert operations when one is asleep and covert operations and reports of them when one is awake . . . in essence, the barrier is impassable. In other words, for the purposes of my theory, one never, under any circumstances, deals directly with dreams. What one deals with in psychiatry, and actually in a great many other aspects of life, are recollections pertaining to dreams . . . (pp. 331-332, my italics).

Interesting language. Sullivan's "covert operations" nowadays would be applied to things like the CIA (Central Intelligence Agency). That, precisely, is the kind of world Sullivan inhabits with his patients. There are security operations and there are covert operations. Sullivan lived much of his career in Washington, D.C.

Kafka, Kundera and Surrealism and the Power of Dislocation

The barrenness of such a modern world in two chambers, the Bureau of Security Operations and the Bureau of Covert Operations, oddly lets loose the modern imagination of the surreal. Perhaps, Kafka is the transitional figure in writing (1883-1924), with his first stories emerging in 1912. Perhaps, Max Ernst is the central figure in the visual arts of the surreal, starting about 1918. Stravinsky had already released into music "The Rite of Spring" in 1912, while Freud's Rat Man (1909, Notes Upon a Case of Obsessional Neurosis) is certainly a surreal composition.

By "surreal" is meant literally "above the real." The term was coined by Guillaume Apollinaire in 1917, and its manifesto was written by Andre Breton in 1924. It succeeded the Dadaism of 1915-1922, which means "hobbyhorse" in French and was supposedly chosen at random from the dictionary. According to the Dadaists like Tristan Tzara,

the only law was chance, and the only reality was that of the imagination (Grolier Encyclopedia CD-Rom)

Surrealism in the hands of Ernst is more than this, although he borrowed some of their tactics of the random and of the collage and of the shocking, for example, in

A Little Machine Built by Minimax-Dadamax for the Fearless Pollination of Female Suction Cups in Early Menopause and Similar Fruitless Efforts (Spies, 1991, p. 14)

The premise was that the real was not to be believed, and the surreal glimpsed the strange broken-up world after World War I. How did you get these stolen glimpses? Ernst has a beautiful suggestion:

When you walk through the woods keeping your eyes fixed on the ground, you will doubtless discover many wonderful, miraculous things. But when you suddenly look upwards into the sky, you are overcome by the revelation of another, equally miraculous world. (Spies, p. 10)

Try it. If you take away the sky, the ground is a strange and dense and intricate world. If you suddenly take away the ground, you are thrown into the sky. Deprived of the usual mixture of ground-and-sky, you see in an utterly different way. This illustrates the profound effect of the horizon on what you can see within it. See Wölfflin's (1932 originally, 1950) discussion of the shift in perspective from classical to baroque painting, for comparison. Very succinctly, the classical perspective is a flat plane in the foreground, while the baroque sets up a series of planes leading into depth on a diagonal. Varnedoe (1990) discusses the next big shift from the baroque perspective to the impressionist perspective. Very succinctly, the elevation of the horizon above our eyebrows puts us right into the foreground plane. Curiously, one could dream in classical, baroque, impressionist, or surreal perspectives. Certainly, they select for what is to be privileged in utterly different lines.

Now, coming back to Sullivan and the departure from the real to the surreal. Once the modern world becomes an exercise in security, in terms of the security operations of a corporation, or academic department, or a military group, its ground-and-sky, if you will, is its routine. It becomes terribly vulnerable to covert operations, of intelligence, of imagination, of art, which simply look at it from a different angle and alter its horizon. It is not hard by this means to expose its ridiculous repetition.

Kafka was a genius at this. For example, in the tiny story of two pages, called "My Neighbor" (1971) (thanks to Michael Moran for showing me this piece), the subject is the operator of a small business:

Two girl clerks with typewriters and ledgers in the anteroom, my own room with writing desk, safe, consulting table, easy chair and telephone: such is my entire working apparatus. (p. 424)

Here we are in the pure realm of security operations, whose content could be anything from legal services to real estate services to literary agency.

Kafka throws us into the surreal simply by doubling the picture, so the subject has a neighbor in duplicate named Harras, by whom he now becomes harassed:

> Sometimes I meet Harras on the stairs, he seems always to be in an extraordinary hurry, for he literally shoots past me . . . Like the tail of a rat he has slipped through . . . (p. 425)

If the double is a rat, the plot hastens on:

> If I wanted to exaggerate -- and one must often do that so as to make things clear in one's mind -- I might assert that Harras does not require a telephone, he uses mine, he pushes his sofa against the wall and listens . . . gets up at the point where the matter has become clear to him, flies through the town with his usual haste and, before I have hung up the receiver, is already at his goal working against me. (p. 425)

Thus, the entirely rational and so-called real is terribly vulnerable to dislocation. It is so empty, that the demonic can flip it over quite like this. It is so dry, it has no weight. Of course, that is why psychiatry gets called upon to prescribe drugs to put these thin souls to sleep, and to get them up again the next morning.

Kundera (1984) (thanks again to Michael Moran for this reference) builds upon Kafka's skill of dislocation, of the horizon. Tomas is unfaithful to Tereza, who says in words,

> I know your infidelities are no great tragedy. (p. 59)

Yet, by telling him the three repeating dreams, of her cats going berserk, of her own execution, of never-ending humiliation after death, she dislocates him. Kundera comments:

> Our dreams prove that to imagine -- to dream about things that have not happened -- is among mankind's deepest needs. Herein lies the danger . . . Tomas lived under the hypnotic spell cast by the excruciating beauty of Tereza's dreams. . . . Dreaming is a game of the imagination, a game that is a value in itself.

In other words, the startling beauty of the dislocation upsets the banal routine and makes it unbearable to resume. If security operations are the group life of mankind in the twentieth century, and define what is real, then only the surreal has a chance to turn it over. Now, we can turn back to Sullivan and see what he is up to with his sudden glimpses from another angle.

Three Dreams from Sullivan

Sullivan's strategy will be to take the dream as an incomplete report of recollection, which needs to be completed:

> I have heard accounts of dreams which impressed me as definitely truncated, as very highly improbable accounts of what happened. In many accounts of dreams there are

areas that are <u>foggy and uncommunicative</u> . . . At those points . . . there is no reason in the world why we should not make the same efforts to obtain completeness. (p. 332, 1953)

<u>Sullivan's Own Dream of the Spider</u>. Sullivan says that he had this dream very early in his study of schizophrenia:

> . . . in order to realize that I had some grave barriers to the task which the gods had brought me . . My dream started with a great series of these beautiful geometric patterns . . . that spiders weave on grass . . . each strand being very nicely midway between the one in front of it and the one behind it, and so on -- quite a remarkable textile, and incidentally I am noticeably interested in textiles.//Then the textile pattern became a tunnel running backward after the fashion of the tunnel-web spiders, and then the spider began to approach. And as the spider approached, it grew and grew into truly stupendous and utterly horrendous proportions. And I awakened extremely shaken and was unable to obliterate the spider, which continued to be a dark spot on the sheet which I knew perfectly well would re-expand into the spider if I tried to go to sleep . . . (p. 335, 1953)

I put my sign for a hiatus (//) halfway through Sullivan's report, for there is the drop-off into the abyss. There is the dislocation, from a beautiful geometric textile that he imagines to be the study of schizophrenia // to a nightmare tunnel of a predator of infinite increase. First, we think we are in location A, of the beautiful geometry, and then we find we are dislocated to location B, of being at the mercy of the predator, as in Figure 6.1.

Figure 6.1

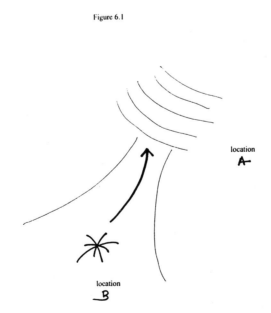

The surreal dislocates the security operation which is not secure, by jumping across the hiatus into the covert, dissociated material.

<u>The Dream of Sullivan's Assistant</u>. Notice the disjunction in the next dream of Sullivan's Assistant who became

> of great interest to a bitterly paranoid woman . . . she seemed to be suffering frightfully from his very casual heterosexual life away from her, and I thought such worries would grow . . . (p. 336, 1953)

> This dream is set at the foot of the Loch Raven dam. There is an island, very small, very green -- a lovely island -- not far from shore, on which this assistant of mine and I are walking, engaged in conversation. He gazes up at the dam and sees his fiancee at the top of it, and is not particularly distracted in his conversation with me. (//) Then observes that the area of water between the island and the shore, over which we had stepped, is rapidly widening. He awakens in terror, finding himself leaping out of bed into a pool of moonlight in the bedroom. (pp. 336-337)

It is secure // it is not secure. The topology is suddenly altered by the covert operation.

<u>The Dream of Sullivan's Schizoid Obsessional Patient</u>. Again, the dislocation is surreal.

> I heard data of how vaguely annoying and depressing his mother had been for several years past. . . about all mother did was somehow to depress and annoy him, discourage him vaguely . . Now this patient dreamed of a Dutch windmill. It was a very beautiful scene, with a carefully cared-for lawn leading up to the horizon on which this beautiful Dutch windmill revolved in the breeze. (//) Suddenly he was within the windmill. And there everything was wrack and ruin, with rust inches deep, it was perfectly obvious that the windmill hadn't moved in years. . . . I said, "That is, beautiful, active on the outside-- utterly dead and decayed within. Does it provoke anything?" He said, "My God, my mother." That was his trouble, you see. The mother had become a sort of zombie -- unutterably crushed by the burdens that had been imposed upon her. She was simply a sort of weary phonograph offering cultural platitudes, without any thought of what they did to anybody or what they meant. (1953, pp. 338-339)

Again, the security operation has been to see the lively outside of mother which is reassuring. Cross over the line (//) to the inside, and the covert operation shows the horror of the already dead. The surreal dream simply is a dislocation.

Laing's Surreal Dilemmas

I will deal with Laing's extension of Sullivan briefly, because it is a simple extension. It doubles the terror, by posing it as a dilemma (see Gustafson, 1995a, Chapter 1 on malignant dilemmas).

> This man was married to a very lively and vivacious woman, highly spirited, with a forceful personality and a mind of her own. He maintained a paradoxical relationship

with her in which, in one sense, he was entirely alone and isolated and, in another sense, he was almost a parasite. He dreamt, for instance, that he was a clam stuck to his wife's body. (p. 48, 1959)

Laing poses the man's position as follows:

> Utter detachment and isolation are regarded as the only alternative to a clam- or vampire-like attachment . . . The individual oscillates perpetually between the two extremes, each equally unfeasible. He comes to live rather like those mechanical toys which have a positive tropism that impels them towards a stimulus until they reach a specific point, whereupon a built-in negative tropism directs them away until the positive tropism takes over again, this oscillation being repeated <u>ad infinitum</u>. (p. 53)

There's horror for you, which is going to become progressively dead as in Figure 6.2.

Figure 6.2

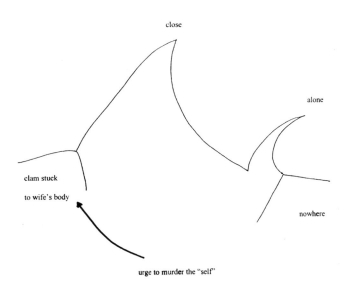

The individual is in a world in which, like some nightmare Midas, everything he approaches becomes dead. There are now perhaps only two further possibilities open to him at this stage:

1. He may decide to "be himself" despite everything, or
2. He may attempt to murder his self.

Both these projects, if carried through, are likely to result in manifest psychosis (p. 147). . . . It is in fact such attacks from such inner phantoms that compel the individual to say he has been murdered, or that "he" has murdered his "self." (p. 158)

Sullivan came himself very close to this self-murder from the gigantic tunnel-spider.

Margulies and Inscapes

Margulies gave himself the project of finding his way in these frightening landscapes of the surreal, which we have introduced via Sullivan and Laing. What he adds is a willingness to sense them in their particular and unbearable detail. The patient will get his acute company.

Red Threads in the Labyrinth

Certain sensory details turn out to be like red threads in the labyrinth of dreams. They link up everything, which is of emotional importance. It is as if the labyrinthine computer had lost access to a huge part of its memory bank. Because it was too unbearable, it was dissociated. Yet it is covertly linked up, after all, by this secret cross-referencing of a bizarre sensation like slipperiness. When we are at the edge of a slippery landscape in a dream, we are about to be dislocated into a surreal world. Surreal seems exactly the right word to me, for this disjunctive world is truly more real // than the everyday real world. However, the patient cannot stand to go into it by himself.

Curiously, Freud had an obsessional patient who came to him in a delirium. The delirium was an entire world of the shameful activities of rats, for which the patient had a rat language (Freud, 1909; Gustafson, 1995a) which plays on the strange linkages of the root word in German:

> Raten is linked to Ratten in German as rats are to installments. Speilratte are gambling debts, heiraten is to marry. . . . The patient's survival is to transform himself into a rat, so he can increase his installments or Ratten, and get pals for gambling or Spielratte, and marry a rat-wife or Heiraten, thereby generating a long line of rats or Raten. (Gustafson, 1995b, p. 46)

Thus, it appears that it is possible for verbal play to be the linkage to the surreal world that is dissociated.

Reich (1930, 1933) later showed that characteristic gestures could perform this linkage as well. They gave away what Reich called "the constant attitude." For example, a patient in a first session

> kept apologizing for the most trifling things; on arriving and on leaving he made several deep bows . . . When he asked for something, he would stroke the analyst's arm (p. 83, Reich, 1933; Gustafson, 1986, 1997, Chapter 4)

This "passive-feminine character" turned out to be the patient's chief mode of surviving his childhood. By seeing where the attitude turned up, Reich would be led down into the entire (de-) file of his troubles. They were linked by the constant attitude that got him out of them. Ordinarily, Reich found that the attitude was borrowed from an admired adult in the child's vicinity. For example, one little boy turned himself into a pompous English Lord, like his uncle (Reich, 1931).

It will turn out that there are several other devices in this category of linkages to a dissociated and surreal world, besides verbal play, gesture and bizarre sensations. Let us turn to Margulies and his discovery, about the latter form of connection.

A Dream of a Slippery Landscape. Margulies abruptly drops us into this nightmare, from which a woman awoke terrified:

> My son and I were going to a park, just for a walk. We were separated -- no, he ran up ahead and I started to go up into a town, a small rural town, and I started to go up the road between two buildings. There was a feed mill and a bridge or a walkway connecting two buildings and there were men hanging from the walkway and grabbing people as they walked that way. And my son was ahead of me and I went another way and I got to the park. And there was this row of doors, and I kept opening the door to see if my son was there and he wasn't -- and I was absolutely terrified and then I woke up. And I kept thinking something had happened to him and he wasn't there. And I thought I wasn't there and if he cried out I wouldn't be there.
>
> The other part of the dream that stands out is the road that was around the feed mill -- it was full of ruts and like covered with shit and very slippery and difficult to walk on. And I remember looking down at it and I was surprised and I just kept walking. I was thinking that it was like the logging road to my son's camp which was covered with mud, and the rains made the ground so muddy. (p. 55, 1989)

Margulies has a hunch that the slippery road will get him where he needs to go, because it had reminded him of a previous conversation in which the patient had told him about being a little girl watching pigs get slaughtered. Margulies comments:

> On the edge of my awareness I had constructed a riveting traumatic inscape in parallel detail to her experience. In a manner of speaking, I had slipped on the ground of her inscape. (p. 57)

It is only six years later that Margulies (in preparation) tells how much this slipping dropped him into, right into the patient's perspective. For the patient, mother had been a kind of fat and drunken pig. Murder of pigs was one terror. Becoming one herself in her own menstrual shit and depression and helplessness was another terror. Father had gone off, charming as he could be in his hunting and gambling, abandoning the mother. The patient had been left slipping in these terrible possibilities -- to kill mother the pig, or to be mother the pig.

> Several years later, it turns out that the patient had been date-raped:
> She went home and washed the blood-semen off of her legs and feet -- the blood was everywhere, she said (and I imagine now that awful slippery feeling) -- and she never told a soul.

Even later as Margulies was preparing the latter account, he realized that the slippery slope was also where she left her own child.

Thus, six years later, Margulies looks back at this case and says that it was more than an inscape, but an entire subterranean city:

> I had developed the term "inscape" to help me explore some of these complex sensory aspects of knowing (Margulies, 1989) -- I wanted to understand better how I enter another's experience through my sensory take on things. Apprehending the world view of another, it seems to me, is less like creating a narrative than it is like encountering a city. We visit the experience of another, gaining a familiarity over time. We reflexively -- and out of awareness -- create an inner map of our encounter with another, implicit maps that are under constant revision (Margulies, in preparation).

Thus, this particular city is a subterranean city of slippery slopes. Strange recursiveness. Surreal.

Inscapes

Let us go back to inscapes. Margulies (1989) introduces the term as follows:
The goal of the poetic imagination was to chart the interior terrain, to establish what Gerard Manley Hopkins referred to as the "inscape." (p. 15)

Let us leave aside for the moment what Hopkins meant by inscape, which was intensely religious, charged with God. Margulies has in mind what he calls "a more prosaic use" (p. 147). Several more examples will allow us to grasp his category.

The Dream of the Ascension. Here is a dream explicitly religious, but Margulies is going to make a familial drama out of it, with marvelous sensory findings:

> I am in a church, standing with a group of people. (The patient begins his narrative slowly, even serenely, his body still.) My father says, "Look at that ray of light coming into the church. Go stand in it." I go stand in the light.

> Suddenly, there is a clap of thunder. (Here, to my surprise, he smacks his hands together loudly -- clap!) Dr. Margulies, it was just like that! (His cadence quickens; he is excited and his body animated as he moves to the edge of his seat.) In fact, I actually heard it and woke up -- but I kept dreaming, strange (said with awe and mystery).

> It was very powerful -- it was a lightning bolt that hit me. (His voice rises in pitch and strength, quickening with excitement and elation.) I start to rise higher and higher in the air and can see the chandeliers. My father says, "Look up." I feel fine, very well, happy.

(Now he <u>drops</u> back in his chair, and his voice <u>ebbs</u>.) But then I get concerned that things will get out of control. I decide to come down, and I do -- and my feet <u>firmly</u> hit the ground. (pp. 23-24) <u>My Italics</u>

This dream is a <u>tour de force</u> of all the sensory modalities, which Margulies conducts us through to culminate in the synesthesia:

> . . . here sight, sound and touch come together in a synesthesia. He is literally "thunderstruck" . . (p. 28) . . . When one is ripped up and out of this early church-womb, there is sudden light, noise, lack of control, and one is smacked (slapped) to breath -- and is never again the same. (p. 30)

The point of all of this seems to be less in the interpretation than in feeling it <u>with</u> the patient in each and all of its sensory dimensions. For Margulies, an inscape is <u>a place you go with the patient</u>.

<u>A Dream of a House Torn Up by Gorillas</u>: A briefer example yields the similar logic:

> A woman has the following dream: "Gorillas are tearing up a house, breaking the windows." (p. 48)

Margulies gets her to give a picture of the house, wrecked, and asks her to open the dream door and walk in. It turns out she has just had an emergency gynecological procedure and had the dream the first night home alone. The obvious violation by the surgeon leads to a previous violation by a therapist which leads to a previous violation in childhood, which leads . . .

> Like Russian dolls, possibilities were nested within possibilities (p. 49)

The house is more than a symbol, it is an inscape, it is a city. Margulies also calls this a "dormant inscape." It has to be brought out of dormancy, by going into it with the patient, and thus bringing it back. It is a world brought back.

The Domain of Dormant Inscapes

We are getting very close to D.W. Winnicott's consultations to children, in which he would, at some point, drop from the shared "squiggles," into asking for a dream (Winnicott, 1971b). We will take this up in Part II of this book, when we are moving to a new general theory of technique. I mention Winnicott here, in passing, because he was the master of an entire series of methods for dropping from the conscious to the unconscious mind. He too wanted to find dissociated worlds, and bring them back.

One of the great tricks of this business is to know when you can do it, and when you cannot. I will come back to the right timing in Chapter 9 on Winnicott. I want to restrict myself here to the question of when a dormant world can be reached at all? I find that the key is whether the patient is able to get a comfort out of my company. But what kind of company do I offer? Balint calls it being a "primary object," like air, earth, fire or water, indestructible, but highly adjustable (1968). Such a primeval object! He says that some patients can use such an object, and some get too little from it. (See Chapters 1 and 2, Gustafson, 1995a, for a full discussion of this difference between malignant and benign regressions.)

I discussed earlier how the transition to a dormant world might turn upon verbal play or on gesture or on sensory attunement. Yet another way is the patient watching my face (Winnicott, 1971b).

A Dream of Disgusting Satisfaction. One of the terrible things about incest is that the patient is extremely likely to go from being a passive and helpless victim to being a perpetrator on someone else. After we bear the evil she suffered, we must bear the evil she promulgated.

I was going to report this dream in the interest of accuracy, but I realize it is too shameful for the public domain.

My point concerns what it is that makes a dream reportable at all? She is so utterly disgusted by it, that she cannot look at me. But she finally does, and I am looking at her with some sympathy as I usually am. This is so relieving to her, that she can burst into tears. She is still accepted. As Winnicott (1971b) put it, she finds herself in my face, and that gets her through. Some patients can get through like this, and some cannot. The red thread in this case, that I simply watch for when she is reporting her disgusting dreams, is when she looks away. Then I know I am needed, to ask what is unbearable?

Inscape as Surface -- to an Entire Set of Surfaces

Transitional Surface

Being-with a patient on a surface of slipperiness, or one of degradation cast out from the face of humanity, or one of a tunnel spider coming on immensely, is necessary. But it is also necessary to have another surface to take comfort upon. Margulies shows this in his Chapter 5, "An Extended Search: Fragments of a Case" (1989),

Early on in the treatment she had a dream of entering a house, holding in her hand a piece of cloth. (p. 64)

This comfort in fabric extends to the old family sofa backward, forward to the couch of Margulies. Even language becomes a texture:

The weave of my words has become palpable. (p. 65)

A red tie of Margulies connects him to her father's snappy Oldsmobile with rockets on the sides. (p. 67)

"My rocket tie."
"Right (laughs) red rockets, red rockets . . . "

116

As she and Margulies weave the connection between her ancient line of comfort from fabrics to her father // it becomes possible to fall back into the uprooted hell of her lurching mother (p. 70). Also, it becomes possible to see where she was left in the lurch by her father, and where Margulies goes too fast or changes his office and so forth.

The patient becomes hugely upset at his failures to be with her. This allows Margulies to slow down, or apologize:

"What would you like me to do?"
"Thank you for asking . . . (sobs and sobs and sobs)" (p. 74)

Thus, the sessions weave between being-alive and being-dead. The two kinds of surfaces are like heaven and hell, and the threads they are weaving will allow them to get back and forth.

The Axis Mundi

Margulies mentions that this patient is like Persephone:

> Without me her world became suspended into the coldness of an internal winter, numb and waiting. (p. 82)

In other words, the entire treatment takes place along a vertical axis between a dead hell below, and a springing of heaven above. This is the "topocosm" (Frye, 1957) of all religion and myth. As in Figure 6.3, the axis mundi connects the two surfaces in a vertical line, with the surface of the earth in between:

Figure 6.3

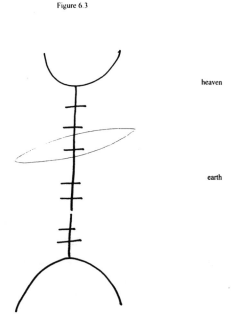

heaven

earth

hell

And so, the <u>axis mundi</u> is divided into three equal sectors, and the distance from earth to the bottom of hell is twice that of the distance from earth to heaven (Kott, p. 5, 1987, originally 1974)

You can see this topocosm in the Old Testament, where it is Jacob's Ladder:

And he dreamed that there was a ladder set up on the earth, and the top of it reached to heaven; and behold, the angels of God were ascending and descending on it! And, behold, the Lord stood above it and said, "I am the Lord . . " (<u>Genesis</u> 28: 12-13)

You can see it in the subsequent Judaeo-Christian tradition, where the entire drama is played out on the vertical axis:

. . . from the creation of man and the hurling of the rebellious angels into the abyss to Christ's Ascension and the Virgin's Assumption. The last chapter, involving the rising of the dead and the Last Judgment, will also take place on the same <u>axis mundi</u> (Kott, 1987, p. 5)
You can see it in the Greek myth, where heaven is Olympus, and hell is Tartarus or Hades, and the earth is the flat "orchestra" in between:

Zeus warns the gods in the <u>Iliad</u> that for disobedience they will be thrown "as far beneath the house of Hades as from earth the skies (Book VIII, 16) (Kott, 1987, p. 5)

Where to Stand

It is not only the patient that needs a surface of heaven, to stand the surface of hell. After I wrote about my patient degraded in her sexuality as if she were cast out from the face of heaven, I could hardly bear it myself. I got away from my typewriter, lay down on my couch, and gladly surveyed with my eye the beauty of my study which is like a ship's cabin. The horror of my patient in hell passed from my sight, to my great relief.

I have to be careful not to take in too much of hell. Like Dante I could faint myself for the pity of these lost lives. This happens over and over in <u>The Inferno</u> (as in regard to the fate of Pablo and Francesca at the close of Canto V). Many times, Virgil has to pick up Dante, and, many times, he has to warn him not to look too closely. Also, Virgil's powers to assist Dante come only on warrant from God. The descent is possible only with an eye to the ascent that will come later. Only because of the overall architecture of hell, purgatorio and paradise is the hell bearable.

In general, the more dire the surface, the more brief the glance, the more distant the standpoint. Notice how Laing discussed the dilemma of the Clam Man as a physical tropism. That is a vantage point of a biologist watching a toy-like mechanism. Notice how Sullivan merely took a glance inside the Windmill filled with rust. That is a vantage point like Virgil often took with Dante, as if to say, "Do not look too close or too long at this!"

Tragedy or Comedy?

The closer in I am to the plight of the patient, the more I feel the tragedy. The farther back I am the more it is likely to feel comical or even farcical. I find that it is useful to my patients that I can sit in both places, for they can sit beside me, and feel both their own tragedy and their own farce.

Dickens was quite a master at changing his line of sight as he went along. For example, the mad Mr. Dick in David Copperfield (originally 1850; 1981) is deeply troubled by the beheading of King Charles the First about whom he is writing:

Because, if it was so long ago, how could the people about him have made that mistake of putting some of the trouble out of his head, after it was taken off, into mine?" (p. 165)

Here we are in his head, in his bewilderment, but soon we will be out of his head in his mad project of using the torn up manuscript as pieces of a great kite:

There's plenty of string," said Mr. Dick, "and when it flies high, it takes the facts a long way. That's my manner of diffusing 'em. I don't know where they may come down. It's according to circumstances, and the wind, and so forth; but I take my chance of that." (p. 165)

So now he is a figure of fun for the boy, David. Yet this fun will collapse, in a literal fall from the heavens, and wring the boy's heart:

I used to fancy, as I sat by him of an evening, on a green slope, and saw him watch the kite high in the quiet air, that lifted its mind out of its confusion, and bore it (such was my boyish thought) into the skies. As he wound the string in, and it came lower and lower down out of the beautiful light, until it fluttered to the ground, and lay there like a dead thing, he seemed to wake gradually out of a dream; and I remember to have seen him take it up, and look about him in a lost way, as if they had both come down together, so that I pitied him with all my heart. (p. 176)

Thus, Dickens puts us with the boy's heavenly hopes for Mr. Dick, and their pitiable collapse. But notice how nimble Dickens has been, like Jack who jumped over the candlestick. He has staged his little drama of Mr. Dick up and down the axis mundi and he has changed the point of observation from inside to outside.

He is in hell in Mr. Dick's head with the King's troubles and bewilderment. He is in heaven in Mr. Dick's head "diffusing" the facts. He sits on the green with the boy watching Mr. Dick ascend, and then crumble. Both of these perspectives are so close in that we feel it all -- the elation, and the despair. Yet Dickens the narrator has kept us way back at the same time so that we can also smile at it all as a boy's fancy.

He opens the passage of the green slope thus:

Mr. Dick and I soon became the best of friends, and very often, when day's work was done, went out together to fly the great kite. Every day of his life he had a long sitting at the Memorial, which never made the least progress, however hard he labored, for King Charles the First always strayed into it, sooner or later, and then it was thrown aside, and another one begun. (p. 176)

So the pathos has been held in a comic framework from the outset. The project of Mr. Dick is an eternal circle. Dickens then slips into the precise language of Ecclesiastes to conclude this introductory paragraph:

> . . . for if anything were certain under the sun, it was certain that the Memorial never would be finished. (p. 176)

This language shades back towards the tragic, preparing the scene on the green slope of rise and fall of the kite and the man -- or is Ecclesiastes stoical?

> I returned, and saw under the sun, that the race is not to the swift, nor the battle to the strong, nor neither yet bread to the wise, nor yet riches to men of understanding, nor yet favor to men of skill, but time and chance happeneth to them all. (Ecclesiastes 9:11)

I would be like Dickens with my patients in this respect. I would be willing to travel the axis mundi with them from heaven to hell and back. But insofar as this is a perpetual journey, I want also to stand back as far as I need to bear the sight.

A Tragic Dream From a Comic Plane. A patient of mine who lives a secluded life as an obscure expert dreamt:

> I am at a play in which the actors come into the crowd and sing with Julie Andrews -- I am with a husband who is perfect, and my perfect parents.

> Then it is all dark, and a funeral.

This dream fell out as she was talking of divorces and deaths, so it meant to her that she had better not delay doing what is important. It fell terrible, in the dream, from light to dark. Yet, what was even more striking is how alive she sprung out of her chair telling me the dream. She was enjoying her own self-parody, from a plane outside the heaven of Julie Andrews or the hell of utter darkness. Herself as nimble, as in Figure 6.4.

Figure 6.4

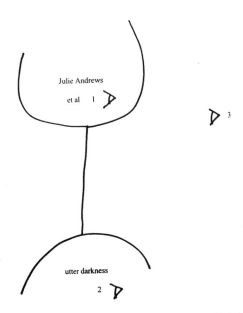

From within the dream in positions 1 and 2, she is much like Mr. Dick, rising and collapsing. In position 3, she parodies herself as a silly minor character. She says I was amused by the dream, and that amused her.

Surfaces in Borges

A lecture by Borges (1984) called "Nightmares" comes the closest to my meaning here about surfaces in dreams, and how we get between them. Borges supposes that dreams travel the axis mundi:

> Each man is given, in dreams, a little personal eternity which allows him to see the recent past and the near future. . . .

> It is not impossible that, during dreams, we are in heaven, we are in hell. (p. 28)

It is not hard to see how this is true of Mr. Dick, and of my patient having a perfect life, and a funeral. A nightmare, in contrast to a dream is a place in hell you cannot get out of. Often, in Borges that is a labyrinth, which is closed.

History as a Nightmare

Yet I believe we need more surfaces than those along the vertical axis, to follow the dream. I dreamt as I was preparing this chapter:

Author's Dream of Ogden, Utah

That I was stuck in Ogden, Utah, without a ticket home. First I went to an insurance agent, which seemed pointless. Next to a football stadium, which looked like a Roman coliseum, but I could not get east past the barbed wire. Turning back west, I met my host absorbed in a boat show, so I didn't think he would be of help either.

Why Ogden, Utah? Well, it is near Promontory, Utah, where the rail-laying crews from the west met the rail-laying crews from the east to complete the transcontinental railway. It was the end of the frontier (Frederick Jackson Turner, 1920 originally; 1994).

So, my little nightmare is about being trapped in a desolate place, in history, like Stephen Daedalus in his famous reply to Mr. Deasy:

> History -- Stephen said, is a nightmare from which I am trying to awake Joyce (p. 34, 1914 originally; 1961)

I would draw this dream along my two axes, the axis mundi and the axis of history, as in Figure 6.5.

Figure 6.5

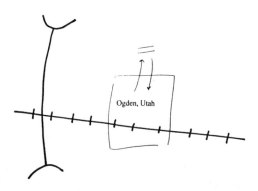

History, or time, is in dreams. Its surfaces allow transitions in some directions. I can slide into hell's blankness from Ogden, but I cannot get to heaven from there.

History and Group Life

This is precisely the subject which Proust (1913 originally) maps in the opening which he calls the "Overture" to Swann's Way. The boy who is talking desperately wants to get to his mother or her to him in his high bedroom. But she is a prisoner of the dinner party, which is a kind of sacred occasion:

> . . . the sacred character in which she invested the dinner party might have the effect of making her decline to disturb its ceremonial (p. 23)

Its surface so repels everything but itself. The interesting passages of their guest, M. Swann, when he is not at the dinner-party are altogether canceled:

> My great-aunt, however, interpreted this piece of news in a sense discreditable to Swann; for anyone who chose his associates outside the caste in which he had been born and bred, outside his "proper station," was condemned to utter degradation in her eyes. . . . (p. 16) Whenever she saw in others an advantage, however trivial, which she herself lacked, she would persuade herself that it was no advantage at all, but a drawback, and would pity so as not to have to envy them. (p. 17)

Two other old ladies of the party actually appear to be deaf to any subject but the topic dear to themselves. It would be futile to discuss anything else, but precious objects:

> So that if my grandfather wished to attract the attention of the two sisters, he would have to make use of some such alarm signals as mad-doctors adopt in dealing with their distracted patients; as by beating several times on a glass with the blade of a knife; fixing them at the same time with a sharp word and a compelling glance, violent methods which the said doctors are apt to bring with them into their everyday life among the sane, either from force of professional habit or because they think the whole world a trifle mad. (p. 17)

Of course, Proust hints through the doctors that this little bourgeois dinner party is indeed mad like all the world. It casts out the heaven of the little boy, and the complexity of M. Swann, and runs its rut as a surface onto itself.

Inscape in Hopkins

If we cannot abide being prisoners of the horizontal surfaces, we had better know how to lift off of them. Hopkins' idea was simply to go contemplate a surface of nature as a work of God. This would transport him, into clouds or rivers, or trees, or ice, or flowers, and so forth. Inscapes are these places. Inscaping is his activity in catching their beautiful structure. Here he is watching the Northern Lights:

> They rose slightly radiating thrown out from the earth line. Then I saw soft pulses of light one after another rise and pass upwards arched in shape but waveringly and with the arch broken. They seemed to float, not following warp of the sphere as falling stars look to do but free though concentrical with it. (p. 96, 1966)

Hopkins puts us back on the vertical surfaces of the axis mundi:

123

This busy working of nature wholly independent of the earth and seeming to go on in a strain of time not reckoned by our reckoning of days and years but simpler and as if correcting the preoccupation of the world by being preoccupied with and appealing to and dated to the day of judgment was like a new witness to God and filled me with delightful fear (p. 96).

Dream as Vertical Departure

If we do not know how to depart like Hopkins in our days, we are going to do so every night in our dreams. I will come back to this in Part II of this book, but we cannot sleep until we find a comforting surface. We are like our cats, pawing the bed until it feels right. This is the creation of a platform for sleep, and for dream.

The Dream of a Crib in Psychiatry. One of my patients had a terrible long night in the hospital watching over her son. She had been badly taxed by the strain. Finally, just before morning, she fell asleep in his room and dreamt:

> I am in a crib in psychiatry. A dachshund-poodle barks at me, and says: "You will have the strength of a horse, and the endurance of a thousand days."

The dog is one she lost twenty years ago, because her parents gave it away when she had left it in their keeping. So he is back after all, and she is in a crib looked after by me. I had not seen her so worn out when she came to this session, but she left renewed by climbing into the surface of the dream.

This dream was uplifting in its vitality, but it also contained within it dire downward currents. When we went into the history of the dog, she cried over how she had been betrayed. All dreams have these opposing currents, upwards and downwards, like a cumulus cloud. Recall Sullivan's dream of the tunnel spider. He gets to sleep in the uplift of the beautiful geometric pattern of the perfectly parallel lines of the fabric of the web, but then falls darkly into its tunnel into the path of the mounting tunnel spider. He has to leave the vertical altogether, which diminishes to a terrifying dark spot on his sheet. He dare not go back into it.

Dreams as a Form of Travel, Limited by the Structure of Dilemma

Once into the vertical, the dreamer like a shaman travels equally in the horizontal. He can go anywhere in anytime. But this is not to say there are no limits. Oddly, in the time-space of dreamers, you get stuck on some surfaces, and you cannot go to others. In this topocosm, to use Northrop Frye's term (1957), travel is quite as it was for Alice in her underworld (Carroll, 1865) -- alternatingly free, and very frustrating.

Now, the vertical is a tremendous source of energy. God, after all, is Rex Tremendae Majestatis. Next to this, a cumulus cloud is a small thing. It lifts, and it crushes. The horizontal gives all the variety of the world. But it can stick you at the end of meaning in Ogden, Utah.

Thus, timelessness and time are both highly ambivalent. This is the dilemma of dreams, for it is both tremendous and terrible, to range in the vertical and in the horizontal. You can be impaled on either horn. This is the structure of dilemma (Gustafson, 1995a; 1995b) which I have argued is the key structure of our existence. In other words, the opportunity of the vertical is a great hazard. Many are prisoners of the vertical. In other words, the opportunity of the horizontal is a great hazard. Many are prisoners of the horizontal.

Dream as a Fulcrum, to Channel the Force of the Vertical into the Horizontal of History

Take Theodore Roethke for example, the poet of my home town, Saginaw, Michigan, and brother of my ninth grade English teacher, June. Ted Roethke was an inspiring teacher. June Roethke was the strictest of teachers. Ted could elevate and dash you. June made you punctuate, exactly.

Listen to Ted describe his craft in "Verse Form" at Bennington College:
As to my particular functions, put briefly, it is a constant effort to recover the creative powers lost in childhood . . . Teaching at its very highest is too much like the dance. Once the moment the class is over, it's all down a rat hole. For instance, during the spring semester, for about six or seven weeks, I was really hot, if I do say so myself, in all three courses, classes conducted, paced and often brought to a real pitch of excitement with genuine insights off-the-cuff, hot improvisational rides, etc. (Seager, 1991, pp. 138-139)

Listen to the metaphor of riding here, like Hearne (1986) on the subject of horsemanship with the horse, Drummer Girl:

Drummer Girl's enormous capacity for precision and elegance was the measure of her capacity for maddened refusals of any lesser communication (p. 43) for whom balance, symmetry and coherence were at the center of her cosmos. What was I going to say to this mare?

Ted Roethke was a similarly maddened horse, or horseman, or both. He had this tremendous talent for coherence, but he had to come back down to the flats:

I once asked him, "Why do you knock yourself out so?" He replied with a snarl, "Ah, I know it's lugging pork up Parnassus" -- here his face brightened -- "but you get 'em up there once, they see what it is. They're better than they'll ever be again." (Seager, p. 140)

Here we are at the juncture of the vertical surfaces and the horizontal surfaces, at the dilemma as I take it of our existence which is built into the structure of our dreams. We need the vertical for its tremendous forces, but we need the horizontal for bringing these forces down to the measure of earth, within its rules of punctuation. Insofar as we can turn this corner from the vertical into the horizontal, gracefully, then we turn on the dream as a fulcrum of divinity in history.

<u>The Author's Dream of Returning to Saginaw, Michigan on New Year's Eve</u>. This very New Year's Eve, as I was contemplating Ted and June Roethke, and this chapter, I dreamt one of my theoretical dreams about the problem I was posing in the chapter I was writing.

> I dreamt I was bartending at the Saginaw Club on New Year's Eve. The strangest thing was that the three ballrooms in parallel had no one in them. I then got a telephone call from a man who claimed that my wife had bounced a check at his business. I told him that was impossible, and I would come right over to demonstrate it to him.

As I worked up the elements of the dream, a few things fell into place. The Saginaw Club was where I first went to dancing lessons in junior high school. It did not consist of three ballrooms but one. The check bouncing has nothing to do with my wife, but with the Roethke's and their greenhouse in Saginaw. Being strict Germans, like June herself, they would never do such a thing. I am being like a mathematician at the end going to demonstrate a proof.

The strange triptych of the dream only fell into place when I drew it as in Figure 6.6.

Figure 6.6

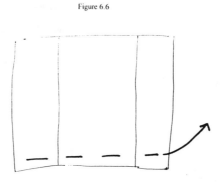

Once I drew the triptych, I knew it alluded to Bosch's painting, "The Haywain," which is in my office, and which shows the journey in the historical axis of time, horizontally, from Eden on the left, Earth and its haywain in the center, Hell on the right.

In the dream, I travel myself in the horizontal across Bosch's triptychal terrain, from Heaven, to Earth, to Hell -- as if the dream is saying, such is the history of man. They danced at the Saginaw Club, and now they are all gone. Ephemera, pass on. Yet I carry something of divine punctuation with me, so I go to make my proof. I have turned a corner from the vertical into the horizontal, thanks to the two Roethke's and Bosch. I always have huge energy after such dreams.

Introduction to Part II, The Orchestral Score,
A New General Theory of Searching the Unconscious

Every practitioner of the art and science of utilizing dreams needs to be able to develop a trade from his map, if he wants to be hired. He has to be able to show his patient that the dream can take him somewhere which is surprisingly useful.

But to be validated by his fellow practitioners, he has to have a map with destinations that are deemed to be correct in their outcome. So, they must not be too surprising, after all. For example, the destination of a psychoanalytic map will be the pain in the past in the family of origin.

Of course, as I have demonstrated in my array of Part I, dreams have many other possible destinations, such as a view on possession by the gods, or a view on excessive elevation or excessive flattening, and so forth. Yet, the practitioner who needs his group to validate him is not likely to stray from the official map. Aristotle figured this out several thousand years ago in his treatise on The Art of Rhetoric (336-322 B.C.), which means the art of persuasion. Persuasion starts from proving you are one of us, and removing any prejudicial hint that you are one of them or foreign. It then sounds the topics of concern to us and our shared welfare. Finally, it adds a small step of departure which might take our group a little farther.

I am bound by these laws of persuasion like any other author. If I defy them, I can be certain of being ignored. How then can I address members of all the different schools of mapping dreams, without being rejected by all of them as foreign to their welfare?

I believe I have to show first that I am proposing a relatively simple method of searching dreams, that is entirely compatible with a psychoanalytic search, or a Jungian search, or an existential search, or with any of their latter variants I have expounded in Part I of this book. You can remain a member in good standing of your association, while borrowing what I have to add to what you already know.

Therefore, I begin Chapter 7, "The Science of Dreams," with what is common to all methods in a relatively simple way. This is what mammals are doing in their REM sleep, without any interpretation at all. As I will summarize the work of Rotenberg and many other investigators, animals seem to be responding to befuddling situations with increased REM time, which allows them to renew their searches for a way through their dilemmas. So, I believe that any mapping of dreams has to be a kind of search, driven by a dilemma. I find that the most common befuddlement of my students and my patients over dreams is in not knowing their starting point -- from what situation is the patient searching, and for what? Just getting that straight is going to lead to a great deal more enlightenment from the dream (whatever the subsequent mapping). An animal that has no notion of what it is running from and running toward is an animal in panic which will soon be an animal in complete demoralization.

However, there is no way that a simple searching theory is going to be very powerful. Yes, it will help a patient in pain with her father in the present to search back to the pain with him in the past, <u>if</u> the doctor's bearing it with her is going to be a relief (half the time this is true). She becomes less panicked, or less demoralized, and her searching for ways to deal with this difficult man will occur under more optimal searching conditions that allow some flexible variations. This is the generic value (the placebo value, as Jerome Frank would say) of all the methods, of searching, with a confident guide at your side. It will settle you down, so you can actually see some new possibilities for yourself. Your own discoveries are more likely, for they are of zero likelihood in a panic or when you have given up altogether.

Yet it is even better and more powerful to have an array of maps which have an adequate dimensionality (Bateson, 1979, Chapter 1) or degrees of freedom to find a way through the dilemma, or more precisely, to find surfaces on which there is a way through. Otherwise, there is a danger that the guide will simply follow the patient around in his own circle of heaven and hell, between converging hopes, and diverging realities. In general, the guide had better have at least one more degree of freedom than the patient, or he will founder with him. While it is useful to have one more degree of freedom than the patient by having a psychoanalytic map of the dimension of the pain of the family of origin, it is more useful to have five other degrees of freedom as well in case the patient needs or lacks one of the other five dimensions. Therefore, I will close Chapter 7 of the "Science of Dreams" by showing in a relatively simple way how the array assembled in Part I of this book yields a set of degrees of freedom to be put to a simple use by a patient searching for a way to be less overwhelmed by his dilemma.

A scientific theory should not only assemble the array of disparate findings that are available, like the last one hundred years of the mapping of dreams, but it ought also to point to new variations not yet thought of. Therefore, I proceed in Chapters 8 through 12 to show how a search theory of the unconscious is a kind of art that relies on transporting oneself to different surfaces, how it is a relief from frozen history into the fluidity of opposing currents, how it is a music that oscillates between the huge and religious forces of ancient man and the necessary compartments of modern man, how it is a tremendous instrument of reading the limitations of society in advance of striking hard against them, and how it is also an instrument for taking back one's own ten-dimensional being while living in a mostly two-dimensional world. Oddly, the EEG varies between 9.7 degrees of freedom in the fully awake subject, 2.05 degrees in an epileptic fit (Schmid, 1991).

Modern man acts a great deal like an epileptic with 2.05 degrees of freedom, getting rid of his other nearly 8 degrees of freedom, in order to fit-in and later have a fit, like Dr. Jekyll and Mr. Hyde (Gustafson, 1995b, Chapter 11, "Visual Maps"). We all have to be ready for him, and we all have to know where the degrees of freedom are to get free of his domination. This is the great dilemma posed by Mark Twain in <u>Huckleberry Finn</u> (1885), indeed all of our most powerful American writers from Hawthorne through Melville to James even until now (Poirier, 1966). It is the American dilemma of being able fit into a correct costume when you need to, and out of it when you can. In the end, it is what we are all up to in this country.

Chapter 7. A Search
Theory of Dreams

A very great deal of ground is now about to be covered in very short order. Allow me to point ahead to what we will traverse. First, I will start from the premise I share with the scientists who study REM (rapid eye movement) sleep in mammals including man in their sleep laboratories: REM-sleep, an objective finding, is needed to renew the animal for searching its way in complex tasks; dreaming, a subjective report, mostly overlaps REM-sleep and has the structure of a search, starting from the dilemma of the subject in its current world. Secondly, I will show that the success of the search depends upon the number of dimensions available to the dreamer. If he has only two dimensions, he will go around in a vicious circle, which alternates between wishful convergence of his hopes, and absurd divergence of his hopes falling apart. If he can find or borrow dimensions outside this perpetual circle of presumption and collapse, he can get somewhere with his dilemma. Thirdly, I will show that there is an overwhelming tendency both in dreamers and in their helpers to be drawn back into 2-dimensional and vicious circularity, while losing the other 8-dimensions necessary to getting somewhere. I will argue why this bifurcation is of such great power, and what can be done to reduce its dire effects. I will illustrate this bifurcation of the 2-dimensional space from the 8-dimensional space by showing the dream spaces of Freud, Jung, Binswanger, Erikson, Hillman and Margulies as special cases or 2-dimensional slices of the 10-dimensional dream space available to us for our searches. In other words, I will fold all of Part I of this book into the conclusion of this chapter.

Searching in REM-Sleep and Dreaming in All Mammals

A general theory of dreams has got to be consistent with REM-sleep in other mammals, for there is an obvious overlap in their activities and ours (Hobson, 1995). Darwin (1899) demonstrated that mammalian emotions are highly parallel. Look at his photographs and drawings of down-turned mouths, sneers, shrugs, terror and sulking in dogs, cats, monkeys and us. When we are awake, we live in mammalian emotion. This is how we can have such rapport with our neighboring kin in the animal kingdom (Hearne, 1986).

When we are asleep, we have three to five periods per night of rapid eye movements (REM sleep), also quite like our fellow mammals. From waking up human subjects in dream laboratories, researchers find that:

> . . . dreams usually last for the duration of the eye movements, from about 10 to 25 minutes. Although dreaming usually occurs in such regular cycles, dreaming may also occur at other times during sleep, as well as during hypnagogic (falling asleep) or hypnopompic (waking up) states, when REM's are not present. (p. 252, Carskadon, 1993).

Still, there is a preponderance of dreaming in REM periods:

> 74 percent of awakenings from REM sleep yielded dream recall, whereas only 9 percent of NREM awakenings yielded recall (another study 80 and 7). (p. 480)

REM periods involve many physical changes besides the rapid movements of the eyes, including changes in heart and respiratory rate, core body temperature, penile erections, electrodermal potentials, and so forth (Carskadon, p. 482).

REM-sleep is thus an altered biological state, which has some nightly importance to the well-being of the mammal. (REM sleep is part of a larger process of sleep itself, in which the serotonergic brain of the day becomes the cholinergic brain of night. See Hobson (1995).) The researchers of the dream laboratories have been able to demonstrate the function of REM-sleep, chiefly by depriving animals of REM-sleep to observe the effect on the animals, especially with regard to complex learning tasks. They similarly deprived human subjects, with entirely parallel results.

REM-Sleep and REM-Deprivation

Essentially, mammals involved in complex learning tasks can no longer perform them after being deprived of REM-sleep. Conversely, when they begin to grapple with such "unprepared learning" like "two-way avoidance" for rats, or "assimilation of a complicated text with a distorted semantic" in humans, REM-sleep increases until the task is solved (Rotenberg, 1992, p. 497, and p. 499).

There is also a vital connection between the daytime search activity of an animal in trouble with his "unprepared learning" (learning for which he is unprepared) and the nighttime REM-sleep. At first, the frustrated animal increases his searching, and his REM-sleep. However, the frustration which is unrelieved eventually leads to a collapse of searching, and of REM-sleep, and of body resistance to disease.

It is dangerous for the animal to be overly frenetic in his search, which will only exhaust him, and it is dangerous for the animal to give up his searching, which leaves him, for example, with no food, or shelter, or defense. REM-sleep seems to keep the animal from getting stuck on these two horns of his dilemma, of panic on the one hand, and of renunciation. Therefore, Rotenberg says that the main function of REM-sleep is:

compensation of the renunciation of search and restoration of search activity (1992, p. 500, my italics)

Quite literally, this means that the frustrated animal on the verge of giving up for the day will have increased REM-sleep in which he increases his capacity to resume search activity in the morning. If he is deprived of REM-sleep, he may not resume search, and his body resistance to illness will fall apart.

Thus, it appears that REM-sleep, with its largely concomitant dreaming, has a huge function of restoring search activity whether or not the animal has any recall of being in REM-sleep or in a dream. Now, what happens when you have both REM-sleep and the recall of

131

dreams? According to Rotenberg, the recall of dream images can be either helpful or harmful to unprepared learning:

> As a restorer of search activity REM sleep increased the effectiveness of mnestic processes, but as a container of concrete information it can interfere with memory process. (p. 505)

It all depends on whether the subject can utilize the dream images to abet his search on his current difficulty, or whether he is just alarmed or baffled or distracted by them.

A Simple Model of Searching with the Help
of Dream Images, from Greenberg and Pearlman

We now come to the critical matter of this book, which is how we turn alarming and baffling and distracting images from dreams into helpful markers for our maps of our lives. Greenberg and Pearlman have a very simple concept, which has the advantage of being borrowed readily.

From waking up patients and subjects in their sleep laboratory, they conclude that the dream is a

> window through which one can see most clearly what the patient is struggling with (1993, p. 297)

It represents

> in pictorial language the problems of the dreamer (p. 297)

For them, a dream is a search into a memory file:

> Thus, when one of us visited his old university for the first time in years, not only did the dreams portray the feelings stirred up by this trip, but also the content contained people from college days with whom there had been no contact over the years and who were rarely thought of. It was as if the pressure of the present stimulus had opened that file drawer and those memories were now accessible for use in dreams (1980/1993, p. 92)

Thus, a dream is a kind of search, and the search is for relevant memory. It pictures the problem the subject is struggling with, and then goes searching into the file from the past of similar struggles. A clinical example will illustrate its logic and its relief.

The Dream of Hiding from Robbers in the Bathroom. The patient was a woman in her twenties, depressed, directionless and deprived of her mother. The parents were divorced when she was six, and the mother died several years later of cancer, and the father just seemed to intrude and control her in an insensitive manner. She reported the following dream after a visit to her father and stepmother, which had gone badly (again). She was telling her analyst something she had been telling her father on this vacation, when she recalled the following dream. In other words, <u>the dream drops into its search from the difficulty of talking with her father, for which it seeks the file of past struggles</u>:

> Her parents (father and stepmother) were in their bedroom in the apartment in Florida. She was in the bathroom, in the shower, smoking. She's not allowed to smoke in the house. Robbers came in the house and started shooting.(//) Suddenly the dream changed so that now her father was away in New York and only her stepmother was in the house when the robbers came in. They came into the bathroom and started to shoot through the shower door. She was hiding behind the bathroom door, and they didn't see her. (//) She then realized that father was coming back. The robbers were in the dining room, so she was able to go out into the hall to meet father and stepmother, who was somehow still alive. She told her father he'd better go downstairs and not risk his life by going into the apartment to try to save things from the robbers. She told him that if he went in she would get herself killed by going downstairs and getting herself run over. So he went downstairs. It was the only way to get him to listen, that is, to threaten him with the loss of her own life. (pp. 300-301, 1993)

The analyst takes the dream very simply, as her perpetual struggle to get through to her father. She had been asking her father in Florida about his life in the past, and he had dismissed her questions. She then has a search back to New York, when she was robbed of her mother. Then, too, he had dismissed her. The analyst simply reflects back to her search for a way to get through to him. This allows her to feel valid in looking for a way, because it is accepted that her father is so important to her. Even if the dream pictures the absurd lengths she would have to go to get his attention, she can get the attention of the doctor to her pain, so it can be shared.

Adequate Dimensions

Such a commonplace dream which could be taken as a useful map to get to an important destination -- is a good test for a theory of searching in dreams. Its structure is so bare, that we can survey easily what is involved.

Also, we can estimate readily how this dream might have failed in getting her anywhere at all. It is so close to a nightmare, and a nightmare with hardly a prospect of relief. But she did get relief from it, with the help of her analyst, so we are in a position to estimate the difference between a search that is only alarming and baffling or distracting, from one that abets the search of the patient to get out of the misery of her dilemma.

Let us start with her misery. She is trying to reach her father to ask him about his past, and is dismissed yet again. This leaves her in her usual dilemma with him. She can get frantic, and force the matter // or she can give up or resign the attempt. Both horns of the dilemma are untenable. Getting charged up is only likely to rouse the old man to put her down even harder. Resigning is only likely to leave her feeling invalid, both in terms of her worth as a person and in her bodily state. This misery is pictured in my drawing of her dilemma in Figure 7.1.

Figure 7.1

"A Bipolar Dilemma"

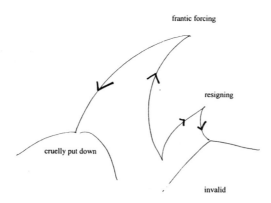

frantic forcing

resigning

cruelly put down

invalid

Let us now follow how the dream searches for a way out of this dilemma. In the session, the recall of the dream inserts itself just as she is recalling her being dismissed by her father in Florida for asking about his past. So the point of departure from the conscious mind for the unconscious mind is as clear as we can hope for. This is of great technical importance. If we know the point of departure, then we can often infer what the search is for.

The search first goes back to Florida, and shows her alienated from her parents in their bedroom, while she is smoking in the shower in the bathroom. Robbers came in shooting. Perhaps, this is her own urge to rob her parents, for defaulting on her. But we can set that aside for now.

Then, there is a hiatus (//) or jump to another occasion of robbery in Florida, with only her stepmother at home and her father away. The robbers really do threaten her to a greater extent, shooting through the shower door which she has just vacated to get behind the bathroom door. She has had to become even more adept at disappearing.

Finally, there is another hiatus (//) so that her father is coming back, and she protects him from taking on the robbers. But she is only able to do this by threatening to go downstairs into the street to get run over. Then, her father backs off and goes downstairs. He listens, only when she threatens to kill herself.

Without any help from the doctor, the patient is hardly arriving at any improvement in her misery. The search moves from her alienation, to her desperate hiding, to her forcing him to listen by the threat of suicide. She has the typical search of any child defaulted on by parents (Winnicott, 1971; see Chapter 9 to come in this book). Such a child feels very hurt, and such a child always has the urge to force recompense in an antisocial way like robbery. She will take back what is due to her (her value). However, such children often get stuck as this child-adult in her dream-text, between lying low and standing up and making or forcing her claim. There is hardly much to choose from, between smoking in the shower, and threatening to walk into traffic to kill herself. She is either resigned, or frantic.

It appears that the text of the dream itself has just gone around the perpetual and vicious circle she has been stuck in since she was six years old. This is a vicious circle of twenty years duration, and countless repetitions, and this gives it its <u>tiresome</u> quality. Entropy is setting in. As Winnicott (1971) pointed out, the vicious circle can go on so long that the child-adult gives up altogether on getting out of it. Help can come too late. Let us picture the vicious circle of this typical abandoned child as in Figure 7.2.

Figure 7.2

"The Vicious Cycle of the Abandoned Child"

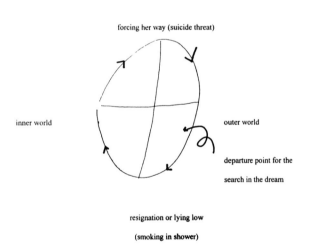

forcing her way (suicide threat)

inner world

outer world

departure point for the

search in the dream

resignation or lying low

(smoking in shower)

You can start at any point of the vicious circle and come full circle back to it. It is a circle of hell, quite as Dante pictures over and over in the <u>Inferno</u>.

Let us start from the point of departure of the search in the dream. In the outer world, she has just been dismissed by her father again (asserting force to open him up has failed again). The search drops into her smoking in the shower. If she stayed dormant in this smoky underworld, she would be giving up altogether like those ghosts of their former selves in endless corridors of the state mental hospitals. She would be like a grey phantom in the wastes of death-in-life.

Somehow, she still has the hope of protesting and claiming her due attention. Like one of Rotenberg's frustrated mammals, she is getting a surge of aggression to try to get her way, after all. The robbers carry some of her antisocial claim, and she finally makes her own claim upon her father to heed her by her suicide threat. This is the updraft in the search, of an influx of vitality.

Yet, it is doomed to fail in the form that it takes. Threatening suicide can force attention, as in the story of the little boy crying wolf. But it is less and less apt to be heeded, as it is repeated. With this tactic, she is like those borderline patients perpetually calling our emergency rooms, and gradually burning out.

Thus, the search looked doomed to fail. The cycle succeeds in activating the animal, as Rotenberg put it:

in compensation of the renunciation of search and restoration of search activity (1992, p. 500)

But the path of the search is a vicious circle, which will eventually tire and wear the animal out. The animal will repeat itself in a more bleary and pointless way, until it gets sick or dies from the decreased body resistance that comes with pointlessness.

The dream images just do not add any useful landmarks or pointers for getting out of the dilemma. This would seem to be the kind of dream imagery that actually detracts from the animal's ability to search in a useful way. One pole of the imagery is about hiding, and is likely to mark the pointlessness of passing time in smoking. No animal is going to get anywhere in such renunciation. The other pole of the imagery is about frantic forcing. No animal is going to get anywhere (for long) by threatening to destroy itself.

The trouble is that the animal, or human being, needs more degrees of freedom, or dimensions, than this to get out of the dilemma, or vicious circle. This is the typical structure of a malignant dilemma, or vicious circle, in which there are only two dimensions. The two dimensions are forcing/giving up, and hiding/going into the world, as illustrated in Figure 7.3.

Figure 7.3

"The Dimensions of a Vicious Circle"

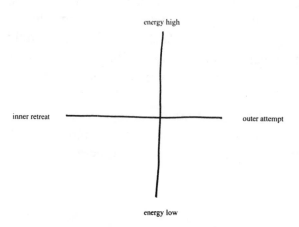

All you can do in such a space with such limited coordinates is oscillate between forcing in fantasy or forcing in reality, or giving up in fantasy or giving up in reality. Indeed, this is the bipolar structure of all mental illness, as I have argued in my last book (Gustafson, 1995b, like the worn out Dr. Jekyll and the unstoppable Mr. Hyde), or all futile and repeating stories, as I argued in an earlier book (Gustafson, 1992, in which I described the stories as strange loops).

It is also the 2-dimensional space of nightmare, as the reader may recall in Sullivan's dream of the tunnel spider. Sullivan's nightmare circles counter-clockwise, in contrast to the clockwise circulation of the search we have been discussing in this patient. For example, Sullivan leaves the frustrating world of his study of schizophrenics for his lovely geometric pattern of the web so perfectly regular that he can fall asleep into it as into a comforting textile (see Chapters 8 and 9 on dream screens as transitional objects for transporting us out of the world into the comfort of sleep). However, as he descends deeper into withdrawal from the world, he falls prey to the tunnel spider ascending from below, and has to flee the web, as in Figure 7.4.

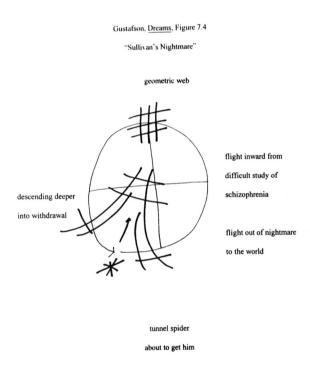

Gustafson, Dreams, Figure 7.4

"Sullivan's Nightmare"

geometric web

flight inward from

difficult study of

schizophrenia

descending deeper

into withdrawal

flight out of nightmare

to the world

tunnel spider

about to get him

The circle is so vicious, that he has to remain awake staring at the black spot on his sheet which was the tunnel spider huge in the underworld of the dream. He dare not risk sleep, which reenters this cycle.

Adding Dimensions

Now let us consider how the analyst described by Greenberg and Pearlman (1993) adds a dimension that is implicit in the dream but undeveloped, and how this makes a malignant dilemma or vicious circle into a map of a difficult but tenable problem.

Simply by recognition of the patient's perpetual struggle to get through to the father, the analyst validates it as an understandable pursuit. The patient takes comfort in this, and cries with relief. If the patient is dismissed by the father, she is not dismissed by the doctor. In a way, he is the missing mother.

Yet, he is not supplying the gratification of a literal father. If the patient insisted on that, the case would remain in hell in a spiral of demands that could not be met (Balint, 1968; Gustafson, 1995a and 1995b). He is supplying understanding of her plight with her father, which is enough to calm her, in what Balint called "regression in the service of recognition" or "benign regression."

The third dimension then is recognition, of how she was failed, and probably will be failed again. After all, the wish for a father in her own father cannot be gratified. It is made absurd, by the lengths required to get his attention. This recognition creates a third dimension, or even surface, of comfort by understanding, which is outside the vicious circle of herself forcing herself on her father, and giving up on him. With the doctor, she is transported to a third dimension, of comfort, looking back at the comfortless realm. Of course, the patient has to be capable of this regression in the service of recognition. Doubtlessly, someone (probably mother) had helped her in this way as a child. The capacity, or dimension, or surface, was being revived, to transport her out of the 2-dimensional hell.

A Dream of Being Dogged to Commit Murder. For comparison, I will now provide another relatively simple example of the transposition from 2-dimensional hell to 3-dimensional relief. My patient is a middle-aged man who is contemplating a second marriage. His fiancee is a good friend, but he is not as attracted to her as he would like to be in sexual terms, and he is not being very creative himself in his work. These two things dog him, and drive his dilemma. If he marries her, he fears their sexual relationship will not pan out, and he fears he will follow her to a new job and be sterile himself on the sidelines. When he feels helpless like this, he has urges to snap her neck off. If he decides not to marry her, he is afraid of being a resigned old man with hardly any company at all. His dilemma has the pole of renunciation, and the pole of forcing the convergence of his wishes with violent energy. Discussing his uncertainty whether to marry, or not marry, he tells me of the following dream:

> He is in bed with his fiancee, but a dog is nipping at him through the sheets. He gets up and goes to the basement, where there is a photographic darkroom, and an old friend who has become a kind of ghostly alcoholic. He develops his film, into a double exposure which shows a skull like an x-ray. The dog keeps nipping him. Finally // he can stand the dog no longer and strangles it with torn strips of white sheets, and wakes up in horror.

I will pass over how we worked up the dream detail by detail, by simply noting that it had the structure I was familiar with in working with him a number of years. He had the tendency to let himself be rendered helpless, and then explode, which is what I call the exploding doormat problem (subservience, Gustafson, 1992, 1995a, 1995b). One pole of this vicious circle is to be nice and accommodating, which is to allow oneself to be trapped, and which drives the urge to flee into hiding (like the friend who is the ghostly alcoholic in the dream) or to explode violently, which is the other pole (strangling the dog), as illustrated in Figure 7.5.

Figure 7.5

"Dogged to Commit Murder"

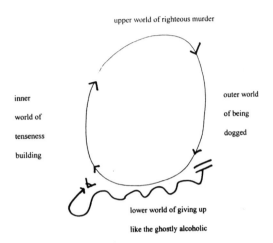

upper world of righteous murder

inner
world of
tenseness
building

outer world
of being
dogged

lower world of giving up

like the ghostly alcoholic

So we are in the vicious circle of the nightmare in 2-dimensions, even after working up the dream and accepting his predicament. In this case, the acceptance of his pain is not relieving in itself. Why not? I believe it is because I only see him occasionally (for financial reasons), so he is really still in the dilemma of going with his fiancee for company, or being a drop out like his ghostly friend the alcoholic. He can stand neither. I am around too little to provide a third surface or dimension of comfort such as an analysis might provide.

Therefore, I need to discover another dimension latent in the dream itself. I simply note that he has been so beset by the dog in the dream at his heels, until he can't stand it any longer, that he has failed to step back far enough to notice that the dog could be tied up or put in a room by itself. He need not let himself be dogged unmercifully. I know he need not, because the last crisis was about his fiancee insisting on having a child. He let himself be cornered by this duty, with ever increasing urges to snap her neck off. I reminded him that that violence had passed, once he had put that dog to rest by telling her that it was not for him to have a child. I was pointing to a dimension that I knew he could summon, as I had just witnessed it and its great benefit to him several months before.

This time, he smiled with some relief that he might tie up the dog. So, what dog is this dog? I asked him. Ah, he said, the sex dog and the art dog, that I am dogging myself to be great in bed and great in the darkroom. Perhaps, I can lay off myself! The tension was broken, that had been driving his murderousness.

The Cumulus Dream Machine, in Terms of Chaos Theory

Let me hasten to add that the hole in the dream text (Gustafson, 1995a, Chapter 13) which had the missing dimension is a commonplace piece of selective inattention in a very commonplace story of subservience. It is routine. It might be turned up easily by many methods for working up dreams. A relatively naive group of patients in a psychodrama or gestalt therapy group might enact such a dream and pick up the oversight about how the dog is <u>allowed</u> to drive the engine of murder (Craig and Walsh, 1993; Delaney, 1993; Natterson, 1993).

A group working up the text of a dream is going to imagine a great many dimensions, which might or might not be helpful to the therapist or the dreamer (Ullman, 1993). What is more difficult is to grasp what the dream forbids, as well as what it might allow. The dream is a map of dynamic forces which can be of crushing power. The key is to locate where the degrees of freedom actually allow a passage, and where the force field just will not allow the passage, at least not for very long.

This estimation requires a just reckoning of the forces of the vicious circle. For it is not so difficult to discover unique outcomes on a group weekend, or in a brief psychotherapy, or in going off to the southern hemisphere, which do not hold up back home in the force field of the daily grind. In other words, new dimensions appear, but most of them get erased. Why is this so? Why is modern man essentially a 2-dimensional creature who gets rid of the other 8-dimensions?

How the 10-Dimensional Space is Bifurcated
Between 2-Dimensions and 8-Dimensions or 30-Dimensions

If we start from a relatively simple search theory of dreams like that of Greenberg and Pearlman, we see that the search is a search of memory. The explicit dimensions are present/past, solution/failure as in Figure 7.6.

Figure 7.6

"Greenberg and Pearlman's Search"

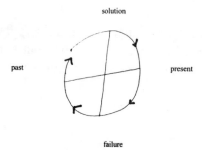

solution

past present

failure

As I demonstrated in my analysis of their example of The Dream of Hiding from the Robbers in the Shower, a third but inexplicit dimension was necessary to getting the patient out of a vicious circle of forcing and resignation.

Freud's search is a little different, because it is a search for hidden wishes, which are censored so that the patient can fit into a correctness in society. The explicit dimensions are present/past as with Greenberg and Pearlman, but the other dimension is censored and correct duty driven by the super-ego/uncensored wish-fulfillment driven by the id, as in Figure 7.7.

Figure 7.7

"Freud's Search"

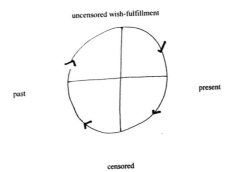

I have placed censored at the bottom, because it is the place of the miserable animal burdened by society's imposed duties which Freud described in Civilization and its Discontents (1930). As the dream delves deeper behind its facade into the past, it discovers the past and its uncensored vigor.

Jung's search is different again, because it is a search behind the persona of the correct mask in society for the huge forces in the vertical of the axis mundi. The dimensions are persona/collective unconscious, and inflation/deflation, as in Figure 7.8.

Figure 7.8

"Jung's Search"

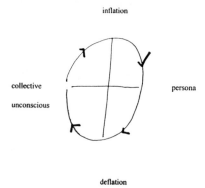

Interestingly, the aim of Jung's search is to balance this wheel in what he calls individuation, which is a squared circle or mandala. Then, one is neither a mere cardboard persona nor possessed by the gods, neither inflated, nor deflated, but more or less centered in this field between these great dangers.

Binswanger's search is quite similar to Jung's, and is concerned with excessive elevation (extravagance) and excessive sinking, with joining society versus being in a fantasy of specialness. Its dimensions are more secular and more spatial than Jung's, namely elevation/sinking, apart/involved, as in Figure 7.9.

Figure 7.9

"Binswanger's Search"

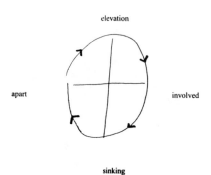

Essentially, its space poses the problem of balance between top and bottom, near and far.

Hillman's search into the underworld is for the ghostly powers that make for the eternal repetition. The outer part is the light of day, which is busy traffic that obscures soul. The inner part is the ghostly light of the underworld and its smoke and its mysteries. Everything rises and dies. The dimensions are light of day/light of the underworld, rising/dying, as in figure 7.10.

Figure 7.10

"Hillman's Search"

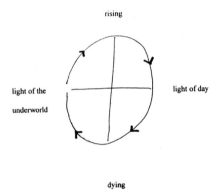

Hillman's search is for sipping the underworld, which yields what he calls soul.

Margulies' search is for the particular sensory quality which is peculiar to the patient's unconscious world, as in the case of slipperiness. Like his predecessors, the existentialists, he is concerned with the danger of elevation, and sinking. His dimensions, then, are the outer role/the inner sensory vitality, elevation/sinking, as in Figure 7.11.

Figure 7.11

Margulies's Search

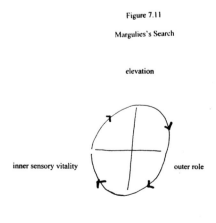

The great problem for Margulies is to provide company in the search for inner vitality, which bears with its updrafts that rise too fast and its downdrafts that are crushing.

Finally, Erikson's search (in a single paper) would seem to break out into a huge array as of 30 dimensions. He is his painterly self of interpersonal configurations, colors of mood, spatial arrangements, temporal arrangements, verbal play, sensory modes, and so forth, and even utilizes the absence of these dimensions to drive through to the convergence of the dream. Then he begins to combine dimensions like in synesthesia, spatial zooming, crowds of characters, actions of the dreamer, and so forth (see Chapter 4).

Like no one else in our series, he brings in history. The dreamer, such as Freud, is beset with fitting into the history of his group. The dreamer, such as the woman of the black and white S(E)INE dream, collides with her group and its culture at each stage of development.

Yet this incredible performance disappears without a trace and no one has built anything upon it. Indeed, Erikson reduces himself to 2-dimensions, and thereby builds quite a following. He proposes that outer man is adaptive, and inner man gets fixated at one of his eight stages of development. The unconscious becomes a chronicle of the progress of man towards full integrity (the culmination of life). Erikson has nicely reduced his art to something in 2-dimensions for Everyman in a kind of Pilgrim's Progress. The outer dimension is adaptation/the inner the developmental fixation. The vertical dimension is the progress through the eight stages of man. This system is pictured in Figure 7.12.

Figure 7.12

"Erikson's Search"

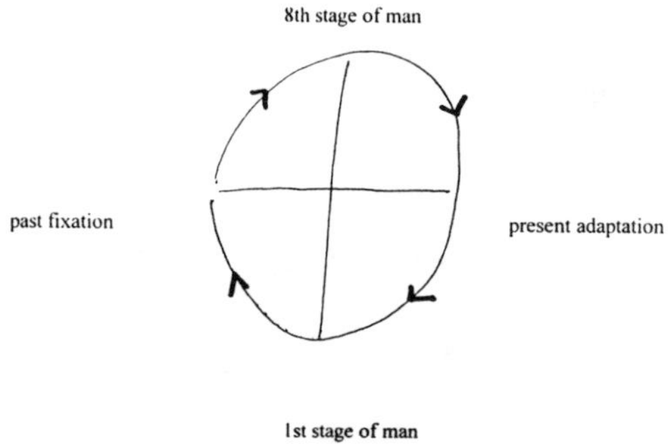

8th stage of man

past fixation   present adaptation

1st stage of man

A Unified Field Theory of the Bifurcation of
2-Dimensional and N-dimensional Space in Dreams

Having surveyed the canon of music of the last one hundred years of dream mapping, we may be in a position to ask how these varying scores fit together in a relatively simple way as different surfaces or 2-dimensional slices of an N-dimensional space which could be the entire subject of one theory and practice. For those familiar with theoretical physics, I am taking hyperspace (Kaku, 1994) as the subject of dreams, and the Klein-Kaluza theory of gravitation as an analogy. For those who are not so conversant with such a difficult topic, let me just say I am lining up the principal maps of dreams of the last hundred years and asking how the array could turn out that way? Bateson calls this the method of Little Jack Horner:

> I shall therefore adopt the method of Little Jack Horner, pulling out plums one after the other and exhibiting them side by side to create an array from which we can go on to list some of the fundamental criteria of mental process (p. 20, 1979)

The great pattern of my array is the reduction of dream space to 2-dimensions, even, as with Erikson most strikingly (students of the other cartographers can illustrate other transient dimensions in Freud, Jung, etc.) who had the potential of 30-dimensions. A general theory has got to explain this reduction as the most powerful trend of the subject. It is the strong force.

A general theory ought to be able to explain how to derive the different 2-dimensional spaces, while not being confined by them. For while it might be useful to have a specialized map of the rivers of the United States, or another of its elevations, or another of its roads, and so forth, it would be far better to be able to use all of the maps so as to have the advantages of different perspectives or slices of dream reality.

A general theory also has to build out of mammalian searching activity into ancient man, and on to the particular condition of modern man. For this is the path by which we have come to the present situation of dreaming. Most of this structure was constructed in the evolution of the mammal, a little in the evolution of ancient man, and only the most recent in the peculiar circumstances we find ourselves in now.

Dreaming as a Machine for Mapping the Subject in the World

The conscious mind is a focal instrument, quite like the fovea of the retina (Gustafson, 1995a and 1995b), of great facility for getting enough focus or intensity on a tiny area. Without it, it is difficult to untie knots (try it with bleary vision caused by glasses suitable for the distance, but not close up), or see into cells, or pound a nail.

The converse is the unconscious mind, which provides peripheral vision like the eye outside the fovea. Without it, we would untie the knot, see into the cell, pound the nail . . . while missing the semi-truck about to run us over from the side, or the chairman of the department bearing down upon us, or the change of a coming thunderstorm.

Thus, a great many of the problems of the mammal are what Rotenberg (1992) and his colleagues call "two-way avoidance tasks." The animal has to focus one thing, while heeding the other thing. This requires what he calls "divergent thinking" (see Schumacher, 1977, and Gustafson, 1995a, 1995b). The attention of the animal has to be in two places at once. A simple example is how to get the feed, while avoiding the predator. The dilemma is about "prey-vigilance" time. How much time to give to prey-vigilance, and how much to putting one's head down to feed? If I do too much of the first, I starve. If I do too much of the second, I am eaten while I eat. This is the central dilemma of the mammal (and of all creatures, one might argue), as illustrated in Figure 7.13.

Figure 7.13

"The Dilemma of Prey-Vigilance"

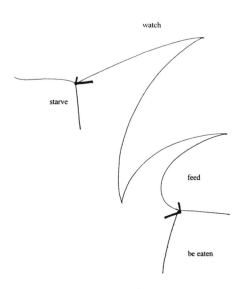

Essentially, Rotenberg and his colleagues have discovered (as we reviewed) that mammals which are frustrated in such a dilemma and in danger of giving up the search for a way through it, will increase their REM-time, which will revitalize their morning search activity.

It is as if the animal gets a surge of energy from an imaginary search at night. In this sense, Freud's map is probably right, insofar as it poses the engine of dreams as wish-fulfillment. From wish-fulfillment, the animal gets his hopes up at night. The other maps suggest that the animal gets solutions, inflation, elevation, rising, progress.

It is quite possible that the animal is also working over the very territory of his dilemma in these rapid movements of the eyes, so he is re-surveying it and looking for ways through his dilemma. Thus, he may get cognitive possibilities, as well as an invigoration of exploratory energy. He may be finding ways through, and sorting them out from going up blind alleys. Of course, we can't see what he is seeing, or ask him about it, so we may never have a way of finding out what he is up to.

Ancient or archaic man is another matter. With the advent of language, we can get a report of the night searches. While we can't go on them with him, we can be taken on a recall of some of the events. As we will see in Chapter 10 on "The Orchestral Score of Levi-Strauss" the waking and mythological mind of archaic man is little different from his dreaming mind. The chief dimensions of his mythological space are top/bottom, and in/out. The myths traverse the distance from heaven to hell on the vertical Axis Mundi, and they traverse the distance from in-group to out-group on the horizontal axis, as in Figure 7.14.

Figure 7.14

"Archaic Dimensions"

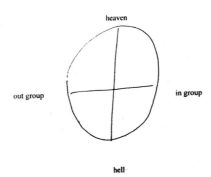

The reader may want to study Chapter 10 at this point, rather than taking my word for what comes out of it. Essentially Levi-Strauss believes:

> . . . the purpose of myth is to provide a logical model capable of overcoming a contradiction (p. 223, 1958, 1963)

Thus, the Zuni have to struggle with the contradiction (or dilemma, an equivalent word for what Levi-Strauss means) between depending on hunting versus depending upon crops (either can fail, and the Zuni perish). Thus, they tell stories (variants of the myth) in which:

> Coyote (a carrion-eater) is intermediary between herbivorous and carnivorous just as mist between Sky and Earth; as scalp between war and agriculture (scalp is a war crop); as corn smut between wild and cultivated plants; as garments between "nature" and "culture;" as refuse between village and outside; and as ashes (or soot) between roof (sky vault) and hearth (in the ground). This chain of mediators, if one may call them so. . . (p. 223, 1958/1963)

Thus, the archaic mind has a tremendous capacity for convergence by mediation, while it has a tremendous capacity for divergence to include every relevant quality or thing in their world. Levi-Strauss constructs his orchestral score such that the variability is read left to right in variants of the myth:

> Divergence of sequences and themes is a fundamental characteristic of mythological thought, which manifests itself as an irradiation (1964/1983, p. 5)

The convergence is read top to bottom by the structural similarities in all the diverging variations, as he illustrated in the foregoing passage about mediation in Zuni mythology taken as one great text.

In other words, the archaic mind is an instrument for handling dilemmas upon which survival depends as for the Zuni between hunting versus gathering. It has tremendous powers of convergence, and of divergence. Thus, it oscillates between its 2-dimensional dilemmas and their necessary mediation, while it brings in countless (N) dimensions that they have to deal with in daily life. Unlike us, they had to be experts in every quality, of plants, animals, housing, tools, weather, etc., etc. This gives them their divergent range. On the other hand, they had to face difficult choices of survival, which gives them their 2-dimensional sharpness.

I think that the dream instrument that we have is essentially this archaic instrument of survival, built upon mammalian searching. The depleted animal or archaic man needs re-invigoration by the hope of convergence (in heaven!), but it also needs sharp clarity about the divergence of its hope (on earth!), so the dream cycles between these two extremes on the vertical axis. The archaic man is also profoundly dependent on his group for survival, so he also cycles between being with his group, and being different from his group. Sometimes, the group has to cleave together tightly, and sometimes it must disperse. The dream traverses this 2-dimensional circuit, as illustrated in Figure 7.15.

Figure 7.15

"The Archaic Instrument"

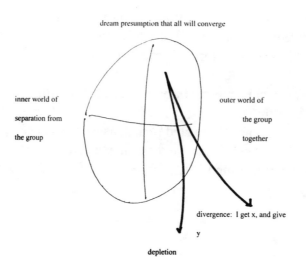

dream presumption that all will converge

inner world of separation from the group

outer world of the group together

divergence: I get x, and give y

depletion

If the reader now looks through Figures 7.6 to 7.12, he will see that they are variants on Figure 7.15. What makes each different is the group that the searcher belongs to -- namely, the school of psychotherapy he both creates and stands for.

I want briefly to discuss how the situation changes from archaic man to modern man, and how this alters the dream instrument. I can only go over the ground of chapters 11 and 12 in rough outline as I just went over the ground of Chapter 10 in rough outline.

Essentially, modern man survives by becoming a specialist, who can trade his contribution for everything else that he needs. This very advantage is also his nightmare, for he dare not lose his standing in his specialty. Levi-Strauss calls this structure "the hot engine" (Charbonnier, 1969). He tends to throw tremendous energy or heat into "getting ahead" and he dreads falling behind and into the cold. This distorts his dream potential like crazy. If he is a Freudian, he has to bring forward Freudian dreams from his patients, etc.

He is extremely vulnerable, either to getting overheated in his zealous attempts to force convergence with his group and to force his own elevation in the hierarchy of his group, or to being cooled out as being no longer of any use. This works upon his mammalian biology we have been discussing, in that he is prone to collapses of morale in any given day. He is apt to get in a heated panic, trying to reestablish himself. As we discussed in Chapter 6 with Sullivan, his chief concern is security within his group of specialists.

Because he is like every other mammal, he cannot search very well either in an overheated panic, or in cold resignation. These are the two pathologies that beset him, and drive him around the vicious circle of convergent hope and reunion with his hierarchy, and divergent reality and separation from his hierarchy. Much of his difficulty is to control his own temperature (heat, energy), so he is not slipping into excessive heat (panic) or excessive cold (resignation). Chen's (1994) model of schizophrenia is just this double failure of temperature, but it could be applied just as well to bipolar disorders of affect, anxiety disorders, and the entire business of psychiatry (Gustafson, 1995a, 1995b; in preparation).

In Summary, the 2-dimensional/8-Dimensional Bifurcation of Dream Space: The Cumulus Engine

Dreams are going to be about attempted convergence, which arouses hopeful energy or heat, but the different schools are going to picture it in their own terms as about solutions, uncensored wishes, inflation with the gods (instinctual powers), elevations, rising, progress, or memory. Dreams are also going to be about coming to terms with divergence, as we turn into the world, to get a, but give up b. They will threaten to turn us cold, as Hillman persuades us in his particular space of the underworld.

That is why I say that the dream machine is like a cumulus engine (Moran & Morgan, 1986), which has tremendous updrafts of heat, and tremendous downdrafts of cold. It takes a lot of agility to ride these forces with patients, and it takes an ability to stand outside such a vicious circle.

A dream can also depart the vicious circle of hot and cold in 2-dimensions, for 8-dimensions, 30-dimensions, or n-dimensions. In general, this is what it means to rejoin archaic man in his plenitude of art and nature. But you also have to be able to get back again, to be ready for your fellow modern man in all his presumption that he is going to win at your expense.

I believe that we get this free passage (Gustafson and Cooper, 1990) in dreams between 2-dimensional worlds of modern man and 8-dimensional worlds of art and nature, by being able to transpose surfaces. If we are stuck on a 2-dimensional surface and cannot get anywhere there, we are likely to heat up or turn cold. There the dream will jump and leave a hiatus // to another surface which will be explored for more fertile possibilities. The set of surfaces in a dream either converge upon the predicament of the dreamer with his group (Erikson's convergence of Freud with the medical grand rounds in Irma), or they diverge from it for searching surfaces with more potential. Also, when fertile possibilities are reached, the dreamer needs to transpose back to the limited black-and-white-reality of his group, as in the S(E)INE dream of Erikson's patient. The great modern difficulty is to live in 2-dimensions, depart into 8-dimensions, and return to 2-dimensions, as I will now illustrate with dreams of two of my patients, and two dreams of my own which broke the theoretical difficulties for me of this chapter.

Dreams of Two of My Patients

The first patient is a middle-aged professional woman, with whom I had worked about five years. She came to me because her previous therapist had chastised her for sexual adventures and even told her G.P. about this material given in confidence. She was extremely wounded by this outright betrayal, and is only now gathering confidence to risk adventures with men again, and risk testing me with my response to this. In the past five years, we have worked through a great many dreams, about incest, about her defending herself in her profession, especially, so that she is considerably better at defending herself.

The Dream of Having Her White Auto Stuck in the Muddy Roads of Greece or Bosnia.
The patient told me that she was interested in looking for a man again, and related this dream:

> She gets her (white) auto stuck on muddy roads in what is either Bosnia or Greece. There are rebellious soldiers everywhere and she is afraid to ask them to help her. She goes into a gymnasium, where men are laying about against a wall, and she fears to ask them also. Then, there is her father, almost in her face, asking if she wants white or chocolate cake?

When I heard this dream, I thought immediately of Hillman's 2-dimensional space of a dim and smoky underworld in black (or brown) and white. Certainly, it appeared to be the eternal repetition of violent men. As she said, it is like a painting with the same thing in the far distance, the middle distance, and the near distance. It looks as if she is prone to sacrificing herself once more to an underworld of man the destroyer of women.

I simply said that it was a hell of a place to look for a husband! She laughed, and said she had always been taken with the romance of this kind of soldierly man. I laughed, and said it did not seem very promising. Just that we could laugh about it, as a kind of painting, was a great thing to my ear, for it meant that part of her was outside this terrible hot engine of war. She was coolly entertaining her own past history even with a sense of humor.

My second patient is also a middle-aged professional woman, who has taken on some stepchildren and a cranky husband. Her entire household is very self-centered, while she keeps hoping they will improve. Her delusion is that self-centered people will stop being ugly, when they don't get their way.

The Dream of Nightmare Baseball. Her husband had had a rare couple of good weeks after a professional success, but got ugly again over a minor event with one of the stepchildren. She was crestfallen. She still cannot quite believe that he has to be this way. I myself am quite convinced of it. She thinks she can bring him around. She dreamt:

> I am playing baseball at night. I hit the ball barely past the pitcher's mound, and start running for first base. But I panic at all the yelling and baseballs flying around and run for third base. Somehow I end up sliding into first from the second base side. Then I am behind some kind of door with my toe barely peeking out.

Her painting of this dream is diagrammed in Figure 7.16.

Figure 7.16

"Nightmare Baseball"

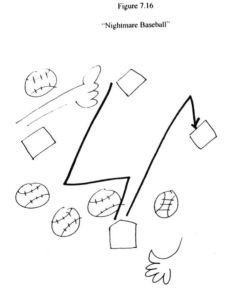

This too is like one of Hillman's underworlds in timeless black and white. Baseball is for her a game in which she was always chosen last, for she never got any help at it. It was a nightmare for her, as in the dream itself. Curiously, the toe behind the door refers to getting pushed into a rush-hour train in Tokyo, by one of those terrifying men with shields who are compressing the

151

passengers to pack the trains. This part of the dream agitated her the most, and she remarked that she'd never get on one of those rush hour trains again.

I replied that they fully grasped the force fields of competitive baseball and of rush-hour trains in Tokyo, but she was still placing herself in the way of similar forces at home. Her husband and her stepchildren play rough ball and they shove her into express trains. If she liked, she could keep getting in the way of their perpetual turning on her. I sent along to her my drawing of the inexorable turning of her household from having their way (presumption) to not having their way (inevitable, and ugly), and her vain attempt to stop this wheel of fire, as illustrated in Figure 7.17.

Figure 7.17

"The Physicists"

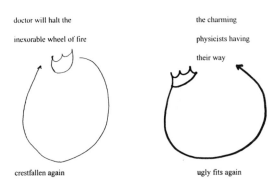

doctor will halt the

inexorable wheel of fire

the charming

physicists having

their way

crestfallen again

ugly fits again

This patient has a tremendous ability to enter the domains of art and nature in 8-dimensions, but she has difficulty transposing back to 2-dimensions in black and white (as if her household were like her) I told her she might want to read Durrenmatt's The Physicists (1962), about a female psychiatrist who tried to set up a hospital for civilizing three mad scientists, named Einstein, Mobius, and Newton, with three lady wrestlers as their nurses. It is a gross underestimation of the physics of these narcissists, who end up strangling all three nurses, quite cheerfully.

Two Dreams of the Author

The Author's Dream of a Fourth of July Celebration. As I was coming to the conclusion of this chapter about the bifurcation of 2-dimensional and 8-dimensional spaces in dreams, I dreamt of their relation as follows:

I am coming down our street on an unusual bicycle in which I can tilt so far back that I am almost looking at the sky. I see our house as if it is in Chinatown in San Francisco for the New Year, three stories, festooned in beautiful colors, like dark green against purple, yellow against orange, and so forth. Its balconies create beautiful planes in different colors. I note I could easily lean back on my bicycle and tip over backwards. (//) Then I notice I am in NYC waiting for a patient of mine who disappeared in an old book shop. Impatient, I go on, and find him looking like death sitting on a toilet. He says it is the only safe place he could find, and that his diarrhea will last three months! All of this illustrated in Figure 7.18.

Figure 7.18

"Erikson's Divergence and Convergence"

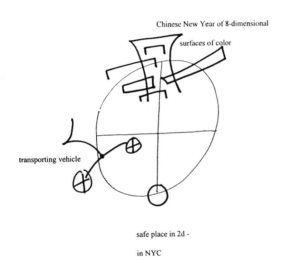

Chinese New Year of 8-dimensional

surfaces of color

transporting vehicle

safe place in 2d -

in NYC

To make a long story short, the house of many colors is my potential dream house in 8-dimensions (colors, surfaces, balconies), the bicycle is my transport that gets me there looking upwards, and the problem posed by the dream is the inevitable transposition back to 2-dimensional reality. It is a dream of spring (bicycle), summer (4th of July in 8-dimensions) fall and winter, or the four seasons of the cycle of time. I must live with it. It is a dream of converging heavenly beauty, and diverging reality, brown in New York City.

The Author's Dream of An Array of Transpositions (Seven). The following night, as I puzzled over why Erikson gave up his beautiful scheme, for his Pilgrim's Progress of banal success, I dream as follows:

My high school class is supposed to go together from the country south of Madison back into the city together, and I am to keep them together. It is like a migration of birds, which disperses in a series of arching trajectories into different sectors of the city (niches). I give up, and take a bus by myself, heading east. (//)

I meet old pals in their high school letter jackets in Southern Ontario, where I have been invited back by them to give a workshop. I shiver as we sit in the snow in our thin jackets at the local baseball diamond they are proud of. I play along, feeling they are living in a frozen past. (//)

I ask to go where they will put me up, and am given the bedroom of the daughter of the host. I look out her patio door, and see an endless corporate farm building without windows. I look back in, and discover a little cage for two worms. I cannot keep the worms from crawling out through a hole I cannot stop. I ask the daughter, and she smiles and tapes them to the floor of their cage with scotch tape! (//)

I decide I have to get out of this place as well, and wander over a little rise past a police car. I get a map, which shows a suburb as an island floating in a sea of nothing, with fancy English names. (//)

I notice a bonfire in this icy city, which seems to draw down a beautiful painting of swallows (summer in Vivaldi's "Four Seasons") in a marvelous array of colors. (//)

I see a little boy (as in "Citizen Kane" directed by Orson Welles) on a sled sliding all by himself down the main street of town turned into a sled run. He crosses the finish line, and a crowd of people burst out of this shack from the 1950s and hug him. This is all in black and white like a film. (//)

I realize I have exactly that run of the little boy, which I do on my cross-country skis, near my house now.

This dream would make little sense, without a theory of convergence, and divergence, and transposition of surfaces. I was only able to pull back many of the scenes, because I felt their logic.

I am heating up in the first scene, working against the migration of my fellows in the American economy. Then, I find them in Ontario (similar), stuck in a static cold. Then, I find them in Alberta on a corporate farm which is vast, and houses tiny worms, readily put to bed with scotch tape by the daughter. Then, I find them in a pretentious suburb, an island nowhere (erewhon).

Finally, I locate a beautiful surface for the migration, in the bonfire of Vivaldi's summer, and in an allusion to a painting by Winslow Homer, in 8-dimensions of color, as illustrated in Figure 7.19.

Figure 7.19

"Vivaldi's Four Seasons"

swallows of summer

bonfire of winter

This transposes quickly back to 2-dimensional black and white in a myth from the 1950s I am distancing here, that the boy-hero will have plenty of company. This sentimental convergence is corrected by <u>transposing</u> from the <u>exact run</u> of the boy's sled to my own <u>exact run</u> of my cross-country skis near my home here. Art and nature are there for me // but company or reunion turns out to be a futile heated effort, or cold and static past, or corporate worms, or pretentious erewhon, or a black and white film from the 1950s.

Chapter 8. The Powers of the Imagination.

The hardest education to get is about how something works in one region, and completely falls apart in another. These are the most wrenching experiences we have to deal with, and the most bewildering. For example, a child is at home on his baseball fields, and is stunned at school when he is cut off the team of the junior high school. Or he chooses an admirable college, and finds himself with barbarians. Or he admires a professor in class, and finds him mad at home.

Spirit is broken by such falls, and can lead to creeping to one's own home with a dislocated psyche. Of course, the mammal in us as we have seen in the last chapter is not going to take this lying down for long. The search will be on to revive oneself with fresh dreams.

The trouble is that a creature ascending again has got to sort out where his climb is secure, and where it is insupportable. In other words, he has to sort out what is workable in one region, and what is unworkable in a second region. If he can sort this out, he can be bold in the one, and bow in the other. Anything else is plain dangerous.

Where is he going to get help with this education? Certainly, religion has been the mainstay. As in Dante's Divine Comedy (1300; translation, Pinsky, 1994) it has mapped out the footing that can be trusted, versus the footing that is treacherous. But religion has gotten less accurate in its mapping since 1300. It is often sentimental about things that will let us down, and too scared to venture out of its platitudes.

Art as narrative and painting and music and so forth has been going over the same ground all along, and holds up better. This is only because it is a tradition of individual works. If society is weakened, art can survive at a high level.

In other words, the sudden shifts that the world has set for us everywhere take imagination to see in advance. Nothing less than imagination will suffice. It turns out that most of us have the very imagination necessary for the job. We are just not using it.

This is because we are modern creatures who believe that will is the great thing (Tate, 1934). As Yeats put it most succinctly, we set will to do the work of the imagination. But it cannot. Will depends upon the focus of the conscious mind. It can see only a little at a time, and misses these terrible fracture lines, where we pass from a sound surface to an insupportable surface.

It turns out that dreams see these fracture lines better than any instrument the world has ever devised. It also turns out that this kind of sighting between one surface and another is precisely the search that goes on in art (of all kinds, narrative, painting, musical, and so forth). So, it becomes necessary for the ordinary man to utilize his own dreams quite like a poet or a painter.

What he creates will be symbols for himself to mark his own terrain. These will allow him to catch himself in these regions where he is apt to go over the edge. For example, the woman whom I described in Chapter 2 with The Dream of the Spiral into the Pit had the vivid image of driving her car into a downward spiral of mud with less and less traction. This terrain was the mess of her mother, whom she could not pull out.

This symbol could be the impetus for a poem or for a painting, but she lacks interest or facility in those forms. It remains a private marker.

The Dream of the Spiral Into the Pit, Revisited. Now, my patient returned a year later in different difficulty. This time, she was entirely spent in her job. For months she had felt less and less like working for them. By the end of the day, she could barely creep home, and fall asleep on her couch. She had no idea of how her vitality had disappeared.

To abbreviate an hour, I did have an idea which woke her back up again. I had noticed that she was very upset about various injustices at work, and I had noticed her remark that little injustices became huge at home. For example, she flared at her son being late for a basketball game and letting down his teammates.

Therefore, I told her that she was spent because she was taking on causes that were beyond her. If she did not want to be worn out, she would have to leave to her son his standing with his team. Similarly, at work, she would have to attend to her own work. "Yes," she exclaimed, "Here I go fixing everything again! How did I forget? I am so exasperated with myself!" She slammed down her fist, and she pointed to her head in self accusation (Gustafson's sign; Gustafson, 1992, 1995a, 1995b).

I replied that she forgot because she was quite taken with fixing things. I reminded her of a year previous, when she was drawn into fixing her mother's situation. I mentioned the loss of traction in the mud.

She exclaimed, "This is like a slap of cold water on the face, that wakes me up again." I replied that she had been lost in the mud. "And choking on it too!" she added. I said that it was interesting that she mentioned water, as a relief from earth, as a kind of baptism. Earth is often a surface, in which my patients get lost.

Memory Maps

As Sullivan (1954; 1956) was wont to say, we fail to learn anything from our experience when it is lost in fog. We had better have these beacons, especially where there are very abrupt transitions. Sometimes, a thoughtful government will mark them for us. As we glide swiftly through a white forest on our cross-country skis, we may suddenly come upon a sign, "Steep slope ahead!" A very great deal of the world's transitions will not be marked for us. We will have to do it for ourselves.

A private memory map is what each of us has got to construct. In the Middle Ages, we would have gotten some help from the Catholic Church (Yates, 1966):

Usually the map took the form of a stairway from the lower Hell, through the intermediate worlds, to the Divine Source. St. Thomas Aquinas had authorized devices of this kind . . "Men cannot understand without images." (Hughes, 1992, p. 20; Gustafson, 1995a, pp. 66-72)

Now we are on our own. Of course, patients can sometimes get help with constructing their own memory maps. My patient now has a more vivid marker of regions where she is going to try to fix what cannot be fixed: a spiral into mud, with no traction. She is less apt to forget this circle into hell.

This we shall see is a first glimpse of the first of three powers of the imagination, which we will need to mark the grave transitions of our daily lives. The first power of the imagination is to see that the surface I am on is hopeless for using my will. The second power of the imagination is to transpose to another surface where I have more free play -- as when my patient got out of the choking mud, splashed by fresh cold water. The third power of the imagination is to come back from beautiful possibilities to the bare staircase of history where political power rules with very little appeal. We will now proceed to these three powers of the imagination, which derive from the dream.

The First Power of the Imagination -- Sighting the Surface I Am On Where My Will Is Useless

Ancient Will

My patient bent on fixing things turns out to be the ordinary case. There seems to be something ancient about a stubborn will. Bachelard (originally, 1938; 1964) calls it

the seduction of the initial choice (p. 1)

and a fascination with primitive material itself, like fire,

the secret persistence of this idolatry of fire (p. 4)

Only if one can catch oneself holding onto such a preference, by standing far back enough to see it and laugh, like my patient, is one going to be free of this presumption.

Medieval Will

But where am I to stand to see myself from the outside stuck on a surface or stage of farce? In 1300, Dante pictures himself lost in a dark wood, at the mercy of a leopard, a lion, and a wolf (Pinsky translation, 1994). The rising sun shows him the road, but he cannot take it, until Virgil comes along to guide him.

Dante suggests that you need to stand back with someone else and with the assurance that there are better places to climb to. Those who have only their own will go around in circles on the same gruesome surface. Yet it is terribly important to witness the entire series of hopeless circles. The idea goes back to Saint Augustine,

"Descend that you may ascend"

as Freccero explains (p. xiv) in the new Pinsky translation of The Inferno. If we try to fly from these things, like Odysseus from Troy, we will be guilty of the presumption that we can rise above them and be doomed to failure (like Dante at the very start). Instead, we must be willing to navigate downward to witness the suction of hell (Freccero, pp. xv-xvii). After such a navigation, we will not underestimate its hold on those who take it lightly.

There is no substitute for reading The Inferno itself. I would just like to note its architecture of disaster. All of its surfaces are circles, constructed by willfulness. The upper circles come from incontinence, that is, from running over limits to desiring things in terms of sexuality, eating, seizing power, and so forth. My patient's presumption to fix things belongs here.

Deeper down are the circles of violence, which beget violence. Then fraud, and finally betrayal, which are the most dangerous. What is good, and sound, and true, is tricked by them.

It is necessary to know the surfaces of hell, for seeing oneself and for seeing others. That is, I can get in trouble when my own will presumes, and I can get in trouble when others are going to go around in their own vicious circles and I presume to get them out.

A Dream of Flying Into Hell. I had been working with my patient for some time concerning her underestimation of the willfulness of her husband and her stepchildren. Her dream of Nightmare Baseball illustrated in Chapter 7 got across to her being lost on certain fields of force, like being pushed into trains at rush hour in Tokyo. Several weeks later, she saw in a dream such a field of force in advance, and, thus, from the outside where she might be able to steer clear of it before it got her. She dreamt:

I am flying from Madison to Milwaukee and I can see out the front of the airplane like a pilot. I see we are in sunlight, but flying toward a kind of wall of dark rain. Oddly, the wall is perfectly vertical (//)

Then I am getting into a bus with women dressed in pencil-thin high heels. We are going to a battle. We arrive at a green field, where soldiers are supposed to clear the way for us. The green field looks like an athletic field, instead of a battleground.

Her dream looks forward to the green fields of summer, when her stepdaughters return from college. It is as if an entire busload of them will be coming in those high heels of their biological mother. She wishes that soldiers would clear the way for them. Alas, she is heading straight into a wall of rain.

Her fiction is her presumption that she can just give to these girls, with no strings attached. Already, she has suffered from this policy, as pictured in Nightmare Baseball. Now, she sights it coming along, and her wishful presumption that soldiers will clear the way to green fields. She decides to see to it that the girls have jobs this summer.

It is very interesting how she would fly and how she would reach green fields (paradise), but that a perfectly vertical wall (surface) of dark rain is directly in her path. It is quite as in Dante. Such a flight is a presumption. Only a navigation of dark rain will be possible. For that I am her company, to see it in advance, and plan for its baleful forces, and keep from taking it lightly.

Modern Will

Modern will is not quite incontinence, violence, fraud, or betrayal. In some ways it is a compound of all of these things, disguised in the form of an allegory of progress. Tate (1934) says that it abounds in two forms of rhetoric: the scientific rhetoric that says we can take what we want in a specialized operation like extracting oil, while ignoring the total situation of the property from which the oil is gotten (p. 112); the romantic rhetoric that says that individual will can stop these things, as if writing a poem about this is going to stop the oil companies. Thus, science consists of

certified half-statements (p. 109)

and romance consists of

fictitious alternatives to them (p. 102)

Together, they constitute our disaster:

The significance of this movement in modern society is perfectly plain: by seizing exclusively those aspects of the total experience that are capable of being put to predictable and successful use, the modern spirit has committed itself to the most dangerous program in Western history. It has committed itself exclusively to this program. (p. 105)

It is rhetoric or the art of persuading others that will can have what it seeks:

. . . rhetoric is a forcing of the subject. "For what is rhetoric," wrote W. B. Yeats nearly fifty years ago, "but the will trying to do the work of the imagination." (p. 95)

The scientist or the poet

. . . ignores the whole of the experience for some special interest. . . For our whole culture seems to be obsessed by a kind of literature that is derivative of the allegorical mentality . . (pp. 99)

An allegory is a story forced to come out right:

> . . . it is an abstraction calculated to force the situation upon which it is imposed toward a single direction (p. 98)

Whether it is in science, in romantic literature, in capitalism, in advertising, in propaganda, in didactic programs of education, in athletics, and even in religion, or psychotherapy, it is going to be a program of winning with the conscious will.:

> For the recognition of that other half of experience, the realm of immitigable evil -- or perhaps I had better say in modern abstraction, the margin of error in social calculation -- has been steadily lost. The fusion of human success and human error in a vision of the whole of life, the vision itself being its own goal, has almost disappeared from the modern world. (p. 106)

Several years ago (Gustafson, 1992) I suggested that there are only three stories that come into my office seeking remedy. The most common is subservience, wherein the subject believes that her servitude will get its just desert. The second most common is delay, wherein the subject believes his postponement of vital needs will get its just desert. The third most common is overpowering, wherein the subject believes his entitlement allows him to seize his deserts without service and without delay.

Following Tate's lucid argument about the modern will, I would now say that all three stories are but one story of presumption

> . . . an abstraction calculated to force the situation upon which it is imposed toward a single direction. (p. 98)

The direction is my deserts, which I will bring about by my ploy of will, which will overlook (Gustafson, 1995a; 1995b) everything which is not fitting with its program by selective inattention (Sullivan, 1954, 1956; Gustafson, 1986, 1996).

A Dream of a Warm Bath // Transposed into a Field of Force. I have worked for a number of years with this patient, helping her to anticipate betrayal. Now, she is better prepared, and interested in having a man in her life after a long foregoing. Her Dream of Having Her White Auto Stuck in the Muddy Roads of Greece or Bosnia was illustrated in Chapter 7, showing her, as I said, looking for a husband in the most unlikely of places. Several weeks later, she related the following dream:

> I am rebuilding my house in the country and decide to take a warm bath. (//) Next I know I am surrounded in the tub by a swarm of onlookers in a field.

The key in the dream is the hiatus (//), wherein her private comfort is transposed to a public field. I asked her how she knew about such a thing, and she could tell me right away that that had been the story of her marriage. She married a very powerful man of science (//) and next she knew she was in the middle of his social circle of the laboratory. He needed his circle, and she became an object of its consuming interest.

She had focused her will upon her private relationship with this man. Bringing this abstraction into focus, she had lost her peripheral vision. The privacy was embedded in a public display. Thus, her dream pictures the actual surface of hell that she is likely to place herself in again when she seeks to follow her fascination with men of power. She would isolate what she wants with her romantic will (//) with the grave danger of missing the dark forest of the beautiful tree. This is the very tragedy of modern will, deceived by its own rhetoric. The dream stands back to sight it as a total picture.

Other Markers of a Surface of Will
About to Go In Circles

My students ask me if they have to be capable of using dreams to sight these surfaces of the vicious circle? I answer that it is not necessary, if you know what to watch for. That is, you need to know the plot, of presumption, its signs, and its oversights.

The Case of Quixote. This man complained of tremendous fluctuation of morale. He could be very high to very low, in seconds. In psychiatry, this is called cyclothymia. This is one of many certified half-statements of truth, which covers up what is overlooked in clouds. Yes, he cycles, but what is the engine?

It turns out to be very simple. He fires up at injustice, like Quixote himself, is drawn into attack, and then withdraws in shame. His presumption is that he is in the world to right these wrongs.

After we had sighted together the entire cycle, through many episodes, he still fell back into it. Why? He felt so stupid about it. He would think he was calm and collected, and a meeting would come up sure to rile him, and he would presume he could handle it. He could not.

I told him he was like one of those basketball players who gets fouled at one end of the floor, and cannot keep from retaliating at the other end of the floor and getting a foul called on him or getting thrown out of the game. I would bench him, if I were the coach, whenever he got fouled. Until he could bench himself.

Can he bench himself? Only if he can see the thing coming. Once he is heated up, he is lost. It is too late, and beyond his control. He dare not presume that he has control, once he has crossed one of those fracture lines from sound to insupportable territory.

I understand this very well from my own athletic career. When I feel that body heat out there, I know I am in a region where I will be pretty useless for a while. I just limit my will to the minimum, until the agitation passes. It is absolutely vital that I know when I am on one of those surfaces, where will only makes it worse. My temperature is too high (see Chen, 1994).

I also answer to my students that I can help patients without dreams that mark the surface of the vicious circle, but I can help them mark it more vividly if I can get to dreams and the first power of the imagination in dreams. Interestingly, imagination need not be visual. I had two dreams about two of my colleagues in two successive nights which consisted of a single word.

The Author's Two Dreams In a Single Word. I had been pondering a colleague, who seemed bright to me as a youth. I dreamt that night a single word:

Incandescent.

In other words, he was like an incandescent light bulb which had had its allotted hours. I had also been pondering a distant colleague who was about to retire, who still smoldered in a kind of mad way. I dreamt that night a single word:

Phosphorescent.

These two dreams helped me to accept that there was nothing I could do about it. These academic surfaces are often circular, and just burn for a while. My will is of no moment.

The Second Power of the Imagination -- The Ars Ascendi, or
Summoning of the Energies of Images, Words, Metaphors

As I wrote, the surfaces of hell can only be seen for what they are if the surfaces of comfort are there to buoy us. The trouble is that they will lull us into sleep, and drop us back in waking up. This is the ordinary vicious cycle. As Bottom says upon waking up from his

Midsummer Night's Dream,

Man is but an ass if he go about to expound this dream . . . It shall be called "Bottom's Dream," because it hath no bottom . . . (IV, I, 204-205, 212-213)

Figure 8.1

"Bottom's Dream"

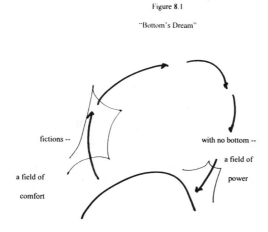

fictions --

a field of

comfort

with no bottom --

a field of

power

Thus, mankind is apt to be foolish in its oscillation between fictions which give it morale, and the bottom dropping out. It is a way to stumble through life, like Bottom himself. It works in this lurching fashion, because it is impossible to live without hope. Yet false hopes get exposed. Hence, the vicious cycle.

A Case of a Relationship as Thin as a Piece of Paper. The ultimate limit to this cycle of uplift in sleep, and downdraft on waking, is the following case which I encountered on a day of being the attending physician for our inpatient service. This thirty-year old woman had a history of countless hospitalizations lifting her up, and countless discharges dropping her into a bottomless pit. I asked her how she managed to keep going? She replied that it was only because Dr. _____, the Professor of Psychiatry, told her he could help her. Otherwise, she had nothing.

Several days later, I discussed the case with the second year residents who were on call for the emergency room. They were anxious seeing her, and fearing it might be their watch when she finally killed herself. I finally said that they were right to fear this "ailment" (Main, 1957), which is often fatal. Often, it is a daughter of a medical family who has the ailment as a ticket, to get something from the doctor as father. This patient did have the air of a little girl, held up by the single thread of the Doctor Professor.

I said that if I were on call, and saw her, I'd ask about how things were with her doctor? The relationship was as thin as a sheet of paper, and I'd look to see if the paper was there or not. Like the woman who jumped off a cliff into the Atlantic ocean after the medical student left the psychiatry service (Havens, 1965), this woman could enter the abyss if the Professor turned away.

Dream Screens

Paper is an interesting example of a surface that holds a person up. It works insofar as there is comfort in it, to let go of vigilance into sleep. In other words, it can have more power than it appears to have. It is invested by the patient with this power, as if the paper became a major carpet upon which the patient could lie at night.

Isakower (1938) suggested that the power of a comforting surface that allows sleep comes from a regression to early childhood. He based this theory upon strange descriptions of patients who were either falling asleep or going into a fever:

"When I'm feverish, I get a curious sensation in my palate -- I can't describe it. Yesterday I noticed it when I was going to sleep, although I wasn't feverish. At the same time I have a feeling as if I were on a revolving disc. Giddiness and a kind of general discomfort. It's as if I were lying on something crumpled, but this crumpled feeling's in my mouth at the same time; the whole thing begins in the palate -- I can almost feel it now when I think of it." (p. 331)

164

Lewin (1973) called this surface the "dream screen." It can be replete with these sensational experiences of a feeding infant, or it can be blank as a white sheet of paper. The dream screen is the backcloth, upon which the content of dreams is played, as movies are played upon a movie screen. The key in Lewin's argument is a particular dream of a patient, in which there was an actual transition between having such a dream screen and losing it:

> The dream screen came to my notice when a young woman patient reported as follows: "I had my dream all ready for you; but while I was lying here looking at it, it turned over away from me, rolled up, and rolled away from me -- over and over like two tumblers." She repeated the description several times at my request, so that I could substantiate the gist of her experience, namely, that the dream screen with the dream on it bent over backwards away from her, and then like a carpet or canvas rolled up and off into the distance with the rotary motion of machine tumblers. (p. 88)

This dream screen is a conflation of the surfaces of a rotary machine, a carpet or canvas, a movie screen and a mother that turns over. Lewin's argument is that the first dream screen is lying upon the body of your mother, and the latter dream screens are just derivatives of the original surface of security:

> Isakower interprets the large masses, that approach beginning sleepers, as breasts. As they approach the sleeper, the breast seems to grow; its convex surface flattens out and finally merges with the sleeper, often to the accompaniment of mouth sensations. My patient's belated waking up was the reverse experience. The flat dream screen curved over into a convex surface and went away. When one falls asleep, the breast is taken into one's perceptual world: it flattens out or approaches flatness, and when one wakes up it disappears, reversing the events of its appearance. (p. 89)

Balint (1968) has very little to say about dreams, but a great deal about these primitive surfaces wherein we rest and renew ourselves. Balint goes back farther than Isakower and Lewin to the fetus in the womb:

> . . . we know that the foetus's dependency on its environment is extreme . . In consequence it is essential for its well-being and orderly development that the environment should be all the time very near to what the foetus needs . . (p. 66)

The quality of this dependence is as follows:

> . . . the cathexis (investment of energy) of the environment by the foetus must be very intense . . . The environment, however, is probably undifferentiated; on the one hand, there are as yet no objects in it; on the other hand, it has hardly any structure, in particular no sharp boundaries towards the individual; environment and individual penetrate into each other, they exist together in a "harmonious mix-up." An important example of this harmonious interpenetrating mix-up is the fish in the sea (one of the most archaic and most widely occurring symbols). (p. 66)

Balint argues that the individual after birth begins to differentiate and distinguish where he is more and less connected:

> . . . libido (energy) is no longer in homogeneous flux . . . under the influence of emerging objects, concentrations and rarefactions appear in its flow (p. 67).

Yet the archaic surfaces remain available:

> We use the air, in fact we cannot live without it; we inhale it in order to take parts out of it and use them as we want; then, after putting substances into it that we want to get rid of, we exhale it -- without paying the slightest attention to it. In fact, the air must be there for us, and as long as it is there in sufficient supply and quality, we do not take any notice of it. (p. 66)

Balint calls air, and water, and earth, and fire, primary objects which are archaic mother symbols (pp. 68-69). The relationship to them is this "harmonious inter-penetrating mix-up." Quite independently, Bachelard (originally published, 1971; 1987) argues that these four primitive materials are the way back to vitality:

> A true poet . . . wants imagination to be a voyage. Thus each poet owes us his invitation to the voyage . . . If the initial image is well chosen, it is an impulsion to a well-defined dream, to an imaginary life that will have real laws of successive images, really vital meaning (p. 21)

Note that the well chose image will act as an impulsion, and that the series set in motion will have real laws of successive images:

> The sequence of images arranged by the invitation to the voyage takes on, through the aptness of its order, a special vivacity that makes it possible to designate, in the cases I shall study at length in this book, a movement of the imagination. We shall actually feel it within ourselves, usually as a lightening, an effortless imagination of connected images, an eagerness to pursue the enchanting dream. . . . It is nutriment for the nerves. It must cause a dynamic induction in us. I shall try to reveal the multiple implications of Paul Valery's profound remark, "the true poet is the one who inspires." The poet of fire, of water, or of earth does not transmit the same inspiration as the poet of air (p. 22)

Notice that the images will have an effect of lightening, of eagerness, of dynamic induction, and that they will move along four different axes: into air, or into fire, or into earth, or into water.

Balint's Two Dreams of the Patient with the Basic Fault. Now it is quite true that many patients cannot allow themselves to enter into the vitality of these primitive sequences. Balint gives two examples borrowed from a patient of his wife's:

> I wish to illustrate this kind of atmosphere by two dreams experienced by a patient during the same night. (1) She was walking in a wood: suddenly a large flesh-coloured bird

swooped down, hit her violently, and made a gash in her forehead. Patient was stunned and fell to the ground unconscious. The terrible thing was that the bird never looked back; it was quite unconcerned about what it had done. (2) Patient was then in a room with a number of friends who were playing games which she used to share with them. Nobody took any notice of her. The terrible thing was she was alone forever because she would <u>never be able to get over the thought that the bird did not look round</u>. (p. 89)

She cannot let herself go in a mix-up with the wood or with a mix-up of sharing the games. She starts to. Then the violent interruption. This is what Balint called "the basic fault" which can only be (partially) repaired by the doctor becoming like a primary substance. That is, Balint has to become like a wood that the patient can walk in without concern for him. Then, the surface can let its dynamic induction go, and the patient come alive in it. But that is a subject that leads us in another direction, which Balint covers perfectly well in his book, and which I have surveyed many times (Gustafson, 1986, reprinted, 1997; Gustafson, 1995a; Gustafson, 1995b) for its ways and its hazards.

My subject now is the second power of the imagination, to summon the energies of images, words, metaphors, and so forth. I call it the "ars ascendi," (Yates, 1966) for the ascendance of vitality. Its literal direction may be into the heaven of the air, or laterally into repose of waters,

He leadeth me beside still waters. He restoreth my soul (<u>Psalms</u>, 23:2-3)

or digging downward into the earth like Seamus Heaney in his early poem by that name, "Digging." As Heaney says in his essay, "Feeling into Words,"

"Digging," in fact, was the name of the first poem I wrote where I thought my feelings had got into words, or to put it more accurately, where I thought my <u>feel</u> had got into words. . . . I felt that I had let down a shaft into real life. (P. 41)

Heaney goes on to "retrace some paths into what William Wordsworth called in <u>The Prelude</u> "the hiding places" -- "The hiding places of my power" (p. 41).

There digging becomes sexual metaphor, an emblem of initiation, like putting your hand into a bush or robbing the next, one of the various natural analogies for uncovering and touching the hidden thing. I now believe that the "Digging" poem had for me the force of an initiation . . . . I was doomed to look for it again and again. (pp. 42-43)

Listen to Shakespeare draw us into the influx of the surface of a fiery world:

Oh for a Muse of fire, that would ascend
The brightest heaven of invention;
A kingdom for a stage, princes to act
And monarchs to behold the swelling scene!
Then should warlike Harry, like himself,

Assume the port of Mars, and at his heels,
Leashed in like hounds, should famine, sword, and fire
Crouch for employment.
(Henry V, I, i, 1-8)

Here is fire upward, or the fire of his ascendancy, which will draw us all in. It is not just image, but it is also sound, or the two together at minimum, or all the senses confluent. Minkowski is quoted aptly by Bachelard concerning this power of reverberation:

> If, having fixed the original form in our mind's eye, we ask ourselves how that form comes alive and fills with life, we discover a new dynamic and vital category, a new property of the universe: reverberation (retentir). It is as though a well-spring existed in a sealed vase and its waves, repeatedly echoing against the sides of this vase, filled it with their sonority. Or again, it is as though the sound of a hunting horn, reverberating everywhere through its echo, made the tiniest leaf, the tiniest wisp of moss shudder in a common movement and transformed the whole forest, filling it to its limits, into a vibrating, sonorous world . . . it is the dynamism of the sonorous life itself which by engulfing and appropriating everything it finds in its path, fills the slice of space, or better, the slice of the world that it assigns itself by its movement, making it reverberate, breathing into its own life (Bachelard, p. 72n)

Dreams seem to set related things in vibration. Heaney is quite clear that his discoveries follow this dream method, and the poems later mark it down. His poem, "The Diviner," is literally about the "stirring" which becomes a "seminal excitement":

> The crucial action is pre-verbal, to be able to allow the first alertness or come-hither, sensed in a blurred or incomplete way, to dilate and approach as a thought or theme or a phrase. (p. 49)

Heaney goes on to give many beautiful examples of this "point of entry" and "point of exit" (p. 52) into a "field of force" which can "encompass" and be "adequate to our predicament" (p. 56).

Three Examples of the Second Power
of Dreams, to Summon Energies

I find I often have to tell my patients who cannot summon dreams to stay down, when their alarm goes off. I say something like:

> Stay down, as if you were six feet under water, looking up. Tag the images you see, like fish, with names. Don't break the surface, and sit up, until you have completed this.

In other words, I am saying that you need to stay in the primitive region which reverberates, in this instance, water. Once you break its surface, you lose its spell to summon. But you can retrace the path into "the hiding place of the power" if you have tagged the images. This keeps the door open. Of course, I could have put my admonition in the air, or the fire, or under the ground.

Thoreau's Dreams, of Rough and Smooth, of the Imaginary Mountain, and of the Bay of Fundy. Thoreau found the society of men to be rough, so he needed to summon a smooth one for himself:

> I thus get off a certain social scarf and scaliness . . . There, in that Well Meadow Field, perhaps, I feel in my element again, as when a fish is put back into the water. I wash off all my chagrins . . . I can remember that when I was very young I used to have a dream night after night, over and over again, which might have been named Rough and Smooth. All existence, all satisfaction and dissatisfaction, all event was symbolized in this way. Now I seemed to be lying and tossing, perchance, on a horrible, a fatal rough surface, which must soon, indeed, put an end to my existence, though even in the dream I knew it to be the symbol merely of my misery; and then again, suddenly, I was lying on a delicious smooth surface, as of a summer sea, as of gossamer or down or softest plush, and life was such a luxury to live. My waking experience always has been and is such an alternate Rough and Smooth. In other words, it is Insanity and Sanity (pp. 210-211, Jan. 7, 1857, Volume 9).

Thoreau's ability to transpose himself is a call to a voyage that inspires many still in America. He is particularly adept at getting from annoying and prickly and fired-up earth, into the other two surfaces of water and air. Frost followed him. Listen to him in "The Figure A Poem Makes" (originally published, 1939):

> It should be the pleasure of a poem itself to tell how it can. The figure a poem makes. It begins in delight and ends in wisdom. The figure is the same as for love. No one can really hold that the ecstasy should be static and stand still in one place. It begins in delight, it inclines to the impulse, it assumes direction with the first line laid down, it runs a course of lucky events, and ends in a clarification of life (p. 18)

As Frost puts it later in the essay, he finds in such a stream "the freedom of my material." It gets him, so to speak, out of the condition

> of kicking ourselves from one chance suggestion to another in all directions as of a hot afternoon in the life of a grasshopper (p. 18)

into a channel

> with the greatest freedom of the material to move about in it and to establish relations in it regardless of time and space, previous relation, and everything but affinity. (p. 19)

Not a bad definition of the search of a dream! Here is a second dream of Thoreau which gathers impetus up the mountain:

This morning, for instance, for the twentieth time at least, I thought of that mountain in the easterly part of our town (where no high hill actually is) which once or twice I had ascended, and often allowed my thoughts alone to climb. (p. 142, Oct. 29, 1857, Volume 10)

It sounds awfully like Dante, and surely is a sacred mountain:

My way up used to lie through a dark and unfrequented wood at its base . . I shuddered as I went along . . . I steadily ascended along a rocky ridge half clad with stinted trees, where wild beasts haunted, till I had quite lost myself in the upper air and clouds, seeming to pass an imaginary line which separates a hill, mere earth heaped up, from a mountain, into a superterranean grandeur and sublimity. What distinguishes that summit above the earthly line is that it is unhandelled, awful, grand . . . It is as if you trod with awe the face of a god turned up, unwittingly but helplessly, yielding to the laws of gravity. (p. 142)

Thoreau says he has had this dream twenty or more times, so he knows somehow the point of entry, back into the exhilaration of this ascent. That is a great gift.

Finally, another and last dream of Thoreau, marking the steps to his place of power:
In my dream I had been riding, but the horses bit each other and occasioned endless trouble and anxiety, and it was my employment to hold their heads apart (//) Next I sailed over the sea in a small vessel such as the Northmen used, as it were to the Bay of Fundy, and thence overland I sailed, still over the shallows about the sources of the rivers toward the deeper channel of a stream which emptied into the gulf beyond, -- the Miramichi, was it? Again, I was in my own small pleasure-boat, learning to sail on the sea, and I raised my sail before my anchor, which I dragged far into the sea. I saw the buttons which had come off the coats of drowned men, and suddenly I saw my dog -- when I knew not that I had one -- standing in the sea up to his chin, to warm his legs, which had been wet, which the cool wind numbed. (pp. 80-81, Oct. 19, 1851, Volume 3)

Quite an unforgettable voyage, compelling in the exactitude of its details as we sweep along: the horses biting each other, the anchor dragged to sea, the buttons off coats of drowned men, the dog standing in the sea up to his chin.

The Dream of the Underwater Chamber. One of my patients has been frenzied with the hot bother of "getting and spending, we lay waste our powers" -- as Wordsworth would put it. She dreamt:

I go to a conference, and meet a woman, and ask her to go out on the lake in a canoe. We do. I decide I want to dive into the icy water, and swim to shore. I do, and she follows me. I reach shore, and do not see her behind me. I dive down and find a room underwater, where her head is caught in a fishnet. I release her, and we make it back.

The dream marked a departure for her, from willing all sorts of things out of her control. I had challenged her presumption the previous week, and she was able to slow down and get much needed sleep. This dream then came, reminding her of the Lake in Madison she had once loved. If she willed less, and had less money, she could go back to the Lake for free. Of course, the dream replied: Not quite free. You do get carried away, and could go too far, and not get back. Watch it. This is divine energy, in a cool surface, but one can get caught like a fish.

The Author's Dream of Sleeping Atop Heavenrich's Department Store in Saginaw, Michigan. I had been feeling a little like Andrew in War and Peace (Tolstoy, originally published in 1869; 1966) that society is all crust, and a joint stock company for profit. And little else. I dreamt:

> I am lying on the bosomy roof of a building in Saginaw, thinking about what a patient needed. A patient care rep comes by briskly and says his five sessions are already used up. I realize from my position, that I am exactly atop Heavenrich's Department Store in Saginaw, Michigan, facing up West Genesse Avenue. The bosomy top is like a billowing sail of canvas divided into four sections, as in Figure 8.2.

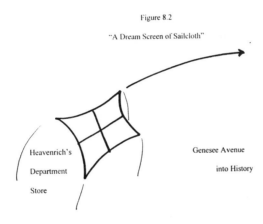

Figure 8.2

"A Dream Screen of Sailcloth"

Heavenrich's is where I bought my first suit, to go to Massachusetts Institute of Technology (M.I.T.) in 1959. In a way, it is where I entered history. It is as if I am getting to back out of it, onto this beautiful, billowing sail of air, lying on my back in full ease. Oddly, I am in Heaven, and seem to be Rich, symbolically, and I must also command a lot of money (in Saginaw terms) to have such a commanding place. Nice dream screen, of the air.

The Third Power of Imagination -- The Ars Descendi,
to Imagine the Limits of Imagination, by
Distinguishing Surfaces, Instead of Confounding Them

Just as it is unbearable to sight the vicious circles of hell, without a way to heaven, so is it unbearable to ascend to heaven, unless you can take yourself back down to earth. I could not stand to be lying on my sailcloth on top of Heavenrich's if I took it absolutely seriously. I am just playing at it, like Scrooge McDuck diving in his bathtub of dollars. I can distinguish play, from history.

It can also be very hard to take the fall, as Thoreau did from his beautiful dream of the Bay of Fundy, which actually began with

I awoke this morning to infinite regret (p. 80)

and ended with a walk with an old friend "reciting grand and pleasing couplets and single lines which we had read in times past," like

"The short parenthesis of life was sweet,"
"The remembrance of youth is a sigh, etc."

These were not the words actually, but the word "memory" was in the phrase. He can catch no more of it, and writes

And then again the instant that I awoke, me thought I was a musical instrument from which I heard a strain die out -- a bugle, or a clarinet, or a flute. My body was the organ and channel of melody, as a flute is of the music that is breathed through it. My flesh sounded and vibrated still to the strain, and my nerves were the chords of the lyre. I awoke, therefore, to an infinite regret -- to find myself, not the thoroughfare of glorious and world-stirring inspirations, but a scuttle full of dirt, such a thoroughfare only as the street and the kennel, where, perchance, the wind may sometimes draw forth a strain of music from a straw . . . how little like a musical instrument my body now. (pp 81-82)

He had to come down from reading "Laing's Account of the Northmen" the evening before, in which he

heard the last strain or flourish, as I awoke, played on my body as the instrument. (p. 82)

This second power of the imagination, of reverberation described by Minkowski, is huge, in the body of Thoreau, but little, in the dirty streets of Concord. Thoreau is obliged to distinguish the two, but it is very painful.

Fiction

If Thoreau did not distinguish the surface of his body, from the surface of the ordinary street, he would be moving in the direction of fiction. Fiction plays with confounding such things, as in Rabelais where Gargantua floods the streets of Paris pissing from a tower. Usually, it is not that gross.

The pleasure comes from taking liberties, as in Rabelais, or more subtly, as in "The Lantern Bearers" of Stevenson:

> Toward the end of September, when school time was drawing near and the nights were already black, we would begin to sail forth from our respective villas, each equipped with a tin bull's eye lantern (p. 213, 1892)

These things were hidden under top-coats, and smelled of blistered tin:

> When two of these asses met, there would be an anxious "Have you got your lantern?" and a gratified "Yes!" That was the shibboleth, and very needful too; for, as it was the rule to keep our glory contained, none could recognise a lantern-bearer, unless (like the polecat) by the smell. (pp. 214-215)

The humor comes as here from the absurdity of the contrast between the inner glory, and the outer smell of the polecat. If the writer can sally forth into the black night with the light of his boys, he can have the delights of their amplitude, which is the second power of the imagination. If the writer can at the same time see how little it looks to the world, he can imagine the limits of his imagination, which is the third power of the imagination. Indeed Stevenson (1888) dreamt all of these stories, and so got his maps.

Now, a great deal goes wrong here. Either, the fiction runs away with the group, or they lack fiction at all and go flat. Boys can become a gang, and boys can forget how to play. Either is extremely dangerous. Indeed, the emptier the reality, the more desperate the fiction which finally hits the wall. The craziest gangs come from the most impoverished places. In his story "At the Auction of the Ruby Slippers," Rushdie describes a world in which everything is for sale in The Grand Saleroom of the Auctioneers. The Ruby Slippers are the most coveted, because they can get you home when no one has a way to get there:

> The presence of imaginary beings in the Saleroom may be the last straw . . . This permeation of the real world by the fictional is a symptom of the moral decay of our post-millennial culture. Heroes step down off cinema screens and marry members of the audience . . . There can be little doubt that a large majority of us opposes the free, unrestricted migration of imaginary beings into an already damaged reality, whose resources diminish by the day (1994, p. 94).

Rushdie himself seems to have a great deal of trouble with this situation. Either the fictions over-run his stories, with their murderous emptiness, or the beauty of actual skill is absent. In

"The Courter," he has both quite along the lines of Stevenson. "Mixed-up," the Indian porter, looks a sorry case, but he is actually a courtier and grand-master of chess. He woos Certainly-Mary into his world of chess, where they have a beautiful courtship. But in the end, Mixed-Up is beat up as the porter, because the fictional men in the house have gone too far with their brutal antagonists.

When I was reading this beautiful but tragic story, I remembered that chess has 8 pieces in the back row with great degrees of freedom, and pawns in the front row with 2 degrees of freedom. Mixed-Up is mixed-up between his beautiful surface in eight dimensions, and his banal surface where he is a pawn. He stands up too tall as the porter, and is smashed. It is desperately important to keep from confounding (courtier + porter = courter) these regions.

This art in the Middle Ages and Renaissance was called the ars descendi, which is to come down the ladder from heaven to earth (Yates, 1966). Actually, the art consists in discerning many ladders coming down from the heaven of the chessboard, where all the powers are united. The powers splinter apart into many specialized worlds: the world of the rook is not the world of the bishop, nor yet that of the knight -- and none of these of the world of the pawn, as illustrated in Figure 8.3.

Figure 8.3

"The Ars Descendi"

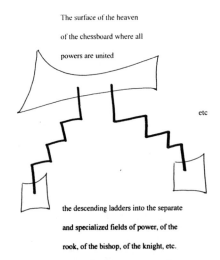

The surface of the heaven

of the chessboard where all

powers are united

etc

the descending ladders into the separate

and specialized fields of power, of the

rook, of the bishop, of the knight, etc.

In more contemporary terms, the banker is one power, the lover is another, and the reliable friend is yet another. We want these powers to go together as in heaven, but they diverge on earth. We indulge in dangerous fiction, when we run these surfaces together. We need to distinguish between the power of our imagination to summon these virtues together // and the power of our imagination to see their ladders diverge as we come down to earth.

Three Dreams Which Depend Upon the Third
Power of the Imagination

The Dream of Noah's Ark. A colleague consulting me about a borderline patient he had seen for many years was excited by some spectacular dreams she had recently brought in. This patient had the puzzling habit of sticking needles in her veins and bleeding herself. It was as if she had to keep her hemoglobin down. While she had just managed to get a very damaging man out of her life, she still seemed to need to bleed herself. I imagined that the dreams might give us a picture, of why she could not bear being full-blooded. The gist of the dreams were as follows:

In the first scene, she was in her apartment, which had the door off its hinge, alone. In the second scene, she was in the hospital with tubes and wires in her, alone, unable to speak, and her heart stopped. In the third scene, she was ready to go to NYC, but had to find someone first, but could not remember the name (//) In the fourth scene, she was in a great big barn with her sister. It was designed to live in, with a nice rustic corner, a warm sofa and animals. A bird sat on her shoulder struggling to sing. An owl, colorful, friendly, nudged her like a dog. Cats were everywhere. There was a four foot horse, that fit her well. A river ran under the barn (//) In the fifth scene, she took live baby pigs to a meat market and handed them to the butcher who cut their throats (sic!). In the sixth scene, she went with her sister to a dress shop. Her sister had become four feet tall, fifty pounds, and 80 years old. She was offered a lime-green, lace dress that was ugly, like everything else there.

My colleague is reasonably experienced in dream matters, and could work it up with the patient, and lay out most of the map. The first and second scenes are her usually death-in-life states of abandonment and intrusion, the third her waking up as she did with a chorus going to Carnegie Hall, the fourth alludes to a period with her grandmother in her early years when she felt loved, the fifth is the bleeding she inflicts on herself, and sixth is back to death-in-life. He knew it went full cycle.

I said to him that I could only add that he ask her about the hiatus between Noah's Ark (//) and the ex-sanguination, for here is precisely where she drops out of heaven, into the abyss, and into a bloodless world of death-in-life where we began. Of course, he could not answer for the patient, but he did remember a hole in the story of the greatest importance. Grandmother's death when the patient was in her twenties was when she began bleeding herself. Out of an end to her world suffered passively, she had made an active vocation. I said to my colleague that he had better be very careful of her improvements. She looks for everything to come together in them, and such things have to come apart into divergent pieces.

A Dream of the Wily Hermes Caught Red-Handed. This patient came to me because he was stuck in a relatively non-sexual relationship with a motherly woman for many years (see his previous dream of "Pablo the Destroyer" in Chapter 5). He had lost his own mother early, and had been very responsible to her. He began an affair with a married woman, who seemed very strong to him. This relieved him, by contrast to his mother and his motherly girlfriend. He brought a very long dream typical of his adventures, from which I will report a couple of striking episodes:

> In the first scene, he is in the lap of a lady psychiatrist. Both are naked, and she is rocking him, and he has an erection. His girlfriend opens the door, and he tries to get under cover, and gets mad at her. (//)

> In a later scene, he is in the bed of the woman he is having the affair with, while she and her husband stand over him. He feigns innocence, which is belied by his books being under the pillow. He feigns surprise. The husband shows him a tonka of wrathful ruthlessness, and asks to whom it belongs. He feigns innocence. The husband picks it up upside down with the patient's name on it also upside down. The patient feigns reading it upside down (//)

> He goes to hide in the garage, which is like his girlfriend's and is locked in. He reaches through a little hole, and the woman of the affair lets him out. The husband is there with the patient's name on paper, rightside up. The husband has a knife, the patient a pitiful piece of solder wire. The husband stabs him repeatedly, but the series of knives are all made of rubber. Finally, the husband gives him a bear hug from behind, and makes him stab himself with a real knife with his own hands around the knife -- so it would appear to be suicide.

This truth calls out, with increasing shrillness, the absurdity of his pretending to be innocent. If he isn't going to come down from his boyish claims, he is going to be brought rudely down. Fortunately, he recognizes the farce. He leaves more soberly, seeing he is going to have to give up his claims to have everything at once. Mothering is one thing, psychiatry another thing, and sexuality a third. It is fiction that he can pull off stealing it all. Only a certain Greek god could do that.

The Dream of the Cavorting Dog. My patient had emerged from a childhood in which she felt utterly demeaned by her mother compared to her princess of a sister. Naturally, her beautiful and even gilt-edged and favorite book was Cinderella. While this beautiful story had given her hope, to endure the evil stepmother so to speak, she had also incurred the hazard of its fiction concerning princes. She fell for liars. Especially if they were intelligent. She would then give them all of the other powers, and she would be in heaven with them. The greatest disaster was her ex-husband by whom she had three children. They were now grown-up. The husband had turned out to be brutal and callous and totally self-absorbed, both for her and for the children. She had divorced him, when the children were teenagers. After the ex-husband, she had had a small and further series of intelligent liars. Why was she still so prone? she had left off with in the previous session. Her dream replied as follows:

> She was in a very remarkable square, which she drew for me on my easel as in Figure 8.4.

Figure 8.4

"The Circulatio of the Cavorting Dogs"

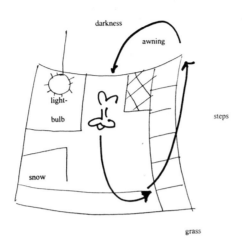

A German shepherd was circling the square counter-clockwise at amazing speed -- first up the stairs on the right, and then leaping down to the left. It was almost like flying. The owner was proud of the dog's agility. The patient was awed, and scared. Two follower dogs couldn't duplicate the feat of the first, but trailed after (//). Suddenly the lead dog caught his foot in the awning and crashed sickeningly down. He cracked his skull and lay against the wall, in snow, and had become a yellow Labrador. She strokes him, puts some snow on him, and asks if he can move his legs? He could. She became afraid that the snow would put him into shock. The owner just laughed and told the dog to shake it off. "Tough guy, tough dog," she thought. She was very anxious. She thought the headline might be, "Amazing Dog comes to a Screeching Halt on His Head." This is one of those big dreams that condenses thirty years into a single night-painting.

We spent much of the hour getting the history of each of its elements. To abbreviate this hour to the raw essentials, the marvelous cavorting went back only to the previous evening when she watched Paul Wylie, the American figure skater. The feeling of awe and fear for the performance came from there. The dogs are big dogs. "Big dogs hang around me. They like me." Yet it is dangerous when they are too wild as in the dream. The brutal owner has the attitude of her ex-husband. This brings her to the grief of these three children of hers. Her oldest is like the Shepherd in the dream, leaping ahead in good company. He has never admitted his pain about his father. She fears he will trip up. Now, she is crying, and scared for her children. Can they manage without a helpful father?

I reply that at least they have had a mother to look after them. They may need to borrow some fathering, on the subject of high-flying. Of course, she is getting exactly this kind of fathering from me on this very subject. The great danger of her last thirty years is her thrill in this kind of circulating energy. Wylie may have the discipline to carry it off on ice, while big dogs crash to the earth. The key is the ability to distinguish one surface from another. Thrill on ice may not transpose to thrill on earth. It is dangerous to generalize from a particular talent in one arena, and generalize it to all virtues. Her ability to summon circulating energy is balanced here by her ability to imagine the limits of this imagination. I am needed to help her bear that pain by facing it with her. We now may see how she falls for intelligent liars, because she is in love with virtuoso performances of big dogs.

Conclusion

The three powers of the imagination turn out to be interdependent. The power of seeing the surface you are on as a vicious circle depends upon seeing another surface with more play or degree of freedom which in turn depends upon seeing the limits of that beautiful surface so you can refrain from over-generalizing its beauty. It is dangerous to lack any of the three powers, and it is dangerous if they are not in relative balance. The first power can leave you overwhelmed in hell. The second power can leave you up too high in Noah's Ark, or in stealing like Hermes, or flying in the circulatio like the cavorting dogs. The third power can be too painful to admit. Some need a fiction about what society will offer them, or they feel entirely punctured.

I have held back the parallel that some readers may have caught before this, which I can finally bring forward. The three powers of the imagination correspond to the three powers of the hero of all myth, which Campbell (1949) calls the monomyth (Gustafson, 1995a; Gustafson, 1995b). The religious hero, the military hero, the artistic hero -- the hero of a thousand faces, as Campbell puts it -- has to imagine where he is lost in circles, where he can transpose himself to summon new powers, and where he can re-enter to the great limitations of history. Fortunately, the dream maps all three of these powers with uncanny accuracy.

Chapter 9. Winnicott's Company.

An animal in a harsh dilemma is going to search for a way out in a dream. He will need to get out of the 2-dimensions he is stuck in, into the other 8-dimensions. He will need company to bear the strangeness of what he finds. This company is now our subject.

This company is very hard to get. Mostly, we get guides who know what they are going to find in advance, to confirm their theories. They have allegories for maps, which foretell the progress of the pilgrim (Tate, 1948). Dreams will turn out to be mere illustrations of their doctrine. Thus, they will find a wish fulfilled, a god in charge, a safe place, and so forth. Whatever is already on the program.

This is mostly what is available to patients, or to penitents in the realm of religion. The strangeness of their difficulty is translated into the terms of the therapeutic community, so they undergo a journey from being lost to saved (James, 1902; Gustafson, 1967 unpublished). Nowadays, this is more likely to be stated in secular terms. The patient's conflict is analyzed, or his possession by a certain archetype has been relieved (Percy, 1975).

A different kind of company is ready to find the strangeness of new dimensions which are at least surprising, usually amazing, and even shocking. The words are fresh, and the images we have never seen before. The reader may ask why this is necessary?

The Necessary Angel

The powers of the imagination I described in Chapter 8 are trivial, once they only embellish what the conscious mind has already figured out. They just give figures of illustration, to fit the allegorical book, of the pilgrim's or patient's progress.

Thus, the results are like cardboard. The patients stand stock still. They are moved, only as they are supposed to be moved, by suggestion. They fit into the doctor's scheme, like a character in search of an author. Walker Percy (1975) described a patient reacting to a curtain fluttering in the breeze with the line from <u>Hamlet</u>

"There's a rat behind the arras." (p. 194)

Soon this is Polonius, and Polonius is a father, and Hamlet has stabbed him, and the patient is delighted to have "discovered" an Oedipus complex in himself. But it was already on the program, and this is only its hiding place, like an Easter egg for a child. Percy remarks:

> Our business is to say what is right and what is wrong here. What is right is that Freud was right and the patient does indeed do well to confront his oedipal feelings. What is wrong is a certain loss of sovereignty by the patient. We must trace out the connection between valid theory and falling prey to valid theory. For is it not true that the patient's chief claim to humanity here rests on the honorable credentials of his pathology?

"Hooray!" he is saying. "I am certified human after all! I have oedipal feelings." (p. 185)

Winnicott had a very simple theory of searching with dreams, but it was a theory designed so that the child did not or could not fall prey to it. How did he arrange it so? And why did he think it necessary? Certainly, he believed with Percy that the child needed his sovereignty, and not to surrender it.

Winnicott's theory was that children surrender themselves to conformity when they are too frightened to stay with themselves. They become false selves (Henry, 1973). They lack spontaneity, because they dare not follow their instincts anymore. Sometimes, they register a protest to this conformity, in an antisocial reaction like stealing or lying or refusing to work. This is a sign of hope, that they want to get back to being themselves (taking what belongs to them).

Therefore, Winnicott's aim was to reach back with the child to the period of strain in which he gave up being himself. They would arrive there together. This was always a region of turmoil which was frighteningly chaotic. If this could be tolerated, and put into the child's own drawing and words, then the child no longer had to be in flight from himself, and lost in his own outer world of conformity. The ease of going by his own instincts could be resumed. This meant a much freer use of others, who would now be in a position to assist him in his own aims. Before, they had been helpless.

Winnicott's (1971b) technique is deceptively simple. He offers "to play a game with no rules" with the child. This leads away from the conformity which shuts the child down. The game is called the Squiggle Game and the only idea is that Winnicott makes an odd line spontaneously, and the child is to "make something of it" by adding his own marks. This pulls for the child to create out of himself onto what the world offers for material. Then, Winnicott reverses the field and has the child make a squiggle, and he, Winnicott, has to "make something of it." This puts child and doctor on the same level as equals, and, at the same time, requires the doctor to put in himself. He cannot hide like Oz, and have the child take all the risks. Thus, they take turns squiggling and having the other make something of it. It is a daring game. It reminds me of that phrase from my childhood when a child is challenged by another child about his dress or behavior or whatever self-expression: "Do you wanna make something of it?" is the counter-reply. Of course, such things are said in hostility, whereas it is meant in Winnicott good-naturedly.

This free-for-all turns out to have a kind of musical structure. It develops in a kind of typical sequence. At first, the child makes conventional pictures of houses, dresses, cars, etc. out of the squiggles. Winnicott is just trying to be easy with the child, and let him enjoy the play. Then the child may just bring out something from deeper down. It may be an odd animal, or a flash of violence, or something unexpected. At this juncture, Winnicott is apt to be interested in comforting objects that help this child go to sleep, as he says, to make the passage from waking to sleeping. His technical term for these is "transitional objects." So now he is getting a departure into the unconscious realm, with the help of transitional objects. The interview is "hanging fire."

When things are at a pitch of this kind of excitement, Winnicott asks the child what he has been dreaming? This dream-drop is apt to take the two into the region where the child was overwhelmed and so they will undergo it together. It is often chaotic, tumultuous, and verging on formless. Winnicott believes in the child's capacity to pass through the chaos when the dream has already "encompassed" it. But he cannot do it alone. When they have "arrived" or "reached to" this overwhelming difficulty, and it is drawn, and spoken, and lived through, they come back up to the conventional area from which they began.

Such a technique goes against all the conventions in the field of psychotherapy. Winnicott has designed it, so that it departs from convention and returns to convention. But in between is all daring. Musically, it is like Mozart. There are quite standard openings and cadences for closing. There is a kind of typical development. But in between it just takes off into free play that is completely unpredictable. This free play also gets dark, in its colorations, and figures, and modulations. It is dealing with the diabolic, and the chaotic, and the overwhelming, within a framework that is classical.

Why is this <u>necessary</u>? Reich (1931; 1933 originally, 1949) explained it very succinctly. He said that an overwhelmed child lifts himself up out of the chaos by identifying with an admired adult. He postures like this adult, and becomes him, instead of himself. For example (1931), one terrified little boy took on the entire attitude of his uncle, an English aristocrat. It made him stilted in every way, but it calmed him down to play-act this part. Thus, history is frozen, and comes to a halt. The child can no longer be touched, because he really isn't there anymore. He has become a character, with a constant attitude of someone else, with an entire array of postures, defenses, and so forth.

In this situation, it is <u>necessary</u> to get past the conventional character, to the fluidity of instinct which has been frozen. This is a tremendous passage to undergo, in an hour. How in the world is a child to trust a doctor he has never met to take him, as Sendak puts it, "to where the wild things are . . ." (1963). Winnicott's reply is that the child has <u>already</u> dreamt of his doctor, the dream doctor, who will go with him:

> I was struck by the frequency with which <u>the children had dreamed of me the night before attending</u> . . . here I was, as I discovered to my amusement, <u>fitting in with a preconceived notion</u> (p. 4)

Usually, this dream doctor is called up in the child hearing of Winnicott from the parents. It is as if the child says to himself, "This is the one I have been waiting for . . ." Then he "discovers" Winnicott and tests him and down they go. But Winnicott mustn't fail the child:

> Either this sacred moment is used or it is wasted. If it is wasted the child's belief in being understood is shattered. (pp. 4-5)

What does it mean to be the dream doctor and to keep from failing the child? That will be the burden of this chapter to show, because you can only get it from the details, as Winnicott would say. It turns out to be <u>necessary</u> to be musical, and artistic, and poetic, to bring a child or an adult out of being frozen in history. Wallace Stevens (1965) called it the job of

"the necessary angel of earth."

I will now take the reader through three of Winnicott's cases from <u>Therapeutic Consultations in Child Psychiatry</u> (1971b), passing from the simplest to the most complex. Then, I will illustrate myself undertaking similar voyages with my own patients. Finally, I will discuss what adults need beyond the needs of children.

Three Consultations by Winnicott

I will take the reader through these three conversations by verbal means alone, but the reader will get much more out of them by looking at the pictures in Winnicott's book (1971b). There are so many interesting turns in the cases that I always see new angles when I read them again.

The Case of Rosemary, Age 10

The beauty of this music is that it is startlingly unexpected even when it is most diagrammatic. The unconscious will have its say, and burst through the technique. This is the simplest case in the book.

Rosemary is brought because of "black fits of depression," "blinding headaches, nausea and photophobia, lasting two or three days and sending her to bed. She had lately become withdrawn. Along with this was a bad temper in the morning." (p. 105)

Winnicott and she begin squiggling, and do a couple of odd girls, and a transitional object of hers named Bruno, and an earlier one, Doggie, whereupon she indicates that she didn't want a brother and that he took her teddy. A picture of her brother is followed by a drop into a dream about she and two friends waiting in the tower to be executed. The girl is making all the transitions herself, which Winnicott often had to assist with more difficult cases.

Now she drops further into an earlier dream which was horrible, and which she needs to reach. It is about "a wicked stepmother who broke the glass slipper, herself being Cinderella" (p. 107). After a picture of Cinderella with a prince on one knee

... She drew with great intensity of feeling and very quickly, showing mother being run over by father's car (p. 108)

Winnicott notes the hate between her and her mother in the context of her father, and she drops the farthest into a third and weird dream:

. . . showing bubbles coming at her, making a funny noise like an ear-ache noise; they are white. This dream is somewhat influenced by science-fiction and links with the idea of comets and meteors which presumably are met with in space (p. 109)

Winnicott simply notes this as a picture of a "coming alive 'inside'," following a phase of "being dead 'inside' . . . represented by the dead mother of the dream" (p. 109). Laconically, Winnicott remarks that

> All these symptoms (noted at the onset of the case presentation) cleared up when she <u>arrived</u> at the drawing of the dream in which her mother got run over. (p. 105)

All Winnicott has to do in this case is to follow the process set in motion by the consultation, while Rosemary makes all the transitions herself. Of course, it is a great thing to know what the child is up to. Essentially, Winnicott knows that a child who has been let down in some very big way is going to go dead like Dr. Jekyll in Stevenson's (1886) famous story. Mr. Hyde will be prowling around inside, and sneaking out in symptoms. By arriving at the presence of the awful Hyde, and at the hurt that set him in motion, he is dissolved, as it were, in comets and meteors. If this kind of knot of melancholia (Freud, 1917) is untied, the child is free to live in all the other 8-dimensions (Stevenson, 1892).

The Case of Ada, Age 8

Now let us see what more is required of Winnicott to travel the same path in a more difficult case. Ada was a girl brought for stealing. He remarks early on,

> I was concerned with getting the patient to give herself away to me, slowly as she gained confidence in me, and deeply as she found she might take the risk. (p. 220)

Let us see what makes Ada slower than Rosemary to gain confidence. She opens with conventional pictures, a vase of flowers, a lamp hung from the ceiling, a pencil too fat, a house, her cousin . . . without hands. "I can't draw hands," she remarks. Already, Ada is dropping like Alice (Carroll, 1865) through a little hole in her conscious conventionality: missing hands. As Sullivan would say, selective inattention is the gap through which it appears. Winnicott already has confidence that they will arrive in the chaos where Ada needs to go:

> I was now growing confident that the theme of stealing would appear, and so I was able to lean back on the child's own "process." <u>From now on it did not exactly matter what I said or did not say, except that I must be adapted to the child's needs and not requiring the child to adapt to my own</u>. (p. 224)

Now Ada says the girl is hiding a present, and Winnicott asks to see it, a box of handkerchiefs. Winnicott asks where she got it, and the girl draws a leading store in London, curiously with a curtain down the middle of it. This curtain turns out to be a recurrent form in the drawings of the greatest importance. It divides the conscious mind, from the dissociated unconscious mind. It is the <u>hiatus</u> (Grinnell, 1970; see Chapter 5, this book).

Winnicott asks to see the lady buying the present, and Ada shows her from the front behind the counter minus hands again. When Winnicott asks to see the lady from behind, the picture surprises Ada:

> "Oh! She has long arms like mine; she is feeling for something. She has on a black dress with long sleeves; that's the dress I have on now; it was Mummy's once. (p. 226)

This drawing (#10) is startling for the hugeness of the hands which look like stars! as I approximate in Figure 9.1.

Figure 9.1

"Hands like Stars"

So Ada is willing to enter into being the thief herself to some extent, trusting Winnicott this much. But Winnicott is uncertain if it will go any farther. In this kind of pause or lull, he asks always for transitional objects to carry them further in a technical sense. He asks the girl about how she gets to sleep. She tells about her bear, and mentions her brother who sucks his thumb. Startlingly, the hand is one of those star hands again, and two breast-like objects like the clouds of the early drawings are above it.

> Our work was now hanging fire. One could say that the child was (without knowing it) wondering whether it would be safe (i.e. profitable) to go deeper. (p. 228)

Ada now draws a "proud climber" and Winnicott grows confident in her daring and asks her about dreaming, "of mountaineering and all that?"

What she said, talking very fast, was something like this: "I go to the U.S.A. I am with the Indians and I get three bears. The boy next door is in the dream. He is rich. I was lost in London. There was a flood. The sea came in at the front door. We all ran away in a car. We left something behind. I think -- I don't know what it was. I don't think it was Teddy. I think it was the gas stove." (p. 229)

Winnicott knows that this bad nightmare is as far as they have to reach. Now she draws a paint brush and box like the fat finger, an aspidistra like a dream of stinging scorpions "walking down in armies, and one big one in my bed" and a muddled house and caravan. Winnicott asks for a sad dream, and Ada mentions one of mother and father being killed but coming out all right. She brags of having thirty-six pencils.

I might have taken the reference to my meanness (pencils) as a sign that her own stealing impulse would be appropriate at this point in the interview. (p. 230)

But Winnicott just waits to see if she is ready to go there.

After a while Ada spontaneously said: "I had a burglar dream." (p. 230)

Now she moves boldly, drawing a black man killing a woman, and another in which the man looks more like a clown. He has one of those star hands again. He is stealing for a present for his wife. She draws the present, a necklace, with a little bow up in the right top corner. Winnicott believes she is ready to have the bow untied, and asks about it. She draws a juggler, with a curtain down the middle (again, as in the department store), and a bow in the middle. Winnicott believes she is ready to have the bow untied and asks her:

Do you ever pinch things yourself? (p. 233)

Ada says no, and draws an apple tree with two apples remarkably like two breasts in the clouds. Winnicott tells her she has reached what she wants, and she serenely draws a picture of mother's dress. It is seen from about knee-high. She concludes by coming up into number games, like the numbers on the dress.

After, talking with Ada's mother, Winnicott learns that her brother was born when she was three and a half, and that this was all right until he became ill and took over the older sister who had been acting as Ada's mother. The stealing that began at seven was an attempt to get the mother-sister back, but she could not admit it until this interview! Now she didn't need the curtain of dissociation. Nor did she need to steal, as she got the "old intimacy" (p. 238) back.

What more has he had to do for Ada than Rosemary? One thing is he has to wait thrice, for her impulse to the interview to come forth like this star-hand, which comes through the conventional opening, the lull, and the sea flooding in the front door. He loses or looses the initiative to her. He is more like an obstetrician than anything else in the medical world, for he waits for her readiness to deliver. He also knows about the bow needing to be untied, and finally asks her for this beautiful little detail. As Winnicott says,

It is for this detail that the reader has been invited to follow the development of the process in the child who has used the opportunity for contact with myself (p. 232)

If Winnicott has a general idea of where the music has to go, he is also alert to the startling detail which holds the door in place. This is a very beautiful precision.

The Case of Alfred, Age 10

Finally, I want to show Winnicott in a third consultation paying attention to the body. The squiggles set in motion not only strange figures and strange words but also strange efforts in the body. He utilized the squiggles as a right hand, to watch for the other movements in the left hand. They will be brought into the music.

Alfred was brought in because of a stammer. Right away, he stammered when Winnicott asked him questions about his father:

> . . . I realized that I must not ask questions, because if I did he would gather himself together to give answers, and there would be a stammer. So I asked him no more direct questions about environmental facts, and during the rest of the hour in which he was in my room there was practically no stammer. (p. 110)

This is very promising, because already Winnicott has crossed over the line between stammer and no-stammer, which is between effort and ease. The first squiggle is a face that looked like a bee:

> As he drew the face he named each feature. I noticed that while he was doing this rather deliberate work that every time he breathed out he made a little push with his breath. This occurred throughout the hour. (p. 110)

With the first squiggle, Winnicott has the trouble in miniature, so he only has to see where it gets big to reach the area of overwhelming difficulty. Somewhere, Alfred needs a huge effort.

> Now he apologizes after turning Winnicott's squiggle into two balloons.
> "That's all I can do," as if I might expect more of him (p. 112)

Next a treble-clef sign, a fish he enjoys, a road-sign for motor cars, and two more in which he complains it is impossible to make anything of the squiggles. Alfred is on the edge between ease and effort, and Winnicott comments:

> One of the aims in this game is to reach to the child's ease and so to his fantasy and so to his dreams. A dream can be used in therapy since the fact that it has been dreamed and remembered and reported indicates that the material of the dream is within the capacity of the child, along with the excitements and anxieties that belong to it (p. 115)

186

So Winnicott now asks about Alfred's dreams. First, he responds by switching from his left-hand to his right-hand (Winnicott had asked about it before) to do a squiggle, which Winnicott makes into a witch (a common transition). The next Alfred makes into a racing track with a grandstand, and allows that he had a frightening dream several years ago.

The next squiggle Alfred muddles all up with lines, and Winnicott knows it is a challenge to him, to make something of it, and so he makes a face. This allows Alfred to tell him about a dream in which witches came and took him away. It's like Winnicott can keep his eye on the boy in the muddle, so the boy can let himself get carried away. The drawing which illustrates the dream is of a witch carrying him away to a den like a coal mine, which Alfred marks as occurring when they moved from another town to the town where his father now works:

> This illustrates the way in which the child's account of the past-history takes the psychiatrist to the period of strain, and gives him the opportunity for accurate understanding (p. 118)

Yet Alfred could tell him little about this period. He went on to a more abstract one in which

> ". . . there are a lot of arrows coming round to the right . . ." In the dream he is whirled round and round clockwise, as if rolled over in bed. "It's not really a frightening dream." (p. 119)

Winnicott asks to see more of the witch's den, and gets a three-legged stool, and a fire, and a tail, and a witch with a tall hat, and Alfred says he would like to see what horrible thing happens, but he always wakes up before he can find out. They are stuck.

> I was being invited to take him to the worst, if only I could find out how to do so. (p. 121)

Winnicott mentions his effort in breathing, and wonders what he is trying so hard to do. Alfred cannot answer much in words, but eases into a drawing:

> Here was a man with a violin case which has a strap round it. Alfred's father plays the violin. He was rather pleased about having done this all himself, but I was not able to use the specific material in the drawing. I said to him. "If you don't try, one thing you have to do is to take a risk, and of course it might be that nothing would happen at all." (p. 122)

Alfred is now done, and Winnicott has a lead to ask the mother about the boy at 6-1/2 around the move:

> The mother said: "Did he tell that at that time his father had a mental breakdown? You see, his father found his new job exacting, and he got caught up in a tremendous effort to succeed and this made him obsessional and he became a case of agitated depression. The

father was worrying all the time, and he went into hospital as a patient for a few months." (p. 123)

Winnicott has only a couple minutes left and invites Alfred back in and asks him if he remembers when his father had a breakdown?

> Alfred's head suddenly went back and he jerked himself into a memory of this illness of his father which he had completely forgotten. He looked immensely relieved. I said: "You see you've been trying all this time, not because of your own need to try, and you have told me things go better if you don't try. You've been trying hard on your father's account, and you are still going on trying to cure father of this worry about work when he couldn't do it well enough. So that's why you push every time you breath out, and as you told me, it's this pushing and trying that interferes with all your work and your talking and that makes you stutter." (p. 124)

After this, Alfred eased up:

> The mother reported that as he left me after my interview with him he said: "You know, I'd completely forgotten that time when Daddy was ill," and he seemed relaxed and relieved. A few weeks later, when my name came up in conversation, he said: "That doctor was bang-on." (p. 124)

If we compare Winnicott with Rosemary just following her through and Winnicott with Ada waiting for her impulse to deliver and Winnicott with Alfred, what else is he up to? Here he is certainly following and waiting as long as he can for the child to come through, but there is a final barrier he cannot surmount. Then Winnicott notes the breathing effort, and gets the beautiful dream of the father with his violin strapped up. Still, they are stuck. He brings in the mother for the material left out, of the father having a breakdown, and then brings the boy back to give it to him, and releases him from its spell. He fills in the gap, so the boy can bridge it. He finds out what is missing. Of a similar gap in the case of Ashton, Winnicott wrote:

> As it turned out this was the main thing in the interview. I felt he had trusted me with something sacred, he had given me the clue to his abstract, although an abstract is by nature a secret hiding place as well as being a demonstration of a constellation in the artist's mind. I felt challenged at this point. Something had become due from me. (p. 154)

"Something had become due from me," is a telling phrase "about meeting" as Winnicott would say, "the challenge of the case" (Winnicott, 1965).

A Summary of Winnicott's Procedure

Winnicott's idea of what he was doing with antisocial cases actually applies to all of the cases in the book: the half that are stealing, lying, etc. (like Ada), and the half that are in some kind of wooden conformity with symptoms like headaches and stuttering (like Rosemary and Alfred):

> Then in these cases there is to be found an environmental lapse of some kind or other as a result of which the maturational processes become blocked, perhaps suddenly. This blockage or the child's reaction to the new anxieties cuts across the life line of the child (my italics, p. 216). There may be a kind of recovery, but there is now a gap in the continuity of the child's life from the child's point of view.

The place that Winnicott has to return to with the child is to this very hiatus which is filled with an acute confusional state that is behind a curtain of dissociation:

> There has been an acute confusional state in the time-phase between the environmental failure and whatever there may be in the way of a recovery. Insofar as the child does not recover the personality remains relatively disintegrated and the child is clinically restless and dependent upon being directed by someone, or restrained by an institution. (My italics, p. 216)

Of course, that is a pretty good definition of psychiatry nowadays for children and for adults. Winnicott's company is much more ambitious:

> It is at this point, the point where hope appears, that the child comes alive and reaches back over the gap to the satisfactory state that obtained before the environmental failure. The child who is stealing is (in the initial stages) quite simply reaching back over the gap, hopeful, or not entirely hopeless, about rediscovering the lost object or the lost maternal provision, or the lost family structure. (p. 126, my italics)

I would add that loud symptoms like Rosemary's blinding headaches or Alfred's stuttering are the same call of instinct looking for its relief (in the initial stages). The job is to follow the child's instinct back over the gap (// hiatus) to the recovery of the lost object. As we have followed Winnicott in the three cases, this chiefly consists in giving the child company with his own instinct to recovery, by believing in it, by waiting for its impulses to deliver the child, and by adding a step or two when he cannot quite reach over himself (when it is clouded for the child by his own selective inattention caused by the painfulness of the loss). This requires a very precise attention to detail, such as Rosemary's white bubbles like comets or meteors, or Ada's star-hands, or Alfred's effortful breathing.

In a way, it is startlingly simple. Yet, hardly anyone can do it. What is going on here? Winnicott gives a clue in his introduction in this sentence:

> It would seem almost as if one has to tolerate the existence of two contrary trends in oneself. (p. 9)

Now hardly anyone can do this anymore. It is a musical capacity, to suspend resolution. You begin in convention with the child which is one trend. You ease into instinct with the child which is the contrary trend. Now, the left hand is moving against the right hand.

> You only set such a freeing up in motion, if there is
> . . . "an average expectable environment" to meet and to make use of the changes that have taken place in the boy or girl in the interview, changes which indicate a loosening of the knot in the developmental process. (p. 5, my italics)

It is better to have a child tied in a knot than to free him up in his instinctiveness when he is only going to get badly hurt again.

Winnicott's Revolution

Winnicott was highly conventional in many ways, being willing to play the part of the correct psychoanalyst. His books of psychoanalytic papers are full of its jargon. Only after his death appear these Therapeutic Consultations (1971b), which turn both psychiatry and psychoanalysis upside down. It is so deceptively simple, but we may miss the revolution. Also, it is very incompletely carried out, by being confined in writing mostly to children. (Actually, he did quite a lot of the same thing with adults as I described in my chapter on Winnicott in The Complex Secret of Brief Psychotherapy (1986; 1997), but it was very secret as his editor, Masud Khan, told me in an interview in London.)

A field of knowledge has a center and a periphery. For example, the center of psychiatry is a set of so-called illnesses, for which its doctors write prescriptions. The patient is an object with an illness, to be set right by a directive. For example, the center of psychoanalysis is a set of wishes, for which its doctors pose the compromises. The patient is a subject with a neurosis which is a compromise-formation, to be set right by letting in more wishes, but still modulated by prohibition of the super-ego.

Winnicott began to practice from a different field with a different center. The field is what he called the transitional field (1971a; 1971b) between the inner center and the outer center. He became the ferryman who gets his patients across this hiatus. That is his job. The outer field is what psychiatrists are trying to fix. The inner field is what the psychoanalysts are trying to fix. The transitional field is the field of the great forces that Winnicott is going to help the patient through, between convention and turmoil. Now, as Hayles (1994) put it very succinctly in a remarkable sentence

> If the criteria defining center and margin change, in a very real sense the structure of knowledge changes as well (p. 144)

For Winnicott, the search of the dream is across this gap or hiatus between being lost in one's own outer world // and finding one's fluidity of instinct in the inner world, as illustrated in Figure 9.2.

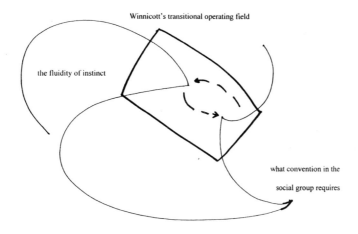

Figure 9.2

"Winnicott's Search Across the Gap"

Winnicott's transitional operating field

the fluidity of instinct

what convention in the

social group requires

Perhaps, it is still unremarkable to the reader that Winnicott has changed the criteria of what defines the center. I have the remainder of this chapter to point out some of the implications, but I can first indicate them in two broad sweeps. First of all, the outer world of convention now becomes a fiction, which psychiatry maintains as a stock reality. Secondly, the inner world of a home on the couch also becomes a fiction and a sentimentality about having a safe place. All the great problems are about riding one's instincts into a sector of the world where one can contribute in (Winnicott, 1971a) out of one's vitality, within some form of the culture. This is the great daring.

The Transitional Field for Adults in the Modern World

The cases I will now bring forth are all adults, who are like Winnicott's children in many respects. Yet there is one huge difference. Winnicott will take children back to their own fluidity of instinct, if the family can be reasonably reliable to refrain from further gross trauma. I, however, have to take patients backward to their own instinctiveness, who have to return to an adult world which is highly traumatic. This is the case because the modern world by and large attends only to the bottom line. Did you win or lose, profit or loss, get recognized or ignored? Thus, all my patients have to cross a hiatus between an instinctiveness that is archaic and 8-dimensional // and a world that is modern and 2-dimensional. Survival literally depends on getting back and forth between these two worlds. In the modern world, you are supplied. In the archaic world, you are renewed, as illustrated in Figure 9.3.

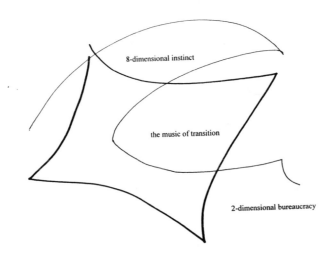

Figure 9.3

"The Modern Hiatus, and Transitional Field"

8-dimensional instinct

the music of transition

2-dimensional bureaucracy

We will come to the dreams of the Zuni in the next chapter, but I want to mention their problem of survival for contrast. They survived by gathering (corn, etc.) and by hunting (antelope, etc.). Thus, a key transitional figure in their dream mythology is the coyote or raven, who both gathers and hunts, in that he gathers dead things. He is their Hermes, who mediates or travels between the extremes they depend upon for their existence.

The modern transition which is a matter of life and death is to be in a bureaucracy to get necessary supplies // and to be instinctive to be renewed. If you fail to be an insider, you are a marginal man. If you fail to be instinctive, you are a shell. So it is quite necessary to get back and forth. Let us look at this music in three cases. Note that the vehicle is not squiggling, but adult sentences. Yet I only exchange sentences like squiggles, in order to watch for gestures, and phrases, and images from the depths.

A Case of Procrastination

This professional woman of age thirty-five had had some helpful psychotherapy in the past that freed her from destructive relationships with men. She married a man from a kind family, and got on with her career and with having children. The residual problem was procrastination. She put off writing assignments, until the very last hours. Her editor was very laid-back, and let her do this. It was an old habit, familiar from college. She came for an intake hoping to get over this old habit, and the resident got just this much information. It was now my turn, with no more than fifteen minutes left.

I had sized up this woman as having a lot of strength. She had a very good-natured look about her, and she had really done very well. So, I simply said to her that the only way to get over procrastination was to stop practicing it and endure the emotions that would soon hit her.

Presumably, she had tried this? Yes, she answered, she had tried to start early on writing projects. She would just sit stuck all day, in a kind of fog. This was worse than working in a last minute panic, because panic actually got her to finish things. The fog just wasted time, of which she had little to spare.

I now had established her dilemma with her. If she starts early, she gets in a hopeless fog. If she starts late, she gets in a panic that mobilizes her to finish. I could see how she had gravitated to the latter solution. She had learned how to comply, out of fear. This had kept her in business, in the bureaucracy.

Now, was it possible to take her to her own instinctiveness about writing? Somehow, I had confidence I could take her there. She seemed to me to have a kind of vigor that was not being used. So, I said to her, "Shall we try to find our way through the fog?" and she said she'd like to. So, thinking out loud, I said, "Well . . . we have only five or ten minutes . . . and how shall we get there?" I was just waiting on the edge with her. After a minute, she said that she had thought about this, and I ought to know her mother. Her mother was crazy, almost totally, but she did attend to her daughter when her daughter was late in getting in reports in elementary school. As she told me this, her eyes moistened, and she said simply that now we were there. She needed some mothering, and this was how she got it. Her editor failed to get after her, so she was really coming to find another mother who would get after her. We could refer her to such a therapist.

Here was a professional woman who looked very independent. Actually, she was longing to be dependent. This longing was hidden in the fog, and I had to help her reach across to it. I simply had to believe she could do it, and wait for her impulse to come up, and it did. I posed the difficulty of emotions in the fog of waiting, in words, and the longing came up from below to moisten her eyes, in the body. This is very, very simple, but most psychiatrists or psychologists would have started to try to fix her procrastination, by more direction from the outside. This would have hidden her instinctiveness, as a power from within.

The Case of the Spiral Into the Pit, Revisited

In Chapter Two, I discussed the dream of a woman driving into a spiral downward of mud in being drawn in to save her mother. The reader may want to refer to Figure 2.2 which pictures this force-field. Many months later, and dreams later, she presented another morass in a dream as follows:

The Dream of Being Trapped in the Basement

She and her husband were going to a graduation party of her son from high school. There were two parties in two houses next door to each other. On the right was a party in which everyone was sitting out of doors enjoying the beautiful day. On the left was a party in which everyone was in the basement. They chose this leftward party, and went down into an unfinished basement. It got more and more crowded as they descended, around more and more corners, and it got darker, and danker, and dirtier. She began to feel frightened.

Then, she saw a big opening to the light of a two-car garage door. She was about to step free into the air, when it slammed shut. Her husband is able to lift it just enough for her to crawl under, but a man tries to hold her back, and a woman to let her go. She manages to break free with a kind of gasp, with the help of her husband, and looks back behind her to see the door slam shut. She is relieved.

The next night she is in this dream again, with her husband and with me. She is very frustrated she cannot understand it, but she is comforted by the sense that I can see her through it.

She glanced at me out of the corner of her eye, when she finished telling this. In my face, she could already read that I knew what it was about. She laughed and said, "So what is it? You know already." I passed her a copy of my last letter from our last session. It read:

The key to being en garde against slipping into the morass is memory, and I hope my map helps. The greatest danger is getting cloudy about your limits when you want to set something right.

I said that this dream is probably a memory-map (Gustafson, 1995a) to show her the force-field which is dangerous to her, if she forgets its power. "Shall we go into it?", I asked, and she was ready to descend.

The graduation party was easy, because she fears her son going his own way with the drinking at graduation, and the two parties was easy, because of the obvious moral contrast between the healthy one and the unhealthy one. The unfinished basement which became more and more crowded and dark and dank and dirty baffled her. She had been in the Cave of the Mounds in third or fourth grade, but what would that have to do with now?

I just stayed with it, and asked her to tell me about it. She said it was silly. I said no matter. Soon she was in tears telling me she had been frightened in the cave and nobody noticed. It had been a terrible experience. So now she knew she was back in something like third grade, which nobody would notice. We went on, downward. The garage door was definitely two-car variety, and that belonged to her parents. Here she said something very striking, which might have gone by the board, but I was watching her. She said that "everyone was watching her" when the door slammed shut. I asked her where that took her, and she said that it was her brother's funeral, when everyone looked at her, and pitied her. Now, she began to cry in earnest. She had been free to leave her parents, but then she had to stand by her mother when her brother died. It suffocated her. We went further. The man trying to hold her back in the dream is her awful boss, and the woman is her friend at work. Now she knows she has to get out of there.

Actually, her feeling now is being free. I say she is out into the air. She says she gasped for breath when she got out. Now, she amazed me. She said the most interesting thing is what is not in the dream. Here she was probing a missing dimension like Erik Erikson. Her children were missing, and that was a great relief, because they were free to go and not take care of her.

She had spared them, what she had been subjected to, the entangling mother. Now, the opening scene of the graduation made a great deal of sense.

Finally, she laughs telling me and reminding me that I was in the final scene of returning to the dream. That was because I had said after the last session that we needed to meet to help her further with the impending anniversary of her brother's death. That had been a great comfort to her after last session that I knew what she needed, and she had told her husband that she didn't understand the dream, but that I would and she would tell him when she got home. I was very amused like Winnicott that I was fitting into a preconceived notion of the dream doctor, just as her husband is the dream husband. Both of us are able to attend to this third-grader going down with her class, and her mother, and her diabolic boss. Then, she takes hold of herself, and can grow up. We have reached across the gap, between her conventional stance which can look all right, and keep up a front // and her instinctive feeling that this is dead wrong for her. Now she is full of herself again.

Of course, she is still in a serious dilemma about work. They need the money of the dreadful place // but it is terrible for her. But now the latter and shadow half of the situation has come forth in full feeling. She can own her own hatred of the place, as it were, objectively (Winnicott, 1947). She is relieved of the fiction that going there is all right with her. Psychiatrists might prop up such a fiction, with pharmacological agents.

This is a common outcome in work with adults. The environment is not all right. It is usually a bureaucracy, that has to be put up with to some extent. This can be withstood if the patient can find and keep her own vitality, in its own domain. The great difficulty, then, lies in the transitional field between the two survivals, of getting supplies, and of getting free.

The Case of Transient Psychosis

The third and last case is a high stakes version of the dilemma of the two survivals. It required all of my agility. Essentially, the psychologist who brought the patient to my clinic for consultation wanted to know if a dream could help them with a very frightening outbreak of visual hallucinations. As the two of them had gotten to know each other better, the patient had had a very strange experience.

She had been feeling mistreated by a boss at work, and one morning she got up to go there and began to feel dizziness coming at her in the air like chunks or clots or clouds. She tried to drive, but she was so distracted by the oncoming dizziness that she feared she would drive into somebody. Cars seemed like they were going to back into her. Terrified, she decided to go on the bus to find her doctor, and when she looked back at her house it was filled with alien people. Somehow, she managed to get to the hospital. In the elevator, there, it seemed as if the elevator doors were bulging in to crush her. She did find her doctor, and she did have this subside in about a day.

About a week after this incipient psychosis, she had a very compact dream:

The Dream of Sitting at the Kitchen Table Alone.

> She was sitting at the kitchen table alone in the house she grew up in. She became uncomfortable, and when she got out of the house she was okay.

I took this dream as a very good sign. Whereas the outbreak of psychosis indicated forces that she could not encompass, the dream a week later indicated that she could encompass them after all in a certain region of her mind. I would work with her and with her doctor in that workable region, and keep an eye out for where the transition was to the unworkable and overwhelming region of turmoil. So I said to the patient and to her doctor that it was a very good sign that she could bend her mind around the problem through the dream. The patient laughed, with evident relief.

As usual in my clinic, I asked the psychologist to give her view, so that the patient and I could discuss it. Essentially, the psychologist told me that their conversation was surfacing the patient's anger at her boss. Obviously, this could be an overwhelming force. Now, I could see about this force with the patient. The challenge of the case would be to see if this force could be encompassed.

Now, the night before the psychosis, the patient had been mad at her boss for giving her a bad recommendation behind her back. She had worked very hard for this woman, and yet she was betrayed. She wakes up in a dream she cannot wake up from, which is a psychosis. A week later, she has a dream she can wake up from, which tells me she can encompass the relevant forces. She already has, and she and I need to find out how she did it, unconsciously.

Now she gives me the dream, and we go through it. The night before this dream she went to a shower with lots of people and got dizzy. She told a friend she had to go, and got out of there short of psychosis. As she tells me this in the interview she shows Gustafson's sign (finger pointing accusingly at the head) (Gustafson, 1992, 1995a, 1995b) profusely, indicating her self-blame for leaving. I ask her about her discomfort in having to go, and she says that her friends tell her she is very successful socially. I respond that she looks good, but feels quite the opposite. Yes, she gets self-conscious, then dizzy, and then in a panic. She laughs with relief when I say that this is the triumph of dizziness. It gets her out of there. I note that this is also the structure of the dream, which we now enter into.

Now we pay our visit to her dream. The house in which it is set is the one she grew up in. She laughs to say she got out of there. I say she may enjoy such a triumph, like Houdini, but now I must drag her back. I say there is a hole in this dream text, after she tells me that sitting alone is something she likes to do. I say that the foreground seems to be comfortable, but the background must not be so or she would not have to get out of there. I say, "Tell me about that house."

She falls silent, and starts moving her shoulders restlessly, and says that she feels tense right now. I ask how? She says it was a house in which you had to do everything right, that is, Catholic. I note to her that we are getting closer to her disturbance. I mention that she is sitting at the kitchen table, in the dream, which is often the altar of the family. What is it like in her family at such a sitting?

She says her father just talked, and the children had to sit. It was very cramped. I ask what her father talks about. She laughs and says she just tuned him out. She is relieved. I say that this is where she learned to be the Houdini who loves to get out. Now I can answer the question, to meet the challenge of the case. The problem for her is that tension builds when she is crowded, by her father, by the shower, by the boss. If she can get away, she is okay. If she cannot, it builds into self-consciousness, dizziness, and finally sheer panic. Now she has a map of the sequence. If it went any further, it would probably be an explosion of anger.

Her doctor now asks me what I think of the psychotherapy getting at the patient's feelings? Is there not a danger of late reactions to the sessions? Just like the late reaction to the boss's betrayal that turned into a psychosis? I agreed there was. The world was going to crowd our patient, and the build-up might be too fast for her to manage. That was the great dilemma of the treatment. If she were just left as she is, she was very likely to get overwhelmed again. If she were worked with about her feelings, it could be too much. I suggested that they see about her reaction to this very conversation. She might find it tolerable, and she just might want to hide out from the world altogether in the mountains of Colorado.

Actually, I felt optimistic, because I could map out the sequence in which things build up. I also relieved her of her guilt (Gustafson's sign profusely) that this is how things stand with her, or fall. This makes it much more likely that she can report to her doctor, when things are getting too much. I remarked that the treatment was like flu shots, that drop the blood pressure. The problem was how much? If not too much, they might strengthen the patient against flu.

As I always do, I wrote the patient a letter after the session summarizing my view. The only different turn of phrase was that I suggested that she was highly allergic to crowding, and that I didn't know if clarification of the sequence -- crowding, tenseness, dizziness, panic, anger -- had felt helpful or not -- nor how she felt about gradually increasing her tolerance to crowding, by facing it in a sequence of dreams? Did she want to stand the heat in the kitchen or get out altogether?

Evidently, the patient felt sufficiently relieved to carry on with a sequence of dreams. Soon after this consultation she was reporting more visits in dreams to this house in which she grew up, with an array of specific difficulties to be encountered there: something that flew at her in her bed, a sister who starts a fire while drunk, a rat to be killed in the basement, having to get out under a bar while the bartender cuts limes in a weird way, and a party in which bombs come out of the sky, and so forth. She seemed relieved to have company to face these devils. As Winnicott would say, the journey can be repeated over and over again, as the patient is ready.

Like my previous patient in danger of being trapped in a morass, this patient is in danger of being crowded. Family, society, work just are going to keep posing these dangers to these two women, by trying to make use of them, take them over, and come down hard on them if they fail to supply what is required. If they pretend it is all right, they get overwhelmed. If they allow for their own instinctive reactions, they have to live with their own intensity. If they can practice the transition, they can become more capable to weathering the harsh crossing between being oneself // and having to fit in.

The Author's Dream of "The General." The night after this consultation I had a dream which put me in this very transitional field of the patient. To help such a patient, I have to be capable of coping with the forces that are pulling her apart. I dreamt as follows:

> I am to play a part in a play called "The General" which is a kind of Durrenmatt play with first class actors. I have not even looked at my lines, but have the book of the play and a newspaper review of the play on top of the book. I go on stage left, and they yell at me to go around the back of the stage to stage right. It is a complete fiasco, as they are prepared to fly at the play in full tempo, while I can hardly find my first line, underneath the newspaper review I am scanning to find out what the play is about! I decide I might as well go out the back door of the stage, and I do.

This stage has me in the place of the patient just trying to be herself // in a world demanding performances. Of course, it is I who want to play in "The General," and have to be prepared for the first-class actors who already know the script and who want to go fast in it. I want to be more impromptu, and childlike, like Winnicott himself, and this is disjunctive (//) with a file of people determined to take power. When you are dealing with the military, at Troy, or in your department // you have to have your lines ready.

Chapter 10. The Orchestral Score of Levi-Strauss.

To get from the beautiful and powerful reach of Winnicott with children, to the full power of the unconscious in adults, we will need a more comprehensive score. The difference is something like that between an accompanied voice and a full orchestra. The reason that you need such a score and orchestra of all the musical colors is that an adult has a much bigger difficulty than a child who has a family that is ready to help him. The adult world is often not ready to help, being often indifferent and downright hostile.

Fortunately, the archaic mind mapped by Levi-Strauss (originally published, 1958; 1963; originally published 1964; 1983) has these very powers of transit between the benign and the malignant, or between life and death. It has also the power to radiate such transitional energy across every possible dimension of existence, from birth and death, to the rise and fall of planets, to the rawness of nature and the cooking of civilization. Its powers are displayed in myths.

These powers of transit remain with us in our dreams, which is what Barfield (1977) called extraordinary consciousness. However, the most difficult transit is between this archaic and extraordinary consciousness // and the modern and ordinary consciousness which is concerned with the defense of property. While Levi Strauss (originally published 1955; 1977) acutely suffered this gulf himself, he did not have a fully developed method for coping with it.

That is because he was looking to a social solution to the degradation of humanity:

> . . . When the spectrum or rainbow of human cultures has finally sunk into the void created by our frenzy . . . (p. 473, 1977, original 1953)

Levi-Strauss feared that this entropy of sameness (speed) was irreversible. The march of western man was and is going to flatten everything into its 2-dimensions. All (and it is very great) that he could hold out to oppose this march was the contemplation of the beauty of our origins:

> . . . as long as we continue to exist and there is a world, that tenuous arch linking us to the inaccessible will still remain, to show us the opposite course to that leading to enslavement; man may be unable to follow it, but its contemplation affords him the only privilege of which he can make himself worthy; that of arresting the process, of controlling the impulse which forces him to block up the cracks in the wall of necessity one by one and to complete his work at the same time as he shuts himself up within his prison . . (p. 473)

Interruption of this "hive-like activity" and "unhitching" from it and "contemplation" discovers

> . . . a mineral more beautiful than all our creations; in the scent at the heart of a lily and is more imbued with learning than all our books; or in the brief glance, heavy with patience, serenity and mutual forgiveness, that, through some mutual understanding, one can sometimes exchange with a cat (pp. 473-474) . . .

is the very sentence on which he ends Triste Tropique. I hear in it echoes from the last several thousand years, particularly, in the despair of Tolstoy (1869) about the hive, and in St. Exupery (1943) about his fleeting opposition of The Little Prince (Gustafson, 1995a; 1995b).

I am more hopeful than this, because I think that the archaic and extraordinary consciousness is already in us, and available to us every night we choose to visit. Therefore, I transpose Levi-Strauss's structural understanding of the archaic powers from the world of myth and from the world of music which is his chief metaphor, back into the world of dream. There are but a few papers (chiefly Kuper and Stone, 1982) suggesting that this could be worked out, which take us in the right direction. Jung was concerned with a similar project, but there is a vast difference in the results gotten by Levi-Strauss.

First, I will expound Levi-Strauss's archaic world of transit between opposing forces, secondly take as my chief example his "Toccata and Fugue" from The Raw and the Cooked (originally, 1964; 1983), and thirdly take us back from the structure of myths to the structure of dreams.

The Archaic Powers of Transit in Levi-Strauss

We will not have a plausible theory of search in dreams unless it is constructed upon the activity of archaic mind. After all, there was no other mind, until the last three thousand years, and very little until the last three hundred years. We will then want to explain the difference made by the addition of modern specialized consciousness.

Levi-Strauss's theory of the archaic mind is encyclopedic in its range, because the theory radiates like the archaic mind itself through every nuance of the aboriginal worlds. Yet, the theory is highly economical because the operating structure is relatively simple.

This simplicity of its mechanism is very difficult for a modern mind to comprehend. We can read a brief account of the structure of this structuralism of Levi-Strauss and think we get it, when we have introduced huge distortions. For example, Kuper and Stone (1982) expound the mechanism as a way to think about contradictions. This is correct as a first step. Levi-Strauss did think that the archaic mind was preoccupied with contradictions, or what he called (in our English translations) disjunctions. For example, the disjunction brought about by heat is that it can be beneficent for keeping warm and growing things and cooking things // but it can be malignant when it is excessive and dries up all the crops and overcooks us.

Yet Kuper and Stone (1982) run this preoccupation with contradiction or disjunction into a mechanism for resolving them by the well-known formula of Hegel:

thesis + anti-thesis = synthesis.

Then, they use this mechanism for analyzing Freud's Irma dream as if they were giving a structural analysis. The gist of it is that Freud's struggle is between a thesis of neurosis as an organic condition +

an anti-thesis of neurosis as a strangulation of affect =

a synthesis of a medical grand rounds in which TRIMETHYLAMIN
> is the solution, because it is a sexual metabolite that would build up in a woman
> as an organic condition brought about by her psychological repression.

The sequence of the dream is solution-focused in the modern sense of driving forward to a successful conclusion, through a series of steps as in the synthesis of an organic chemical compound. As Kuper and Stone put it

> . . . We stress the movement from the initial problem to its resolution and suggest that this movement is coherent and orderly . . . (p. 1233)

The reader may refer to their original paper for the details, which demonstrate the dream as an argument (not as a wish-fulfillment as Freud himself would have it). The gist of it is that the

> sequence follows the model of diagnostic medical rounds in a hospital (p. 1229) . . . If the examination sequence carries, as it were, the melodic line of the dream, then the dialectical permutations are the harmony. Their development occurs through a distinct process of contrasts and reconciliations. We have already stated the first opposition, between the diagnoses of hysteria and organic illness. This is only the most superficial aspect of what is the dialectical structure of the dream, the opposition between the physical and the psychological domains (pp. 1229-1330).

Now it is true that the story in a myth can arrange a resolution, just as coitus can be a resolution of a sexual tension, and a cadence of a musical discord. This archaic transition between opposites is not the same, however, as the synthesis of an organic compound like TRIMETYHLAMIN (either literally, or symbolically as a solution to a theoretical problem).

The difference is that the mythical, sexual and musical tensions recur as divergent problems, while an organic chemical compound like TRIMETHYLAMIN (literal or symbolical) is a convergent problem which remains fixed once it is synthesized (Schumacher, 1977; Gustafson, 1995a and 1995b). In Levi-Strauss's language, the mythical, sexual or musical disjunction is resolved by a conjunction, but only temporarily. The Hegelian machine of modern progress synthesizes stable objects. The modern improvement in the direction of stability has the disadvantage of putting an end to the excitement of the disjunction. Once a solution is found, the problem is dead, trivial, and repeatable for a kind of dull learning. A fresh antithesis may not be able to rouse the monumental synthesis in stone. Entropy has set in. This is the wasteland of the modern world.

Therefore, I think that Kuper and Stone have made a dreadful mistake in reducing the archaic mechanism to the Hegelian mechanism and in joining Freud in synthesizing his result. They have followed Freud's Hegelian logic with great accuracy. Indeed, it has proved to be the main myth of psychiatry a hundred years later. Its chief research is the synthesis of metabolites like TRIMETHYLAMIN, which are now called the neurotransmitters. The doctor's job is to regulate them as best he can, quite as Freud imagined in his dream. As Jung would say (1974, originally, 1945), Freud's big dream is one of a gifted dreamer that is taken up by his group.

Levi-Strauss's archaic mechanism of thinking retains the disjunctions, which the modern and Hegelian and Freudian mind would resolve forever. Kuper (1989) is clearer about this in his article on Levi-Strauss versus Freud. For example, this would lead to a very different perspective on the Irma dream. The reader should please read it now, if he or she is not entirely familiar with it (Freud, originally 1900). The opposition or tension in the dream, the disjunction, is between a woman who will not get better // and a group of men forcing a solution upon her.

The men are in a nasty competition with each other, in regard to diagnosis, and treatment. The text is shot through with Freud's rivalry with Fliess, Dr. M. (Breuer) and Otto (his pediatrician friend, and doctor of the Freud family, Oskar Rie (Schurr, 1966)). Indeed, the men are so caught up in their findings and in their battles with each other that the woman disappears. In this sense, the drive towards convergent solution is the same as the drive to be ascendant among doctors. Is that not an accurate picture of the hierarchical modern world?

If we return to Levi-Strauss's theory of the archaic mechanism, we see that his view is that

> The truth of the myth does not lie in any special content. It consists in logical relations which are devoid of content or, more precisely, whose invariant properties exhaust their operative value, since comparable relations can be established among the elements of a large number of different contents (p. 240, 1983, originally, 1964).

Thus, the meaning of the set of myths is not the story-line of melody about arranging one convergence or another in the horizontal plane. The meaning lies in the vertical plane of the harmony, in which the divergence of great opposites are recognized. In the case of the Irma dream, the divergence is between a raw woman who refuses to get better, and a group of doctors cooking up solutions. Levi-Strauss also utilizes a mechanical term for this mechanism of thinking, which devalues particular outcomes (resolutions, convergences) for recognition of the constant oppositions:

> I propose to give the name armature to a combination of properties that remain invariant in two or several myths: code to the pattern of functions ascribed by each myth to these properties; and message to the subject matter of an individual myth . . . . I can define the relation between the Bororo myth (M_1) and the Sherente myth (M_{12}) by stating that when we move from one to the other, the armature remains constant, the code is changed, and the message is reversed. (p. 199, 1983, originally, 1964)

"Armature" is an interesting word with a gamut of meanings, in which there is a constant idea:

> 1. Armor, esp. that worn for the protection and defense of the body; hence, a covering suggestive of such armor, as a. A covering of flat wire would about a cable. b. Biol. An organ or structure for offense or defense, as teeth, thorns, etc. 2. A piece of soft iron or

steel used to connect the poles of a magnet or of adjacent magnets. 3. Elec. a. The movable part of a dynamo or motor, consisting essentially of coils of wire around an iron core . . . b. The movable part of a relay or electric bell, moving in a variable magnetic field (Webster's Collegiate, 1941)

The electricity is created by the connection of the poles, and that is the dynamic power that interests Levi-Strauss, and it is a kind of ancient armor, or armature, as it were. The power is set in motion by the gap or disjunction between the great opposing powers, like life and death itself. Particular solutions or messages are relatively trivial by themselves, but important as they point to the pattern that connects them (the armature). In this precise sense, Levi-Strauss is not interested in myths per se, but in the sets of related myths which allow him to characterize the engine of the archaic mind.

The "code" of the myth is simply the sensory category, taste, hearing, smell, feel and sight, and its contrasted pair which can be drawn from different sectors of the aboriginal world like the cosmography of rising and setting planets, which is visual, or the growing or rotting of plants, which is olfactory.

Before I illustrate the archaic engine at work, I want to summarize the difference between such a "cold engine" and a Hegelian "hot engine" in the hands of a modern man like Freud, or his interpreters like Kuper and Stone. The "cold engine" generates stories or melodies full of strange transformations between the poles it is concerned with, like life and death, sky and earth, raw and cooked. The messages in the stories are amusing or frightening or whatever, but they are not to be taken literally as the truth of the matter. The truth lies in the mighty disjunctions that remain, coldly, and must be negotiated all the time. Things live, and die, rapidly, in an aboriginal world. The masters of such worlds are masters of these transitions, and are often coded as animals, like the opossum, or the crow, or whatever animal can negotiate the distance from one extreme to another that must be undergone.

The "hot engine," by contrast, of the modern world is built upon a fixed difference in power between those who have it, and those who serve it

Thermodynamic machines . . . such as the steam engine, operate on the basis of a difference in temperature between their component parts, between the boiler and the condenser; they can do a tremendous amount of work, far more than the others, but in the process they use up and destroy their energy. (p. 33, Levi-Strauss, with Charbonnier, 1969, originally, 1959).

In summary, a hot engine uses up its raw materials, as in a steam engine, while a cold engine recycles its raw materials, as in a cumulus cloud.

Thus, Freud's hot engine operates on a tremendous difference in temperature between the heated-up doctors // and the patient's cold reception of them. This disjunction is not the truth, however. The truth becomes the message which is concocted, or the rhetorical solution to the convergence of power upon cold objects, which makes them respond (Tate, 1934). The code is no longer of much interest, since the engine works the same on all its specialized objects, as in the different disciplines of the university. Their form is remarkably the same, whether they are producing the solution in feminist short stories or in hoof and mouth disease. The problem is to administer the world, and the technologies are selected for their ability to manage things. This makes for a convergent world, of administration, which destroys its own energy, and flattens into being everywhere the frenzy and exhaustion. It is a world of entropy production.

Myth as Musical Mind: The Overture as Introduction

Let us visit the opposite world of the cold engine, and see how it works to protect the great polarities of its armature, its variegation of code, and the humor of its transformations. I particularly like Levi-Strauss's "Toccata and Fugue" which is number three of part IV of The Raw and the Cooked (1983, originally published, 1964), and the book itself is Volume I of the four-volume Mythologiques.

I like this chapter best because Levi-Strauss as a writer is being carried away by the very beauty he is describing. His composition gathers up the same powers, in parallel, as the myths he is describing. Thus, writing can be like myth and like music:

> . . . the exceptional position occupied by music is brought out still more clearly. In making the comparison, I referred at the outset to an attribute that the myth and the musical work have in common: they operate through the adjustment of two grids, one internal, the other external. But, in the case of music, these grids, which are never simple, become complex to the point of reduplication. The external, or cultural, grid formed by the scale of the intervals or the hierarchical relations among the notes . . . already wholly cultural objects in themselves . . . The inner, or natural, grid . . . constituted by the visceral rhythms. (p. 27, 1983, originally, 1964)

The art of this composition is beautifully explained in Levi-Strauss's "Overture" to The Raw and the Cooked as follows:

> The musical emotion springs precisely from the fact that at each moment the composer withholds or adds more or less than the listener anticipates . . . If the composer withholds more than we anticipate, we experience a delicious falling sensation; we feel we have been torn from a stable point on the musical ladder and thrust into the void, but only because the support that is waiting for us was not in the expected place. When the composer withholds less, the opposite occurs: he forces us to perform gymnastic exercises more skillful than our own. Sometimes he moves us, sometimes he forces us to make the movement ourselves, but it always exceeds what we would have thought ourselves capable of achieving alone (p. 17, 1983, originally, 1964)

Naturally, this could be taken as the art of teaching or the art of making love or the art of walking in the woods. They are all related, yet they remain very distinct in their sensory codes:

204

Divergence of sequences and themes is a fundamental characteristic of mythological thought, which manifests itself as an irradiation; by measuring the directions and angles of the rays, we are led to postulate their common origin, as an ideal point on which those deflected by the structure of the myth would have converged had they not started, precisely, from some other point and remained parallel throughout their entire course (pp. 5-6)

Music is privileged for Levi-Strauss, the very key to progress about the nature of man (p. 18), because it can <u>integrate everything</u> into what Bateson (1979) called "the pattern that connects." Thus, time as a forward progress and timelessness work together in music:

> ... this relation to time is of a rather special nature: it is as if music and mythology needed time only in order to deny it. Both, indeed, are <u>instruments for the obliteration of time</u>. Below the level of sounds and rhythms, music acts upon a primitive terrain, which is the physiological time of the listener; this time is irreversible and therefore irredeemably diachronic, yet music transforms the segment devoted to listening to it into a synchronic totality, enclosed within itself. Because of the internal organization of the musical work, the act of listening to it immobilizes passing time; it catches and enfolds it as one catches and enfolds a cloth flapping in the wind. It follows that by listening to music, and while we are listening to it, we enter into a kind of immortality. (p. 16, my italics)

With this overture in mind about what to look for, let us now follow the music of Levi-Strauss's "Tocccata and Fugue," if only in very broad outline. The pleasure itself is to take it up for yourself, while I am just serving as a musicologist. The density of detail and range of reference can be daunting to a modern mind. I will try to keep your eye on the cold constants, which are its great message.

The Toccata and Fugue
Toccata

The first section of this piece is called "a. The Pleiades," which is the toccata. Let me briefly say that a toccata is

> A brilliant composition, usually for organ and harpsichord, in free fantasia style (Webster's Collegiate).

and The Pleiades are or were

> The seven daughters of the Titan Atlas and the Oceanid Pleione . . . The Pleiades were so distressed at the death of their sisters the Hyades that they all killed themselves, and Zeus placed them in the sky as a cluster of seven stars. It was also said, however, that Zeus turned them into stars to save them and their mother Pleione from Orion, who had chased them for seven years. He too became a constellation which appears to be ever pursuing the Pleiades . . . The word Pleiades is derived from a Greek word meaning "to sail," because the seven stars are visible during the summer months, comprising the season which the ancients reserved for navigation (Grant and Hazell, 1993).

So this will be a toccata of the Pleiades, which plays a set of variations on their origin. The first is as follows:

M_{131a}. Mataco. "The Origin of the Pleiades." Formerly the Indians used to climb into the sky by means of a huge tree. There they found an abundance of honey and fish. One day, after they had returned from the sky, they met an old woman at the foot of the tree. She asked for a small share of their provisions, but they refused. In order to be avenged on them for their greed, the old woman set fire to the tree. The Indians who had remained in the sky turned into stars and formed the constellation of the Pleiades.

Levi-Strauss at first makes no comment on the familiar oppositions in the myth: sky/earth, abundance/poverty, young/old, male/female, greed/revenge, wood/fire, Indians/stars. I will not quote the next four variations, taken from tribes in the same region, but only note the emergence of "floating viscera" in several of them from a murdered person halfway, as it were, between sky and earth. Levi-Strauss himself comments:

The preceding myths suggest that as a code term the theme of the floating viscera fulfills two distinct functions and is, in a sense, bivalent. In the "aquatic code" the viscera are congruous with fish and marsh plants. In the "celestial code" they are congruous with the stars, and especially the Pleiades. (p. 244)

Levi-Strauss then summarizes this little series by noting two fundamental points about their structure. The first is that any variation is going to have "gaps" which are "punched out" of the entire set of possible elements for the story. For example, the first variation did not have the "floating viscera." The second is that it is as if

. . . the sign system had its own built-in resistance to the buffetings to which the things signified have to submit from without (p. 245)

Thus, the floating viscera in the Guyana area connects the appearance of the Pleiades in the sky with the appearance of fish in the rivers, while in Bororo country the appearance of the Pleiades signifies the ending of the dry season. They have a festival to "burn the feet of the Pleiades" to slow down their leaving and prolong the dry period suitable for nomadic activities.

Thus, the theme of the Pleiades is buffeted wildly, as it heralds different things in neighboring regions, such as the coming of the fish or the ending of the dry season. Levi-Strauss is not averse to extending his composition all the way around the world. His readers may have heard the Greek meaning of the sailing season before he even began. He slides into North American (Wyandot, Eskimo, Zuni, Navajo, and Blackfoot) and Polynesian variations. This is a brilliant composition in free fantasy style, that is, a toccata of the Pleiades.

206

Fugue

The second section of this piece is called "b. The Rainbow," which is the fugue. A fugue is

A polyphonic composition, developed from a given theme, according to strict contrapuntal rules. (Webster's Collegiate)

While the Pleiades allowed Levi-Strauss to let loose the powers of heraldry, the Rainbow theme will allow him to tighten the powers of precise adjustment. I could say he is playing these opposite musical powers against each other, the radiation of its energy in a free fall and the multiplication of its precision, like Bach, but then Levi-Strauss would have rightly replied that Bach was capitalizing on the archaic vitality itself. Try Bach's Toccata and Fugue in D minor for organ, for comparison. My wife happened to read three poems of Emily Dickinson to me last evening as I was preparing to write this, and I was astonished to see how her world is quite like that of the Bororo Indians, and Bach, and Levi-Strauss. I will come around to demonstrating this before we finish this chapter, and I will also come around to showing this vitality in the dreams of patients. It is our mainspring, or armature.

Levi-Strauss begins his fugue with a digression, to state the definition of the rainbow: In South America the rainbow has a double meaning. On the one hand, as elsewhere, it announces the end of the rain; on the other hand, it is considered to be responsible for diseases and various natural disasters. In its first capacity the rainbow effects a disjunction between the sky and the earth which previously were joined through the medium of rain. In the second capacity it replaces the normal beneficent conjunction by an abnormal, maleficent one -- the one it brings about itself between sky and earth by taking the place of water (p. 246)

Levi-Strauss is already operating in strict counter-point: rainbow as disjunction, beneficent // to rainbow as conjunction, maleficent. This music loves inversion, as in a variation which quickly follows:

In the Gran Chaco the Vilela have a myth (M_{173}) about a shy, solitary boy who used to hunt birds and who changed into a multi-colored and deadly serpent, the rainbow (p. 246)

The Author's Dream of Caruso in Milwaukee. I often dream of the very powers I am writing about, and last night was no exception in its economy of means. I dreamt

Enrico Caruso was singing in Milwaukee.

and later

We had adopted a tame lion in our family and he pounced on me in play, which made me acutely aware that we couldn't keep him around for fear he would go over the line from play to preying on us.

The first variation is the toccata, of the operatic powers in conjunction with the popular stages. Caruso was so well known in the 1950s that the cliche for taking down somebody singing with gusto in the shower was: "Who do you think you are, Caruso?" The first variation associated myself with Caruso, because I just had done what seemed like a beautiful demonstration of the archaic powers of the archaic mind in the dream of a patient in consultation in my Clinic with an appreciative audience behind the mirror. So Caruso can radiate even into Milwaukee, so to speak.

The second variation is an inversion of the first, in which I suffer being on the bottom of a great force, instead of on the top. This alludes to my daughter's huge Malamute, Elko, visiting us for the summer, who loves to get over our little Shetland Sheep Dog, Athena. The strict inversion is the beginning of a fugue. It says that conjunction can be maleficent, especially if you are on the bottom.

This tiny toccata and fugue illustrates the great radiation and tight circumspection that Levi-Strauss is bringing us to consider. The radiation is exhilarating because the stops are out, while the circumspection by inversion takes my breath away. I am obliged to make the transition from being on top, to being on the bottom, of a great force. It helps me to appreciate why people run away from me when I am full of great (playful) force. To feel ourselves as others feel us, to play on Robert Burns, is a gift which we get from the power of inverting the theme. We get into the shoes of the other. For the archaic man, this is absolutely essential to help him refrain from injustice to those he must depend upon as his brothers:

> . . . issues are only settled by unanimous decision. It seems to be believed that if, at the time of making an important decision, there existed, even in the tiniest fraction of society, feelings of bitterness such as are normally associated with being the loser in an election, resentment and disappointment at not having been supported would produce a powerful and almost magical effect and jeopardize the result that had been obtained (Levi-Strauss to Charbonnier, p. 35, 1969; originally, 1959)

Nowadays, this jeopardy wrecks every cooperative project such as seminars and teams and marriages. This is why Western man, out of touch with the archaic powers of inversion, is such a failure at these matters which insist upon equality. This is why his power grid exhausts itself.

Let us go back from my digression to Levi-Strauss's fugue. Having stated his first inversion from beneficent disjunction to maleficent conjunction, he will now multiply his powers of inversion. Thus,

> The food-bearing tree in the myths of Guyana and the Gran Chaco can be identified with the Milky Way. This would give the following equivalence
> (a) Milky Way: rainbow :: life: death . . .
> The nocturnal counterpart of the rainbow would therefore be the non-presence of the Milky Way at a point it would normally occur, hence the equation:
> (b) Rainbow = Milky Way (-1)

Now he will show how the rainbow becomes the mother of diseases:

> It will be remembered that the guilty woman's brothers cut her body into two pieces, one of which they threw into a lake in the east, the other into a lake in the west. (p. 247)

The two ends are two snakes for the Timbira, which is the "dual" aspect of the rainbow. The Katawishi

> distinguish two rainbows: Mawali in the west, and Tini in the east. Tini and Mawali were twin brothers who brought about a flood that inundated the whole world and killed all living people, except two young girls whom they saved to be their companions. It is not advisable to look either of them straight in the eye: to look at Mawali is to become flabby, lazy, and unlucky at hunting and fishing; to look at Tini makes a man so clumsy he cannot go any distance without stumbling and lacerating his feet against all the obstacles in his path, or pick up a sharp instrument without cutting himself (p. 247)

The Dream of the Wake of the Whale. The very dream consultation I alluded to in my dream of Caruso in Milwaukee is apt to cite here because it picks up this "duality" of the rainbow from which "distance" is of absolute importance. The patient is a middle aged woman seen by one of our staff psychologists, whose story has been the difficulty of getting out from under a powerhouse mother, and later a powerhouse husband. I had first seen her four years ago in consultation when she came in for being acutely suicidal. After several years of work with one of our best residents, the patient believed in herself enough to limit her self-destruction to minor crises. Now, the psychologist had the patient and wanted to know what it would take to get out of minor crises, which continually interrupted their contemplation of her huge feelings. They had gotten out of the region of death's door (A) into the region of continual minor crises (B), but how could they stay in the region of stable work (C)?

> I will drastically simplify the epic dream text which we dropped into when we were discussing the patient's vulnerability to being run down by her husband's criticisms. She dreamt

> Of going to an aboriginal peninsula in Australia where her hosts were being tampered with by western sailors. The shepherd dog of the natives stood up to them, and got his nose broken. Then a whale came up the inlet and his wake smashed most of the intruders and swept them away. A couple survived, and raped her daughter, and cut off her clitoris. An old lady and the patient and the people then come to comfort the dog and her daughter. The old lady sees a bone-button fall off, and niftily sews it back on.

The patient and the psychologist had already translated a number of elements: the old lady refers back to her "duality" of grandmothers when she was twelve, one critical and cutting and driving her mother from her father, and the other saving them from destitution, when the patient was twelve; the clitorectomy refers to her own hysterectomy, which seemed to rob her of her entire sphere of autonomous power of having children, which occurred the year before this consultation.

I was able to show her her own archaic vitality getting mobilized to handle these life-long intrusions of the violent critics. First, she was taking great distance to the southern hemisphere and to aboriginal time and to the intelligent sociality of these whale-people. Secondly, she was having trouble borrowing this whale power because it tended to be so huge or so unable to protect small things like the shepherd dog and the child. It's like having nuclear weapons, and no conventional defenses. The western sailors keep tampering with you, and breaking you. Probably, this was why she was still in continual crisis.

The armature of the dream is:

whale-power: western intrusion :: grandmother-sewing: fallen bone-button
In other words, the refuge in the whale-people is still vulnerable to the critical intrusion, especially for her children. Thus, her urge to get distance from the malign power of criticism is not entirely protective for the small creatures. Only when the whale-power is distanced and scaled down to her grandmother's eye and needle can the bone-button be mended. As she said of her husband's power to criticize,

He is subtle.

Thus, she needs the power to recognize subtle undermining, which has been continually throwing her into crisis. The power of the whale-people is scaled down to the power of the eye and needle. When she has this, she will have stability.

Fugue Continued

Having left from the Fugue of the Rainbow at the variation of the two brother rainbows, Tini and Mawali, and in the theme of the need to distance their full powers, we pick it up again with the next variation. Levi-Strauss now transposes from the pair of rainbows in the Katawishi to the pair of rainbows in the Tucuna and then on to the Indians of Guyana:

> Similarly, the Tucuma differentiated between the eastern and western rainbows and believed them both to be the subaquatic demons, the masters of fish and potter's clay respectively. . . . At the same time the Indians of Guyana establish a direct link between potter's clay and diseases (p. 247)

Levi-Strauss describes how they have to get their potter's clay at night during the commencing of the full moon, or it will break and bring diseases to those who eat of the dishes (pp. 247-248).

So now he is describing how they keep in mind to distance the powers of disease, as he transposes into a Bororo myth:

> The Bororo heroine (mother of diseases) is the opposite of a pregnant woman, since she is the mother of a young child. Like the western rainbow of the Tucuna, she assumes, or rather usurps, the role of mistress of the fish. She is a bad mother and leaves her child on a branch (therefore in an external position, whereas a pregnant woman's child is internal)

and causes it to turn into an ant heap--that is, into hard, dried earth, the opposite of the supple clay found in the streams. At the same time as she enters into physical conjunction with the water in order to feed on the dead fish drifting on the surface, she creates a disjunction between the sky and earth, as the myth indicates in two ways. (p. 248)

Namely, the child who had been high in the tree goes low to become hard earth. It becomes raw, like ants the natives fed on in nature.

Meanwhile, the mother of diseases has stuffed herself with fishes which she will exude from her body as diseases. Levi-Strauss now compares this to the opossum of the last section (see "The Opossum Cantata") and obtains his transformation of the Borora heroine into an opossum:

... the Borora heroine is an opossum whose positive modality (nursing) is transformed into its opposite (stinking), and whose negative modality (stinking) is raised to a high, although indeterminate power. She is an opossum whose stench (which has become fatal to the whole of humanity) completely cancels out her qualities as a nursing mother (p. 249)

He goes on to note that the Guianian Indians call the rainbow "opossum" because of the reddish color of its fur:

The opossum is characterized by ambiguity: as a nursing mother, it serves life; as a foul-smelling or rotten beast, it anticipates death (pp. 249-250)

Now Levi-Strauss has nearly the "maximum significance" of the opossum which is quite like a serpent. By this, I think he means how transitional it is between all the great powers. The great thing for the archaic mind is to be able to undergo these transitions, imaginatively, which must have prepared them to undergo them in their lives. Modern man fixes himself to a lever. Archaic man is the master, like the opossum, of transitions, of weather, of life and death, of sky to earth, of sweet beneficence to stinking malignity.

The last two variations are so dense in their voicing that I cannot possibly reproduce them without overburdening this chapter. The first of them adds the astronomical dimension, and the second is about the sacrifice of a girl. Oddly, or not so oddly, they both have elements in common with the dream of the wake of the whale. The first ends with a flooding of the world, as Venus (a male) is carried up into the sky by a whirlwind. The second ends with a gang rape of the girl by a flock of birds, who dismember her body, and take pieces of her vulva for shelter.

Levi-Strauss's interest in them is in the wealth of transformations. In the first, Venus is covered with malodorous ulcers. He is thus a kind of opossum, because he stinks so much that the people turn up their noses at him. The wretch is taken by a man, whose daughter lets him sit on her thighs and wash him. The transformations (from other myths in the set) include: star to opossum, female god to male god, nursing mother to passive nurse. Finally, the male god

(Venus) afflicted by ulcers rapes the virgin, and saves the lives of the people under his protection.

In the second variation, the transformation from the set of myths include: a shift from the vertical axis of high and low, to the horizontal axis of water-earth -- the girl tries to cross a river on the back of an alligator, on consideration that the girl will insult him afterward! -- a shift from woman as a star come down to earth, or a rotten fruit that has undergone metaphorphosis, to a woman that disappears to benefit the birds! -- and finally, a third inversion, from a woman whose pieces were hung up inside huts as wives for the men to the same pieces put up outside as roofs!

When I first read these myths, I was astonished by the reveling in sheer violence. Levi-Strauss has a very different idea, which is the tremendous interest, and play, of transformation. Of course, the two levels are related, and people too alarmed by the potential of their own violence are not going to play easy with symbolic transit. They are going to fix themselves, and go around in dead circles, exactly as pictured in Dante's <u>Inferno</u>.

From Myth to Dream With An Orchestral Score in Hand

Now it is time to ask about the relationship between the myths analyzed by Levi-Strauss and the dreams of my patients. A myth is something passed around by a group, while a dream need only be known to one dreamer. Yet, a dreamer may give his dream to a group, and the group makes it its mythical property. Thus, Freud's Irma dream becomes a myth for psychoanalysis about its creation from a rounds in the medical world. Similarly, Jung's dream of the Crusader becomes a myth for analytical psychology about its creation from a dying psychoanalysis.

Jung argued that the dreams that remain private are about matters of no concern to anyone but the dreamer, whereas those that become mythical property are seized for their relevance to the life of the group:

> Not all dreams are of equal importance. Even primitives distinguish between "little" and "big" dreams, or, as we might say, "insignificant" and "significant" dreams. Looked at more closely, "little" dreams are the nightly fragments of fantasy coming from the subjective and personal sphere, and their meaning is limited to the affairs of everyday. That is why such dreams are easily forgotten, just because their validity is restricted to the day-to-day fluctuations of the psychic balance (p. 76, 1974; originally, 1945)

Jung contrasts the "big" dreams coming from a different and deeper level of the unconscious:

> Thus, we speak on the one hand of a <u>personal</u> and on the other of a <u>collective</u> unconscious, which lies at a deeper level and is further removed from consciousness than the personal unconscious. The "big" or "meaningful" dreams come from this deeper level. They reveal their significance -- quite apart from the subjective impression they make -- by their plastic form, which often has a poetic force and beauty . . . For example,

a young man dreamed of a great snake that guarded a golden bowl in an underground vault. (p. 77)

In other words, the big dreams from the collective unconscious

> . . . employ numerous mythological motifs that characterize the life of the hero, of that greater man who is semi-divine by nature. Here we find the dangerous adventures and ordeals such as occur in initiations. We meet dragons, helpful animals, and demons (etc.) . . . which in no way touch the banalities of everyday life (p. 79)

Now it is certainly true that it is possible to divide dreams into two groups by this categorical distinction between personal banality / divine adventures. Jung even reifies the distinction into two different spheres or levels in the unconscious. They become two different places, literally. It is even plausible that groups ignore messages from personal banality, while attending to them from semi-divine sources.

I take a position about dreams closer to Levi-Strauss's position about myths. I think that dreams take place in the space-time of the group, but with gaps in them that obscure the armature of the set that they belong to. Just as any myth utilizes a fraction of the armature of its set it belongs, so an individual dream will have

> gaps, so to speak, punched out of the fabric (1983, p. 245; originally, 1964)

or dream screen in which it is embedded.

How are we to know the set of myths to which any particular dream belongs as an outrider, like an obscure and highly punched out myth? How do I even know that this is the situation? Well, I don't know, but I propose it as a working hypothesis. Its plausibility is this. We are very recently descended from archaic man, whose preoccupation (if we believe Levi-Strauss, and I do) is transformation between extremes. For this humanity, which I take to be us, suffering comes from disjunctions that keep us from going where we want to go, and conjunctions that keep us in toxic realms. Thus, the relief of suffering is a matter of transit, by disjoining (||) or distancing things that injure us, and conjoining (=) things that benefit us.

Thus, the unconscious mind is a great searching and mapping instrument of transition between all the extremes like life and death. This raises the next question of what extremes are relevant to modern man and woman? Here I have to depart from Levi-Strauss, who did not deal with this question very much. In general, I am taking as a working hypothesis that the relevant extremes for modern humanity are between the specialized foci by which one earns a living in the modern world by fixing and repeating oneself // versus the vitality of the archaic world wherein we are renewed. We all have to operate at the first extreme to have resources, whereas we all have to reach to the second extreme to have vitality.

Therefore, I think that the archaic consciousness has undergone a shift from its perennial polarities, which we visited in the Toccata and Fugue, to getting back and forth between all of them // and the means of modern survival. This is the matter of life and death for us. It sets up the structure, of the armature, of dreams. In general, I map any dream onto this armature, by means of the kind of orchestral score utilized by Levi-Strauss. The particular variant is written in the horizontal like a melody, while the vertical of the harmony is constituted by two long lines, the right one in red to represent the emergency of specialization in the modern world, and the left one in green to represent the vitality of which we are constituted. The divergence or disjuncture between the two is represented by two yellow lines which start together at the top and move in opposite and downward directions. All of this armature is illustrated in Figure 10.1.

Figure 10.1

"The Armature of Modern Dreams"

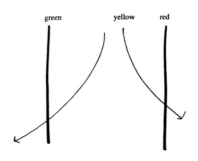

Now, I will close this chapter illustrating the use of this score with three examples, a dream of one of my patients, a dream of my own, and a poem of Emily Dickinson.

The Dream of the Flying Chair. My patient, a doctor, had just given a test to her students. She had taken precautions against their cheating, but was still amazed that they did not seem to care what they were doing. They seemed amoral and amotivated. Since she is quite the opposite, she had trouble bending her mind around them. She dreamt

She was weaving a seat for a chair, but the ballast and cornices would not come together This is illustrated in her drawing, which is Figure 10.2.

The great puzzle of the dream was about "ballast" and "cornices" which do not belong together in any ordinary sense. "Cornices" turned out to refer to the anatomy of the "cornu" of the thyroid upon which she was testing her students. "Ballast" turned out to refer to an item in hot-air balloons, which had thrilled her on the fifth anniversary of her marriage.

The tear in the fabric of the dream began to appear at this point as tears. Because she could not get her husband to do such things anymore. He was pulled into his specialized medical world, while she was in both places, and unable to bring the two together. I will not complicate this description with the richness of allusions in this dream, all of which fell into this set of divergent problems. The green world of her beautiful ideas, and the red world of emergencies, did not come together for her.

The Author's Dream of the Jekyll/Hyde Problem. The very night after the dream of Caruso // and the Lion, while preparing this very text you are reading, I dreamt what my unconscious has to say about this conscious text. I dreamt

Scene 1. "Baby-Faced Johnson," a murderer, like his father, also named "Baby-Faced Johnson."

Scene 2. I am a very passive patient in a medical assembly line in a big room with glass walls, looking out onto Massachusetts Avenue in Boston, or the Seine in Paris. I am to have an inguinal hernia repair, and a Dr. Welch comes to have the cursory look and go. I am amazed that I just took whatever doctor came along.

Scene 3. I get off my bed and go outside to have a look, and circle a large set of green playing fields, which are like soccer fields, but some are up high in mountains and some are contracted. I am reminded of Machu Pichu in Peru, of a rifugio in the Italian Alps called Roda da Vael with its green helicopter landing strip, and of soccer fields in Europe foreshortened by the speed of the train. The last of these playing fields is more like a basketball court, surrounded by bleachers which are like a maze that ascends. I enter it at the top and walk around the top and see one of my female patients as the only spectator of the game sitting down at the level of the court. I wave good-bye to her, and leave at the top.

All of this complex space is pictured, if cryptically, in Figure 10.3.

Figure 10.3

"The Space of the Author's Dream of the Jekyll/Hyde Problem"

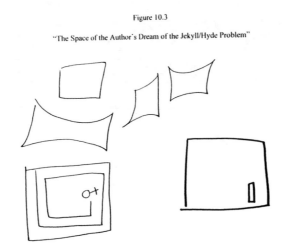

This dream begins with the problem of sterility in Western culture, which Stevenson mapped in The Strange Case of Dr. Jekyll and Mr. Hyde (1886) and which I discussed at length in my last book as the quintessential problem of my patients (Gustafson, 1995b, Chapter 11, "Visual Maps"). I had just had several cases the day before, in which I was immersed in this Jekyll/Hyde world, such as that of the patient who had the dream of The Wake of the Whale.

The first scene of this dream simply means that conjunction with a world in all innocence (baby-faced) gets you wrecked like my patients // while disjunction from this world as a killer (whale) destroys what little you have. You lose double. Thus, the first scene is about the hopeless predicament in which so many end up lost.

The second scene makes me into one of these overly trusting patients, who is going to entrust his creation (inguinal area) passively to any surgeon who comes along. It is an inversion of my usual caution, which allows me to put myself in the position of my patients. I come to my senses, so to speak, to get free of this dangerous conjunction, and depart for "green fields" as it goes in the song

Once there were green fields lit by the sun.

I now move freely in very beautiful and even sacred fields that I have known, which is the conjunction with the archaic mind that is my blessing. But I must come back, and I do into a playing field in which one of my female patients is down below where I began. I stay up high, in this maze, and wave to her, and depart. I am mindful as I leave of a line from Yeats,

> Horseman, pass by.

This is the noble rider (Stevens, 1965):

> It is a violence from within that protects us from a violence without. It is the imagination pressing back against the pressure of reality (p. 36).

In other words, I distance myself from passivity too easily conjoined and too low to what is awful, but I return from on high to oppose it.

Emily Dickinson's Poem. This is precisely what Emily Dickinson was forever doing, as in her #229 (Ruth Gustafson, personal communication):

> A Burdock clawed my Gown -
> Not Burdock's - blame
> But mine -
> We went too near
> The Burdock's Den -
>
> A Bog - affronts my shoe -
> What else have Bogs - to do -
> The only Trade they know -
> The splashing Men!
> Ah, pity - then!
>
> 'Tis Minnows can despise
> The Elephant's - calm eyes
> Look further on!

In other and less words, it is our own trouble if we allow too much conjunction with Burdock and Bog // we must take our disjunction and see them from the perspective of Minnows who can despise (look down on something smaller!) and Elephant who can look by (overlook). Are we not in the same armature, and seeing it by the same orchestral score?

Chapter 11. A Search for Survival on the Frontier.

Now I can pull my method together, to show what it can do for survival. With an adequate armature, the animal has a much better chance. I will reserve the full vitality of this art for the final chapter.

In this chapter, I begin with an exposition of how I work up a dream. I will show how the orchestral score alters the outcome. Essentially, the music of the hot engine is exhausting, while the music of the cold engine is a fearful renewal. Survival depends upon modulation, between these great extremes. For such transitions, it is absolutely necessary to know what can be done, and what cannot be done.

This brings up our second topic, which is bogus transitions or conjunctions. A very great deal of harm in this frontier culture of ours comes from buying tickets that take us nowhere. For example, the railroads sold the seeding of the barren West as a Paradise in the 19th century (Raban, 1996). Nowadays, every product is a pair of ruby slippers to take us home (Rushdie, 1994): A Lexus, a lawnmower, a beer. All promise happiness. Almost all of our psychopathology can be generated from bogus conjunction, and almost all of our survival depends upon reading it before falling prey to it.

Finally, our third topic is the search for adequate bridges between our natural vitality in the green world of the cold engine // and the power to command resources in the red world of the hot engine, over this hiatus (//) between them. I utilize the engineering mind of Thomas French (1970), to show what is typical of science for building an "integrative span" to carry the "strain" of the load. I will show why this secular dependence on a single metaphor is fine for business, but inadequate to the great difficulty of renewal in the Western world.

The Search for Modulation

I begin the work-up of a dream as Jung did, by locating what the dream is reacting to from the previous day and by establishing the patient's knowledge of each element of the dream from how he came to know of such a thing. I differ from Jung in that I take all the movements of the composition as variants of the contemporary struggle of modulation between the cold engine of the archaic mind // and the hot engine of modern adaptation. Like Levi-Strauss, I believe the patient cannot but compose within the limits set by his group, so that every dream is a variant of the group mind.

Tolstoy has given us the clearest pictures of the void out of which we must construct our lives (Gustafson, 1995b, Chapter 15, "Tolstoy's Fate"). On the one hand, we live in a social world of ceaseless and specialized struggle for status. Anna Scherer's drawing room at the opening of War and Peace (Tolstoy, 1869) shows us the men who have the status to pontificate and to give places to subordinates, as well as the women who get places by flattering them. This is dull and exhausting and wears out whatever grace its actors had to start with. Such a hot engine cooks us into feverish activity, and dries us up, finishing us off.

The counterpoint comes from the cold engine of perpetual childhood and its self-delight in pure play. Tolstoy calls this samadovolnost or self-absorption (Gustafson, 1992). The children and the young people are the saving grace of War and Peace.

The adults are all mixed forms of status-mongering and self-absorption, most of them relatively trivial, some comical, some tragic, and a very few finding their way through to keeping their vitality // and their place. Kutuzov sleeps through conferences of his generals and retires to his tent // knowing he must just bow to the tide of Napoleon's surge from west to east, and waiting for it to spend itself.

The novel is this vast set of variations upon the theme set out in the overture of the young Andrew and Pierre colliding with the machinery of Anna Scherer's drawing room, as illustrated in the orchestral score depicted in Figure 11.1. Notice that the hot and red engine of status diverges increasingly from the cold and green engine of play, as time marches in the music from left to right and top to bottom of the score. This is what I call Tolstoy's abyss.

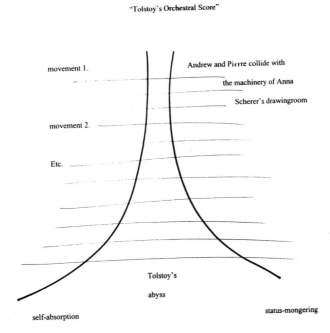

Figure 11.1

"Tolstoy's Orchestral Score"

Of course, I could be wrong in my argument that this is the structure of the score for all modern music, literature, art, psychology, and dreams. I am persuaded I am right, by trying it out, as I illustrate in the case of Tolstoy's novel. Now, let us try it out on the first dream of a patient. I believe it will prove to be a variant of what Tolstoy and I are talking about, just as any myth-story found by Levi-Strauss in South American Indian oral tradition turned out to be a variation of the set of myths of the region.

The use of locating the particular dream as a variant of the set I hope to make obvious. In general, it orients the patient to the vast power of the force field in which he must get back and forth between fitting in to get the supplies he needs // and getting free to keep his vitality. He has to read accurately where he can modulate in such a free passage (Gustafson and Cooper, 1990, Chapter 7, "Free Passage"), and where there is no such passage and he is going to be stuck and cooked on the inside, or stuck and frozen out on the outside.

A Dream Variant of Lord of the Flies. In her third session, my patient in her late twenties brought her first dream. She slipped into it just after asking me if I knew about the Fisher Divorce Scale she and her husband took as a test, which showed she hadn't changed much in her marital therapy with a previous therapist. She felt it was funny. She also prefaced the dream by telling me about her oldest sister, the family martyr who stayed in her marriage subserviently as God's duty. I had asked her in the second session to look for a dream to show up, which would comment on her dilemma discussed in that session: to stay in her marriage because she "should" make restitution for hurting her husband by an affair // or go with the affair which she felt like doing. My concluding sentence was:

> As Vicki Hearne (1986) would say, _____ (your husband) has trouble asking something of the horse, and you, the horse, are very dubious after ten years of distrusting the rider (so to speak -- I am aware of the dangers of the metaphor). Your dreams will reply.

She dreamt, two nights later:

> I saw this dream from the outside, as in a movie. A young boy was with his mother who was making dinner, while they waited for the father to come home from work. The kid waited in agitation and anticipation, and was excited, when the dad did come. They sat at a table, father and son, across from two men, a dark one and a fair one. Then the dark man came and stood behind the father, and the mother came up behind him also. Now I noticed a knife on a stick on a plate in front of the father. They dared him to put it in his mouth, like swallowing a sword in the circus. The father rolled his eyes in fun at the son. When he put it in his mouth, the mother jammed his head together (she gestured with her hands, to show an upward thrust from one hand below on the jaw, with a downward thrust from the other hand on top of the head). Blood spurts all over.

Because she started from the distant position of a movie-goer, I first asked her to draw the scene on an 18" X 24" pad of paper which I guessed would draw her into the dream. Her sketch was as faint in a light brown color as could possibly be drawn. It looked roughly like the following Figure 11.2.

Figure 11.2

"Lord of the Flies: A Variation of a Dream"

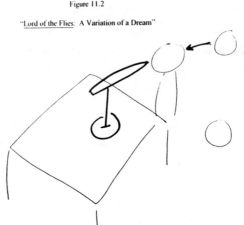

I asked her how she knew such a room, and she replied that it was a room of a poor family. It was like the room of the family of a girl she adopted in college. To make a long story short, the girl had prospered under her tutelage, but fell apart when the patient left to get married. She had grieved this, but derived some consolation from the girl keeping some of the interests engendered in the period of being looked after.

At first, she thought that the mother and father could be any mother and father, until she reflected a little longer and said this scene was quite like her family of origin. The father was the figure of fun for the children, and mother in the background. This shook her a little, to find herself in a diagram of her own family. Mother cooked and did the laundry, and slept on the couch. "I know because I was appointed to look after her. I didn't think she was angry! She seemed depressed. Later, after we grew up, she got her own job and was rejuvenated like a teenager." I simply replied to her that flight often takes the place of fight.

The light and dark men also seemed nondescript to her, until she stayed with them a while. Now, the light one reminded her of her husband, and the dark one of a brother of her husband's who had lived with them and been their partner in business. They tried to help this brother, but he dragged them down into his depression, drinking, and irresponsibility.

The knife on the stick on the plate was dark, rusty, used, and fit the poverty of the room. She had not seen it in the opening sunlight of the dream, as if it were in shadow. She knew about such knives from . . . Lord of the Flies (Golding, 1954). I asked her to tell me about the story. She replied that the boys in the story "lost it and killed a pig and had its head on a stick like it was their god." At last we had reached over the gap of her distance, for now she felt upset for the poor kid having to witness this horror. She felt helpless, and she looked tearful. "I feel like I should do more for children like that, but I don't really want to be there."

As we were near the end of the hour, I simply said that we seemed to have a long line of martyrs in her family, from her mother to her sister to herself. She added, ". . . and my father, too, who didn't do what he wanted in work, and is not doing well now." In my letter to her after the session (see Gustafson, 1995b, Chapter 12, "Official Documents and Generative Letters") I wrote:

> About your dream of the set-up for Lord of the Flies: it seems to pull together the unwitting sacrifice of so many lives . . . . // versus you wishing to get distance on all this martyrdom which pulls you so strongly in the family tradition.

What is new about the interpretation of this dream? Certainly, the work-up of its elements is classical, and entirely in keeping with Jung's recommendations. Like Jung and Winnicott, I use the drawing to draw the patient in, and reach to her felt distress. They, in turn, were making small, but decisive, modifications in Freud's procedure as I have already discussed.

What is new here is not in the work-up, but in the placement of the dream into the series in which it belongs as a variation. The series of stories in which it belongs long preceded her in Western culture, in her family tradition, and thus draws her into its force field. Some of these are mentioned by her and by me before she recites the dream, many are literally in the dream, many are context for the elements of the dream, and several more appear after we finish our analysis.

If we line these up as a series as Levi-Strauss did with myths, then these stories which are recited left to right in the horizontal lines of music show up in the vertical lines like the harmony of music. Not all the variants have full development of all the elements, but have gaps punched out in them. The vertical columns then look like those ghostly columns seen in strips of paper chromatography. Oddly enough, the cover of one of my last books has this very pattern (Gustafson, 1995a), even though I never talked directly with the artist that did the design. This is not synchronicity as Jung would have it, but the power of the pattern to come through. In any event, consider the series in the order that it arose:

> her dilemma of whether to divorce or stay married
> her sister as martyr to marriage
> Vicki Hearne's tales of "asking something of the horse"
> the idealized family in sunlight, and murder in shadow
> (I think here of Jekyll and Hyde, duty and murder)
> the poor girl helped, and then abandoned
> her mother's subservience, and fading into the couch
> (like Jekyll, spent by duty)
> their friend the dark man that weighed them down
> the boys who lost it and became primitive killers in Lord of the Flies
> her own horror at a child having to witness the murder of its father
> a long line of martyrs in her family
> she adds her father

I put one more story or set of stories before this series, in this chapter, and that was War and Peace. I would say it fits. For all of this is about duty that wears a body out, and builds up the urge to murder or flee. I have crudely summarized it elsewhere (Gustafson, 1995a, 1995b) as "the exploding doormat problem."

What advantage have we derived from placing the dream in this series? If we consider her variant in the context of the series, we can grasp the strength and weakness of her grasp on the force field she is in. We can see what gaps are punched out in it, which are the holes of her selective inattention (Gustafson, 1995a, Chapter 13, "The Dream as an Individual Map of Dilemma").

First of all, the sunlight idealization is in stark contrast to the shadow of murder. The transition is one she is barely prepared for. This is due to her idealization of fathering, fun, helping, quite like Dr. Jekyll, or the line of martyrs in her own family. Like her own father rolling his eyes in fun at the circus stunt about to be performed, she is totally or almost totally unprepared for the violence of her subservient mother. We are talking about a family cover-up, but this is a family behaving as an idealized American family. Actually, it is in the wider set of Western Culture. Think of Thomas Mann's (1929) story, "Mario and the Magician," about a naive family falling into the hands of a killer-sorcerer when they are on vacation in Italy. Or, coming back to America, think of Flannery O'Connor's story, "A Good Man is Hard to Find" (1955).

As my fifteen year old daughter just said to me coming up to my study to discuss starting a dream journal, dreams are not only about imagination, but about conscience: to-wit,

unconscience // conscience

When the conscience is getting all the light, then the unconscience is likely to burst out of the shadow. Here we are back in Freud's Victorian world, or Dickens' or R. L. Stevenson's. In such a world of duty (super-ego) // chaos (id), the trick is to be able to modulate to mixed forms or balance of duty and impulse. I suppose that is why I quoted Hearne to her about asking something of the horse, this, a metaphor, quite enamored by Freud, for the ego.

The Author's Dream of the Hamlet Variations. I would like to add one more dream to our series which began with War and Peace and ran through Lord of the Flies and ends up back in the Renaissance with myself in Hamlet. This one is relevant, because I dreamt it while I was clarifying the theory for this chapter. It is my own unconscious in reply, and it composes, oddly, a static piece of music. It is a dream of a situation in which I do not have a move. I am like Hamlet returning from his studies at Wittenberg, to his home castle of Elsinore, and standing in the front door. In other words, it is picturing a regime in which nothing can be done. It is as clear as possible about a class of situations in which there is no transition between being a cooked insider // or frozen outsider. In other words, there is no modulation, and this is absolutely critical to judge. Otherwise, you get into Hamlet's messes, and helpless and murderous rage, because Claudius has already taken over with his low ways, and because Hamlet's noble father is already forgotten. There is a complete disjunction between the actual corruption // and the recent ideal. I have long felt about the play that Hamlet never should have come back from Wittenberg, and now I dream about it as a theoretical statement about the force field of the modern world. I dreamt:

M1. It is a very cold and unrelenting polar wind as in Kenneth Brannagh's Hamlet I have been listening to on audiotape. There is nowhere to go, but into those tiny rooms in the rifugio in the Alps.
M2. I am standing at the door of a building that is a composite of the church I grew up in in Saginaw, Michigan, the University of Wisconsin Field House, Elsinore Castle, and a chess board (like negatives of photographs laid on top of one another to yield the composite). While I have been outside, the teams have changed for the worse. One is in black uniforms, one in red, and they are circling the track of the Field House non-stop. I cannot get through the track to my old dressing-room (an actor? an athlete?), which is also covered by a canvas tarp shaped like the new moon. I am aware that the temperature in the Field House is over +100°F/ while I have just come from a polar region which is -100°F. I can only stand stock still.

All of this is pictured in Figure 11.3.

Figure 11.3

"Hamlet Variations"

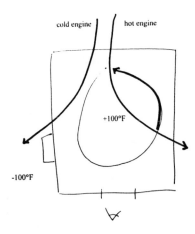

A few associations are necessary. The rifugio refers to places our family has stayed in in the Alps, for which we were very grateful in inclement weather. The red and the black uniforms refer to Stendhal's novel, The Red and the Black (1830, originally published; 1961), in which red stands for the army and black for the clergy, as the two routes or careers available to power for a young man from the provinces.

While it could be rightly said that dreams are nothing more than imagination, it is also true that it is an imagination with the power to shock us. Mine is mapping a region in which I really am not going to get in, a region of my old First Congregational Church, the Wisconsin Field House, Elsinore Castle and a chess board. The military and the clergy, or these desperate people in careers are not going to let me in at all.

A week later, I began reading C. Wright Mills's The Sociological Imagination (1959). In the very year I graduated from high school, Mills argued that it was absolutely necessary to set the record straight by connecting individual biography to the great sweep of history. Otherwise, people would be trapped in forces that made no sense to them. Mills argued that the fragmentation of sociology into narrow-minded schools was going to wreck the record, while furthering the careers of professors. Mills's counsel went entirely unheeded, and sociology has become utterly useless for the record. Here, my dream replies. You, too, will be unheeded. The careers, of the red and of the black, will lock you out. When you are in the Academy, you get heated up in their sweat. When you are not, you are out in the cold.

The church, Field House, chess board is a 2-dimensional space going around in an endless circle and cooked at 100°. In other words, it is a Hell. It is a hell of circling careers, which merely repeat their findings once set in motion. It is the Academy itself.

Insofar as it is also a chess board, it alludes to Rushdie's story discussed in Chapter 8, "The Courter" (1994), in which a grand-master of chess (in its 8-dimensions) is helpless as a porter in the family lodging in London to being beat up (in 2-dimensions of having to answer the door as a pawn for the corrupt Majarajahs living there, whose enemies do show up and take out their rage on the porter). The Courter is a courtier (in 8-dimensions) who is a porter (in 2-dimensions), so "courter" is a mix-up between his transcendent capacities and his lowly immanence. Indeed, he is called Mixed-Up.

So, I am pausing at the Gates of Hell, and seeing I don't have a move in it, as in a hopelessly truncated game of chess in which the only move is circular, as in the game of monopoly to go around the board and do more of the same buying and selling, as Wordsworth would say, "laying waste our powers."

Finally, the canvas tarp shaped like a new moon covering my dressing room is very striking. It alludes to the shadow side of the brightly lit hellish scene in red and black, with its color of green-brown canvas, and with its moon shape. It is slit-like, female-like, and an entrance to a world below. It alludes to Jung's discussion of the sacred marriage, or Conjunctio, of opposites discussed in his last book (originally published, 1955-1956; 1963). If we take this dream from Jung's perspective on the state of the Union, so to speak, we see that the Male Rat Race is entirely dominant, so much so that the Female has been obliterated by the tarp of the Male Field House shoved to the side to uncover its track. It only shows through in the shape taken by the tarp. In other words, the Academy has destroyed the fecundity of the underworld. The athletic specialists circle the track endlessly, and they are the winners who know nothing about how the world is put together.

In this precise mapping, my unconscious is setting the record straight by connecting my individual biography to the great sweep of history. If in 1959 C. Wright Mills could discuss within the Academy the need for integration of the sociological with the psychological and the historical imagination, then in 1996 this is completely impossible. I might as well go hiking in the Italian Alps to talk with Selvini-Palazzoli, or with the ghost of Hamlet's father. Increasingly, the integration of our culture is diverging from its disintegration in the hands of specialists, as illustrated in Figure 11.4

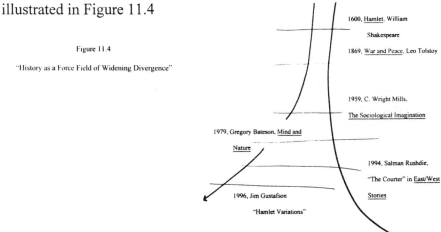

Figure 11.4

"History as a Force Field of Widening Divergence"

1600, Hamlet, William Shakespeare

1869, War and Peace, Leo Tolstoy

1959, C. Wright Mills, The Sociological Imagination

1979, Gregory Bateson, Mind and Nature

1994, Salman Rushdie, "The Courter" in East/West Stories

1996, Jim Gustafson "Hamlet Variations"

If the unconscious searches for possible modulation between its ancient instincts // and its modern adaptation, it can be extremely clear where (the Academy) there is no such Conjunctio (n) possible. In this precise way, we are warned about attempting the impossible which will jeopardize our existence. We map our individual trajectory onto the force field of history, whose currents are mighty and will bear us where they are going if we step into them. Often, survival is only possible by maintaining a circumspect distance. I can decline to be a courtier treated as a porter, which is to be a very Mixed-Up courter.

The Frontier of Bogus Conjunction

Almost every patient I see has some of the bad taste of a soap opera, and some dignity, nevertheless. A man I saw on the inpatient service this morning was a spent bus-driver worn down by responsibilities, but kept alive by one thing: "I keep my word." A woman I saw an hour later was a spent single-mother worn down by responsibilities, as her daughter said, "like a boxer lying on the canvas not wanting to get up."

This is what comes of the great promises of the frontier in America, which are by and large, bogus. Marriage turns out to be servitude, and so is bus-driving and key-punching. It is all exhausting. Hopes that start up these people again, listening to country western songs, end up cheating them. They literally do not know where to turn.

An intern from Pakistan who witnessed these two hours of Mr. and Mrs. America in his first week in psychiatry was distressed by their fates. I replied that it is indeed very distressing, and it is an epidemic. I said it had occurred because the old bonds of the extended family, as in Pakistan, had been weakened by migration to the West in hopes of economic opportunity. That sacrificed the connection that means something, which became restricted to the nuclear family of a spouse and a couple of kids. Then, the marriage becomes embittered by its daily and boring struggle, the kids leave, and the work is trivial. This results in the man who only has his work left, and the woman who lies on a mattress in the seclusion room and refuses to get up.

It is completely unfashionable in psychiatry to say anything like this is wrong with the patients, who are supposed to be suffering from a myriad of semi-medical disorders catalogued in DSM-IV, or the Diagnostic and Statistical Manual Number Four of Psychiatry. In my opinion, this entire set is simply generated as variations on broken promises (Gustafson, in preparation). The cases are all the same case, with the exception of those who have complications from the further deterioration of their liver, or blood pressure, or stomach, or brain. The body ends up being cheated with the soul.

A few surmount the epidemic, and some have their pleasures and their alcoves of meaning. Most wear out in circles, and develop the variations noted in the catalog. Don't take my word for it. Just leaf through Studs Terkel's Working (1972) and look around you. Terkel gave us one of the few samplings we have on the despair of America, and things are much worse twenty years later. How did we get to this pass, and how can dreams map a way back through Cumberland Gap from a pseudo-promised land?

For this, we need to recount a little history, about three thousand year's worth to be exact, of the Western world. America then just runs through the same sequence in about three hundred years, from plenty to poverty. By and large, the average person has no conscious idea of what is ploughing him along with his species. Oddly, his dreams do know. They are maps of our history. Let us take one from a contemporary colleague, and then line it up in a series from Homer to Star Wars. Somewhere back in the 1970s or 1980s there was an article about nuclear weapons that included this summary of our history:

This, finally, is the punch line of our two hundred years on the Great Plains: we trap the beaver, subtract the Mandan . . . harvest wave after wave of immigrants' dreams and send the wised-up dreamers on their way; plow the topsoil until it blows to the ocean . . dismiss the little farmers, empty the little towns; drill the oil and the natural gas and pipe it away; dry up the rivers and the springs . . . (and so forth)

We started doing this sort of thing back at Troy in about 1000 B.C., and have a great many plans for carrying it much further. Now let us see what our dreams know about it.

From Homer to Star Wars

Let us begin with a contemporary immigrant's dream, for we are all lost immigrants from East to West (Rushdie, 1994):

Else, . . a Norwegian photographer in New York on an assignment. While here she had an affair with a black musician who worked in Harlem. The dream occurred toward the end of her stay in New York (Ullman, p. 26, 1993).

Else's Dream of the Black Man in the Dirty Brown Pond. Else dreamt:

There was a small pond of dirty brown water. It seemed to be connected with industrial waste or farming. I was passing it on my way somewhere. There was a man bathing in the pond. To me he seemed white. He is drunk. There are others with him. It's a kind of party. They are all drunk. A voluptuous woman is also in the pond bathing. She is very white and naked. The man dives down. He doesn't come up. I know he has drowned. The woman tries to find him.

I have almost passed by as this was happening. The thought came to me that perhaps I should go back and try to rescue him but I don't.

Then one day later someone who I think is my mother or secretary phones the drowned man's mother on my behalf to offer my condolences. Then I see that his mother is black, an African, so at this point I realize the man was black. His mother is dressed like an African. She has a lot of people around her and says she doesn't need my condolences. (Ullman, p. 26, 1993)

I will summarize five pages of associations to this dream by noting only a few key points: the pond is Norwegian where she grew up and recalls a bull roaming around it she feared would push her in // and it is the industrial wasteland on Harlem about which she was composing a photographic piece; she is the white Madonna by moonlight // and she is polluted Whore; the man is her boyfriend whom she had loved // and the man ruined by being cut off from his roots.

The dream helped her correct the bogus union or conjunctio, of Old World and New, White and Black, Female and Male, by seeing its impossibility. She could pass by something beyond her powers, which had been caught up in this dangerous illusion. Ullman concludes:

> The Madonna is the ideal, pure nurturer. The Whore is the plaything, the pleasure-seeker living for the moment. The integration of these two polar opposites is not just the problem of the dreamer. To a greater or lesser degree, it is a problem of all women living in the twentieth century. (p. 31, 1993, Ullman)

Ullman is right but his scope needs to be widened from a hundred years by thirtyfold. Helen of Troy and Peneloppe, the wife of Odysseus, were caught in the same dilemma about 1000 B.C., and it simply runs on and on as long as women are basically property. It may even be much more ancient, as women are also property in aboriginal culture of South America (Levi-Strauss, 1964, originally published; 1983) and by and large all over the world.

On the Western Circuit

The tragedy of women as property is no more clearly drawn than in the short story, "On the Western Circuit," which Thomas Hardy wrote in 1891. At the exact same time, Breuer and Freud were putting it more clinically in their Studies on Hysteria (1895) as the strangulation of feeling. On the opening page of Hardy's simple tale is allusion to Homer and Dante, as if to say how old a tale it is indeed.

The man of this western circuit is no Odysseus, but a young lawyer who travels with his brethren lawyers from one small county seat to another west of London to try local cases:

> . . . no great man, in any sense, by the way (p. 455)

The gist of the story is that he falls in love with a beautiful and utterly simple country girl who is riding on a merry-go-round in one of these towns in their autumn carnival. A very brief interval is quite sufficient to lock them up forever:

> Each time that she approached the half of her orbit that lay nearest him they gazed at each other with smiles, and with that unmistakable expression which means so little at the moment, yet so often leads up to passion, heartache, union, disunion, devotion, overpopulation, drudgery, content, resignation, despair (p. 458)

The man leaves to continue his circuit after court, and writes back to the girl of his interest in her. She, unable to write, asks the lady of the house in which she is the maid, to write for her. This lady has already fallen in love, witnessing the love of this young couple, and takes up writing on behalf of the girl.

Well, the long and short of it is that the man falls in love with the grace of the letters, the girl gets pregnant, the marriage is arranged, and the man realizes too late that he has been tricked by the lady into thinking the simple girl is his true correspondent. The lady has taken her revenge. What is her motive? She had married safely to an old wine merchant. Coming to the end of her twenties, she felt utterly robbed of company. Then comes along another man to court another woman. She actually falls in love with his modest sensitivity, at least a little compared to her stolid husband who is totally out of touch with anything but himself. But she is going to ruin him, by fooling him into a pointless marriage like her own.

The Structure of the Frontier

A frontier is a border region between settled and unsettled. While we tend to locate it ever further west, it can occur back of this historical edge in pockets, or in fields, or in individual lives. Thus, Hardy's story is of a man from a settled region (London) becoming tedious from its typical quality of repetition. When things are settled, they hardly vary.

Looking for renewal he attempts to go backward out of the city, and he is looking at the old Cathedral in the dark when he is introduced to us. Often, the frontier is backwards of us in time. Looking or rather listening to the old cathedral in the dark, he hears the roar of the carnival flung back upon him off its walls. There he goes and happens upon the country girl, upon the mechanical contraption.

Like a Wordsworthian romantic, he looks for renewal in the past and in the country and in innocence. But these ancient green things are all mixed up with the roar of the carnival and driven by the machines of steam. This is the typical frontier mix-up, of green and red, of cold and hot engines.

This mix-up of the frontier is what is so confusing. It is hard to tell what anything is, from its shell. You join up with something or someone because of a quality you like, and find to your chagrin that it is joined to a quality you cannot stand. All conjunctions are hazardous, but forgoing them all is also hazardous for leaving you altogether alone in the lurch of an essentially anonymous society. Because nothing is half as desirable as it first appears, or one-tenth, it has to pretend to be much more than it is to be bought. Thus, the stretched truth, or "stretcher," as Mark Twain (1880) calls it, is the standard currency, which is more harshly called a hoax, or a bogus currency.

A frontier, therefore, selects for shysters to take advantage of the confusion, and for skilled men who are not deceived (Williams, 1925 originally, 1956; Williams, 1934). Once the cities get everything in their grip, these frontier types disappear in favor of the eminently safe man who is all routine (Melville, 1853). Thus, Kafka has an ape address an Academy about how he learned to become a man. Essentially, he had the dilemma of being locked up in a cage, or imitating the men so they thought he was one of them. He really wanted the freedom of space in all directions, but he could no longer have it so he took the only way out he could by going forward in time with the dubious progress of men. He comments wistfully:

> I could have returned at first, had human beings allowed it, through an archway as wide as the span of heaven over the earth, but as I spurred myself on in my forced career, the opening narrowed and shrank behind me. .
> . . . the strong wind that blew after me out of my past began to slacken; today it is only a gentle puff of air that plays around my heels . . . (p. 173)

Society then is going to be a mix-up of these settled regions which are essentially dead, and frontier regions which are essentially confusing.

Fortunately, our dreams map this space, and give us our precise location every night like a control tower at an airport provides for its airplanes otherwise flying in confusion. The point out the settled regions which are hopelessly settled or cooked (Brecht, 1920 originally; 1976) and the unsettled regions which are wild, and the frontier between them where everything is mixed up and hard to track where it is going to end up. In this frontier, small differences end up making huge differences in time. The great problem of orientation is to know what to be near for its actual benefit // and what to distance for its harm. Since a given thing is often a mix-up of benefit and harm, it is vital to know of both to do as best you can with it.

A Dream of Going Back to New York City. A patient is contemplating a return to New York City, where he grew up, for his brother's wedding. He is dreading his toxic parents, and he is anxious about getting around a dangerous city with his children in hand. Yet he'd like to enjoy himself. He dreams:

> M1. I am going to some kind of test. I am taking a taxi in NYC, and I am shoeless. I look up front and see that the cabby in his enclosure is completely naked and comfortable. He is Indian or Middle-Eastern. I have three shoes, a pair and an odd one. I end up wearing one of the pair and the odd one. I am looking down the hallway of a hotel, barefoot again after the test. I look in on a corporate meeting, chaired by a schmuck who is just firing people. I confront him very matter of factly, although he becomes irate.

> M2. I am in an open area like Woodstock, helping with the sound system. I accompany Billy Joel, playing "New York State of Mind."

> M3. I am with my friend at an airport. His wife calls and something has not gone right again. We run into her and she's complaining.

Going back to NYC is to go into a frontier with the East. Having been a grim and driven Westerner like his parents, he is beginning to have the humor of a Buddha whom he actually follows in his meditation. Like Arjuna in the Bhagavad Gita (3rd century BCE), he rides to his battle with his god driving the chariot. He would like to go perfectly naturally.

The shoes he translates for me as two formal black ones, and one tan informal one. He compromises to one black formal one, and one tan one, bowing to the formality of the occasion. He is able to confront the chairman, and keep his composure. He visibly delights in this.

Oddly, the second movement or melody is about a conjunction with Billy Joel's harmonious "New York State of Mind," yet he becomes tense in association with it. He wants to take his children to the Statue of Liberty, but they must pass through the Port Authority terminal, and he makes a fist unconsciously telling me about the journey. He cannot fool his own body here about staying mellow in NYC, in the presence of danger to his children.

Finally, he is tense all the way talking about getting away from his friend at the airport, because the wife of the guy is always on the guy's back. He just cannot separate the good of this fellow's company from the bad of taking on the incessant problems of the wife.

I note the progression of the three musical variations for him as delighted in the first, becoming tense in the second, and cross all the way in the third. He laughs, and says that that wife is like his parents. The Buddha just means for him to have to put up with certain things. If he wants to honor his brother at the wedding (a good), then he has to suffer his parents (a bad), but he has to be very careful not to stay around too long. He has to watch for the very build-up that is sure to come. This is a man who has been prone to exploding out of nowhere, who is becoming much better oriented to the green of his ancient ease, and the red of being run over, and all the mix-up of this strange West/East frontier we call New York City. He is thus ready to conjoin with what suits him, and disjoin when he is getting cooked, and to see how the first modulates rapidly into the second even when he would keep them altogether distinct.

Adequate Bridges

I happened to come upon Thomas French's classical (1970) contribution to the interpretation of dreams as I was preparing this chapter, and I found much to admire in its clarity of engineering. I thought that if I was right about the armature of dreams in the West as a frontier structure between cold and hot engines, it ought to be perfectly evident in French's material. It ought to fit into my series, and I ought to be able to show its virtue and its limitation. I was especially interested in its scientific line of thought, for the advantage and disadvantage of that point of view. After all, it is the engineering mind that has built most of the structures around us.

French's Theory of Dreams as Integration

French is simple to summarize, because his theory is highly schematic. Essentially, he starts from the disjunction which is classical in psychoanalysis and derived from Freud that the patient's sexual urges conflict with fitting into society. If the strain of integrating these oppositions is too much to bear, the patient will reduce the load by reducing the gap between the primitive urges and the social demand. He can do this by getting rid of the urges, or displacing them into urges less forbidden // or he can get rid of some of the super-ego of duty so less is asked of him. The chasm (hiatus) between the two sides is made less of a gap, so the integrative ego can span it without breaking down under its load.

One of the great advantages of this kind of civil engineering map of the dream space is that it prepares us for reading successions of dreams, as they increase the strain and decrease the strain that the patient is bearing. A pair of dreams from French will illustrate the virtue of this point of view.

The Dream of Going Into the Hall. French notes by way of preface to this dream that the analyst had been interpreting the patient's fearfulness as a reaction to threats from his father about masturbation. The patient admitted some threats of this kind, but insisted they did not mean much to him at the time. The next session he brought a dream that the analyst could not make much of. Typically, he had reacted to any fearfulness, by trying to make the analyst fearful of him. Again he had succeeded in putting the analyst in the weak position (turning passive into active, as Weiss and Sampson (1986) would say (Weiss also, 1993)). Now he dreamt:

Patient is fixing a velocipede with his brother. The brother asks patient to get something out of a hall where a meeting is being held. Patient refuses with playful politeness on the ground that his brother is younger. Finally the brother straightens himself up to go but indicates he is afraid. Patient is distressed on learning this and says he would have gone if he had known that this was the brother's reason for not wanting to go. As patient gets up to go he meets people who are coming out of the meeting. There is a black cloud in the rear of the hall of which the patient feels very much in awe. One man as he comes out of the hall puts his hand on his pocket and another says: "They have taken in five hundred marks." (p. 109, 1970)

Dream of Yellow Boy Urinating on Patient's Yellow Coat. The next dream was reported four days later after two intervening analytic hours:

Patient is in the toilet and a small boy who is yellow urinates upon patient's yellow coat. (p. 110)

French works up the dream with the patient from his associations to its elements as follows. The hall is the one where the patient's father preached. The velocipede is one he owned with his brothers, which his father took over once and made him very angry. The five hundred marks refers to cheating his brother by getting him to endorse a loan for a small amount and then filling in the large amount. Essentially, French tells the patient the brother in the dream is the analyst, who failed to understand the dream two days before, because he is afraid:

His insight has only one defect. It is projected. (p. 110)

The patient's second dream is the patient's reply to the analyst giving him back his own fear. It says, essentially,

The analyst just urinated on me (p. 111)

In other words, <u>he</u> is yellow, and he is degrading me with his fearfulness. <u>I</u> am just wearing a yellow coat.

Engineering as a Kind of Music

I like French's ability to modulate from a wide span to a narrow span along with the patient. I believe he is right that we do this when we cannot bear the integrative strain. This is a lovely piece of insight. The weakness is that French himself stays stuck in his single metaphor for his entire career. It would be as if Hart Crane admiring the engineering of Brooklyn Bridge could not modulate from it into all of American civilization, but took it literally. Then, he could not have written:

> Then, with inviolate curve, forsake our eyes
> As apparitional as sails that cross
> Some page of figures to be filed away
> --Till elevators drop us from our day.

And further on:

> Again the traffic lights that skim thy swift
> Unfractioned idiom, immaculate sigh of stars,
> Beading thy path -- condense eternity:
> And we have seen night lifted in thine arms. (Ellman, pp. 663-664, 1976)

Can we have French's engineering sense for the quantitative, without reducing the span to infantile sexuality? In a sense, the patient is only doing a parody of French's parody of his dream. Surely, this black cloud is more than the father, but something as well of the terrible wrath of an Ancient God. Perhaps, it can be taken in our series as a collision between the little engineer with his modern velocipede // and the Old Dispensation about being truthful. Melville would have more feel for the abyss between these two powers (Olson, 1947).

A Dream of Murder with Moose Antlers on a Frame. My patient who dreamt of going back to NYC was able after that session to lead a kind of palace revolution in his company to unseat the board of directors. He knew he was right, he knew he had the shareholders all behind him, and yet he was disturbed the night before the meeting of the board in which he would spearhead the attack to get them to resign. He dreamt (with some abbreviation):

M1. That he was working for a guy that owns a restaurant, and his wife somehow injures herself and comes in at one point and tries to kill him by throwing a small sledge hammer at him . . . The scene becomes very confused, with the hammer being thrown by all parties trying to kill each other (and two other people). . . . He (somehow) has a wooden frame with two pair of moose antlers on it, and slides it under her rib cage to impale her. "I am not looking as this happens. Although I know it had to be done (having seen her kill me or someone else in the future) it makes me sick."

M2. Driving with this or another woman, waiting to turn and a pickup flies by. Imagines it hitting someone, and feels a mixture of anger and fear.

M3. Pull up in front of a diner, and a woman is chaining or unchaining her bicycle. I get mad at her and say, "Nice face, what do you sit on?" A slimy couple standing there threatens us, but I am holding a gun and they back off.

As we go through the dream together, the first movement makes him sick again. While it begins with Thor's hammer of justice, it degenerates into a Hobbsian war of all against all. All moral bearing is lost, like in the jungles of the Vietnam War. It returns again with the flying and murderous pickup truck, in his fear and anger. By the third movement, he has got his "hit and run" New York wit back, which delights him in his ability to strike and get away.

The moose antlers refer to a comic gag of the Three Stooges he had recently watched again, but the attempt at comic perspective is dissolved in the horror of hand to hand combat. The modulation from horror to righteousness to readiness turned out to be a pretty good map of what happened several days later in the fire fight itself. After it, he felt empty, and unsure of what he had done. It took several days to recover his perspective about having done what was necessary. I summarized the modulation as follows in my letter to him after the session,

About your dream of Thor's hammer: fine, when you are ready with "hit and run" wit and clarity of rightness // and nauseating when it is just one righteousness against another. It is not yet possible to enter into the first, without some slide into the second, but comic perspective reestablishes the day.

This is a remarkable traversal for a man who several years ago was continually losing his temper at everyone he felt to be in the wrong, from authorities, to bad drivers, to his wife. He had a shallow sense of his own righteousness, and terror of helplessness. Whenever threatened, he would let loose his thunderbolts. He was owned by a division of the Thor Corporation. This was a bogus conjunction of his own vulnerability linked to righteous intolerance. It is all too commonplace in our CEOs like himself.

Now, he is able to experience the moral ambiguity of being in a struggle for power, and to doubt his own urges to wreak violence. He is sickened by it, yet he does not run away from the battle. The huge gap that yawns between having a moral purpose // and being in a primitive struggle for your life is now something he can tolerate. They are not the same, but one slides from one to the other in any kind of dangerous politics. This armature is pictured in Figure 11.5.

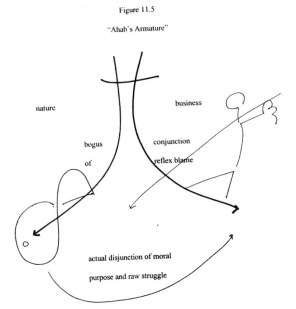

Figure 11.5

"Ahab's Armature"

nature

business

bogus

conjunction

of

reflex blame

actual disjunction of moral

purpose and raw struggle

I call this Ahab's Armature, in reference to Melville's character who lost a leg to Moby-Dick (originally 1851; 1956). Thereafter, he was pledged to annihilating the whale, and took a great many down with him. My patient was doing a minor version of this with his own crew. Part of the virtue of the armature is to see that his kind of captaincy is one of a large set common to our captains of industry. They do in whomever they need to, and they count it right.

The Author's Dream of King Lear. Finally, I want to put French's right sense of the quantitative into the full sense of the qualitative with a dream of my own which is another one of the theoretical dreams I have had. This one was the night after my "Hamlet Variations" discussed earlier in this chapter, in which I had no move but to stand stock still. That night I read and contemplated French's "integrative span" and "load" and so forth and dreamt the following:

M1. I am stuck on one of those rotarys on the outskirts of Boston going around and around, as if on the cross. I have either to go out into the Wilderness alone, or to follow this fallen woman into the city of Mahagonny (I am also reading Brecht's play, 1930 originally; 1976). I take the latter course.

M2. I am visiting a couple, and the husband, an engineer (like French) shows me his absurdly elongated velocipede for two. I think to myself that the span could never carry the stress of any load at all. When I take off my transparent Dutch clogs to fit my feet into the tiny rear straps, I realize the second seat is constructed for a kind of Madame Butterfly by a kind of Pinkerton (Puccini's Opera). The rear turns out to be utterly weightless (no wonder the elongated span was possible, if the wife imposed no load on it at all! Q.E.D.). I rise up into the air so high I have to push off the power lines from my head. I am now in the force field of The Southern Cross.

M3. I am visiting a mental health center run by a friend of mine. I am afraid to go in it among the desperate wretches, and have to be led by the hand by a black woman. I am carrying my infant, and fear the creeps of this underworld shaft, which is like a tunnel of concrete under O'Hare Airport. It's going down at an angle, and is utterly bare, but for an occasional street person leaning against the wall. I hurry by them, but they prove harmless, grotesques, or gargoyles, like Lear's retinue of knights (I had just seen Peter Brook's movie version with Paul Scofield). I pass through the transept of this underworld cathedral whose arms are cut off, where my friend is conducting some kind of service. I find myself in a room of natural light falling upon beautiful American Indian artifacts (like the dream catcher in my office, which also has beautiful light from the East).

These three movements can be superimposed upon one another to show the common lines of force. All three work on the diagonal (Wölfflin, originally 1915; 1956), like the paintings of Christ carrying his own Cross to Calgary, as shown in Figure 11.6.

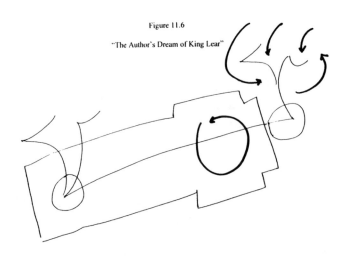

Figure 11.6

"The Author's Dream of King Lear"

I will not go into great detail about the wealth of allusions in this dream, except to note how they fit in the same set. The unconscious mapping has a tremendous ability to group things that belong together. This dream is a set of bogus conjunctions which I have known in my fifty years on the frontier in America: the Boston rotary of Harvard power which is a static field, the literal marriage or conjunctio of the inventive man and his weightless wife, and the underworld of the mad looked after by some of my friends. I do not belong on any of these crosses. After all, a cross is the conjunction of the vertical axis of the gods, and the horizontal axis of man.

Any of us who finds his passion, so to speak, is going to carry a cross to join the sacred to the profane. But it is extremely dangerous to carry one that is not of your own calling. You can go to waste in a Boston rotary, or on The Southern Cross, or in an abortive underground cathedral. So here I am being shown a set of things that could have been the end of me, in a kind of retrospective. It is absolutely important to know where a small step can carry you off into dreadful currents, that is, as Bateson (1979) would say, where a little difference makes all the difference. In my armature, the cold and hot engines start near each other and diverge rapidly as pictured in Figure 11.5. This is the gist of a non-linear force field which is the usual one on the frontier. Tremendous energies roll between warm fronts and cold fronts, when they cross each other at different elevations (Moran and Morgan, 1986).

Even when you can handle such tremendous forces as Melville did in Moby-Dick (1851), there is no assurance that you will keep the ability with its vitality, for long. Thus, our subject of the mapping of survival in this Chapter 11 carries over into our final subject of Chapter 12. An existence that develops tremendous dimensionality (powers of integration) must manage the humbler acts of mere survival on the frontier.

Chapter 12. A Search in History for Rebirth.

Imagination in the sense of the poets is not a luxury. Without it, we dry up fast, like fish out of water. With it, we have the chance of continual rebirth.

A dream can be taken as an attempt at rebirth. It is a creation. It is what poetic imagination flows from, or painterly imagination, or musical imagination. The force field of rebirth is essentially religious. That means that it depends upon a relationship between the sacred and the profane.

There are many possible relationships between divinity and the world, as there are varieties of religious experience. In general, the religious experiences of an individual are going to be heavily constrained by those of his family, his community, his region (James, 1902). As I argued along with Levi-Strauss in Chapter 10, the individual is apt to have variations of these myths, with gaps punched out in them.

If this is the case, then it becomes extremely important to understand the religious situation of our times. In other words, imagination depends upon rebirth and rebirth depends upon religious vitality and religious vitality depends upon the historical struggle between opposing ideas of the sacred. While it is commonly thought that religion is on the wane in the Western world, with some throwbacks to various forms of fundamentalism, I do not think this to be the case at all.

I will be showing in this final chapter how the dream searches in a profound and religious context for a way to cope with the oppositions that our history requires us to deal with. Essentially, I think we are trying to handle the difficulties generated in the Renaissance by the collision of the Goddess of Complete Being, the Virgin, with the Puritan Dynamo (Adams, 1904, 1907; Hughes, 1992). This is most clearly seen in Shakespeare's imagination about 1600, and transposed to the American democracy by Melville about 1850. It is still the great strain on us, and I will try to demonstrate how it shapes all of our dreams.

Of course, this is another way of discussing the cold and the hot engines of Levi-Strauss, and of the frontier, now placed in a religious, historical context. But the main subject here is rebirth or renewal by a search in dreams. I want to show how it is achieved. After explaining the dynamism of the Renaissance in Shakespeare, and bringing it to the New World with Melville, I will show it here in my patients as the simplest form of musical counterpoint. It is about getting out of the sham of words into the flow of the body.

More complexly, dreams will search for a way between an accommodation to the militant Puritans who run everything by narrow formula // and the imagination's power to reach by metaphor. This wealth and this vitality are divorced, as illustrated in an extraordinary and current movie, "Il Postino (The Postman)." I will show variants of its dream-like structure in my own patients. They try to have some wealth, without becoming its prisoner (Marx, 1843-1844; Ollman, 1971).

Finally, I will illustrate a musical progression in several of my own dreams over the last several years, to show how the vitality of the cold engine of the Virgin is found, and brought into close proximity with the hot engine of Puritan commerce, to generate tremendous energy.

Shakespeare, Melville and Us in a Religious War

Shakespeare's Dynamism. A greater imagination will comprehend a lesser imagination, as Hamlet can parody Polonius or Rosenstein and Guildenstern and all the other denizens of Elsinore. It is a matter of range. Some can only play a little pipe, and some can play every instrument in the orchestra, and direct it as well.

This range is emotional as well as intellectual, for it means being able to witness everything that is going on in the castle. Most have to avert their eyes, so they have great gaps of selective inattention. Most are so vulnerable (Henry, 1973) to the new regime of Claudius that they just have to smile and nod and not think too much.

What is going on in the castle is a sham (Henry, 1973) to cover up a murder of the good old king, Hamlet's father. This is essentially Shakespeare's view of history. One coup d'etat leads to the next. Jan Kott in Shakespeare our Contemporary (1964 originally; 1974) calls it "the grand staircase of history," on which a deadly game is played like king of the hill. The next aspirant is always rising to push the current king off the top, and he will suffer the same in his turn. Lest we think this has little to do with us, consider the role of fashion in any field or specialty. Those riding it dominate, and will soon be gone.

The game of history is played by different rules at different times. When the rules are changing, the violence is tremendous. Everyone is desperate. For if the wave you are riding goes down, you are utterly ruined. This is the abyss that yawned open in the Renaissance, between the old medieval order based upon the worship of the Catholic Virgin, and the new modern order based upon the worship of Puritan asceticism.

Each side had tremendous energy. Shakespeare commanded both kinds. That is why he could dramatize their life-and-death struggle. Ted Hughes has conducted a tremendously detailed argument quite along the lines of Levi-Strauss in his book, Shakespeare and the Goddess of Complete Being (1992), that all thirty-six plays are generated by this collision of the Catholic myth and the Protestant myth.

By the Catholic myth, Hughes means the story of the Goddess of Complete Being who becomes jealous of the latitude of her son. She becomes transformed into a wild boar, and kills him. Thereafter, he spends half the year in the underworld with his deathly mother, and half the year in the upperworld with his mother of procreation. In other words, she is split into the goddess of the fall into oblivion and the goddess of the return of spring. Christ is a typical son in a mythical series of this kind.

By the Protestant myth, Hughes means the story of the stern son who will not be sacrificed to the Goddess of Complete Being. He will see that she is killed, and return no more.

To do this, he has to cut himself off from her tremendous sexual attractiveness. He will narrow himself into the typical Puritan hero, who finds a band of brothers as narrow as himself to make an army and flatten the world.

If I may seem to digress into Sartre's Critique of Dialectical Reason (1960) (see a good exposition by Laing and Cooper (1964)), it is because Sartre has captured the mechanics of the Puritan engine over three hundred and fifty years later in all its pure savagery. If Sartre is difficult to read, it is because of the sheer redundancy of slight variations on the same idea. This idea is as follows.

Once there is no cold engine society in which everyone has a relatively equal place, within the reign of the Goddess of Complete Being, then we enter the modern arena in which some have a lot and some have very little. There is scarcity, and every body is potentially one too many. Your freedom to take for yourself could rob me (Marx, 1843-1844).

The way out of this is for a group of us to pledge ourselves to stay the same. This is what Sartre means by becoming practico-inert. By this means, we rid ourselves of the danger of any of us claiming our freedom to be different, and thus endangering the group. This is the dynamic of the Puritan army, and the bureaucracy, and the professions. It is the specifically modern thing. In Winnicott's terms discussed in Chapter 9, it is a matter of cutting off your own life-line and surrendering your sovereignty.

A nice and savage little example from our times is the short story by Kinsella (1987) called "Apartheid." A writer joins an English faculty in a large university, whose regime is the usual of petty specialization. He is warned by a colleague that his status will be black, among these whites, and that he'd better be careful about his liberties. To make the short story shorter, the writer allows his wife in his class discussions and she goes farther by attending upon one of their colleagues who has to go into the hospital.

His colleague warns him of the impending trouble with a parable:

"Jomo Kenyata, the old lion of the veldt, used to carry a moonlight-blue machete, which he used to chop up Britons like a chef cutting beans." (145)

When the chairman summons the writer to tell him the rule against his wife being in his class, and when he returns to his office to find a poster of Kenyata on his door, he savagely slashes it down with his ball point pen:

The stroke of his pen had created a long blue welt in the pretentious varnish of the door (p. 146)

This is precisely what Sartre meant by a deadly group pledged to being practico-inert, and regarding any liberty, any breadth or depth of integration as needing to be cut off. In this sense, Puritanism is a highly fervent religious point of view.

So here we are after a slight detour through Sartre right in this contemporary story in the middle of the religious war in which Shakespeare found himself. The Puritan specialists will kill the Goddess of Complete Being, and the Goddess will send her man with the moonlight-blue machete to chop them up like a chef cutting beans.

Let us go back to Shakespeare's versions of this four hundred years ago, for little has changed. In Hamlet (1603), the Renaissance hero of the old order of humanism is walking into the new order of Machiavellian, specialized creeps. He totally underestimates his adversary, Claudius, and his grip on his vulnerable subjects who will make themselves sham subjects of a sham king.

By 1611, in The Tempest, Shakespeare presenting the very same opposition of the old beauty and the new power now has the protagonist, Prospero, knowing exactly what to watch for. The story is that he was Duke of Milan. Preferring the study of liberal arts, he put his brother in charge of the government. The brother usurped him. So far, we have the usual plot of history, quite like Hamlet's father usurped by the Machiavellian Claudius.

Prospero got away to a strange island, in charge of a monster-man called Caliban. Prospero usurps his government, and becomes its Faustian ruler with an array of magical powers. A shipwreck of the court of Milan onto the island, brought about by Prospero's magical staff, sets the play itself in motion for the four hours from two in the afternoon when the storm breaks the ship, and six o'clock in the evening, when Prospero forgives them all their trespasses, and has them to a quiet supper. Between two and six, the court and Caliban attempt a series of murders, which are averted by the intervention of Ariel, the sprite governed by Prospero for the time being. At six, in the Epilogue, Prospero surrenders all his magical powers, to return quietly to Milan.

Jan Kott calls his essay on The Tempest, "Prospero's Staff," because the key to this last of the thirty-six plays is the limitation of the old powers of air, earth, fire and water to the staff of art. It commands from two to six, in a theater called "The Globe," which stands for the entire world. The power to show the eternal struggle of the world is not going to alter history at all:

Prospero's island, like Denmark, is a prison. Antonio's and Sebastian's plot repeats scenes from King Lear:

"If that the heavens do not their visible spirits
Send quickly down to tame these vile offenses,
It will come,
Humanity must perforce prey on itself,
Like monsters of the deep. (IV, 2)" (Kott, p. 312)

In other words, the hopes of the humanists of the Renaissance, Montaigne, Da Vinci, Galileo, are coming to a crashing end. The heavens do not send their visible spirits, and the Virgin is made powerless:

The bankruptcy of the Italian Bank of Scala, registered by almost the whole of Europe, coincided with the outbreak of the Hundred Years' War (1346). Religious architecture was replaced by military architecture. The time of thick walls had returned. (Herbert, p. 99, originally, 1962; 1985)

From 1346 to 1600, they rose and fell many times, but time was running out on the old ideal of Heaven interceding on earth, on humanist learning that knows about everything as Da Vinci did, and is honored for it by the powers. Kott writes:

In none of the other Shakespearean masterpieces -- except Hamlet -- has the divergence between the greatness of the human mind on the one hand, and the ruthlessness of history and frailty of the moral order on the other, been shown with as much passion as in The Tempest . . . One could dream that it would change. But it did not change. Never before had people felt so painfully the divergence between dreams and reality; between human potentialities and the misery of one's lot (Kott, p. 318) (my italics)

Art remains, of writing, of painting, of music, to show the old powers of the Imagination at the mercy of the new powers of the sham and Machiavellian Puritans.

What Kott says of this last show at The Globe, I will try to bring out in the continuing show that goes on in the globe of our heads which are called dreams. First of all, the plot structure of The Tempest is the plot structure of dreams, quite in the same musical logic as we have seen from Levi-Strauss:

Shakespearean dramas are constructed not on the principle of unity of action, but on the principle of analogy, comprising a double, treble, quadruple plot, which repeats the same basic theme; they are a system of mirrors, as it were, both concave and convex, which reflect, magnify and parody the same situation. The same theme returns in various keys, in all the registers of Shakespeare's music; it is repeated lyrically and grotesquely, then pathetically and ironically. The same situation will be performed on the Shakespearean stage by kings, then repeated by lovers and aped by clowns. (p. 303, Kott)

Secondly, the visual structure of the dream is of mixed forms, of blessedness and bestiality, quite as in the two paintings of Bosch in my office, "The Haywain" behind my chair and "The Temptation of Saint Anthony" behind the couch:

Such worlds (as the island of The Tempest) were painted by one of the greatest visionaries among painters, precursor of Baroque and Surrealism, the mad Hieronymus Bosch. They rise out of a grey sea. They are brown or yellow. They take the form of a cone, reminding one of a volcano, with a flat top. On such hills tiny human figures swarm and writhe like ants . . . Under the tables shaped like big tortoise shells, old hags with flabby breasts and children's faces lie embracing half-men, half-insects with long hairy spider-like feet . . . That island is a garden of torment, or a picture of mankind's folly. (p. 310, Kott)

It is also the kind of picture the dream makes, searching between rebirth and a cruel world.

Much more is said by Kott that I would like to repeat but leave to readers to find for themselves. I will only state a third implication for the search of dreams, and that is that youth, Ferdinand and Miranda in the play, are outside the grinding history:

> They are dazzled with each other. They represent the world's youth. But they do not see the world. From first to last they see only each other. They have not even noticed the struggle for power, the fratricidal attempt, the rebellion and plotting that have been going on around them. They are enchanted with each other. (p. 337, Kott)

Indeed, it takes a very long time for the youth in us to face history in our own dreams. We resist it as long as we can.

Melville

A wide-angle lens is needed to take in the scope of Creation itself, and no one in the New World has had this power like Melville in Moby-Dick (1851). He is the very successor of Shakespeare, not only figuratively, in carrying forward the music of the collision of the cold and hot engines, but also literally in that he studied all of Shakespeare just before composing his book. Charles Olson (1948) managed to borrow Melville's six-volume set from Melville's descendants and discover the very lines he underlined. Olson called his momentous book, Call Me Ishmael (1948). Just as Ishmael is the chorus for Moby-Dick, so is Olson the chorus for the rise and fall of Melville himself.

I am bringing up Melville now, because he gives us the scope of the space of dreams, quite like Shakespeare, but differently because of the New World. I sensed this writing my first book, The Complex Secret of Brief Psychotherapy (1986), which I composed while reading Moby-Dick. I borrowed from Melville the ambition to ride the main currents of the field as if it were the ocean, and to build a mighty ark, and to thrill in its rhythms. I had Melville's admiration for the Nantucketers who could be at home on the sea as if it were a great prairie . . .

> With the landless gull, that at sunset folds her wings and is rocked to sleep between billows; so at nightfall, the Nantucketer out of sight of land, furls his sails, and lays him to rest, while under his very pillow rush herds of walruses and whales (Melville, 1851, p. 68; Gustafson, 1986, p. 253)

and yet they were Yankee enough to earn their living with whale-oil. I hoped to ride the seas myself, and get paid with the precious oil of brief psychotherapy.

I did and I was, but I could not help noticing I was out there myself, while the colleagues were in port running their machines, their protocols, their programs. They were Yankee to the core, and knew you could get the profit without the voyages. They were not very keen on what I was doing, having little acquaintance with the ancient unconscious, as I was not of what they were doing, these thoroughly modern men, and so I became acquainted like Melville with the reality of who is actually running the world.

Now, over ten years later, I am back with Melville because his <u>Moby-Dick</u> tells us more about the <u>space</u> of dreams than any book ever written. This is a space like Shakespeare's that yawns open behind the backs of the English Puritans (write Yankees in America) into the full dimensionality of the Goddess of Complete Being, here, in the closing sentence of the first chapter of <u>Moby-Dick</u>, as Ishmael says:

> By reason of these things, then, the whaling voyage was welcome; the great flood-gates of the wonder-world swung open, and in the wild conceits that swayed me to my purpose, two and two there floated into my inmost soul, endless processions of the whale, and, mid most of them all, one grand hooded phantom, like a snow hill in the air. (p. 27)

Now how did Melville get this space, and how did he surrender it? Olson (1948) tells the tale, and I apply it to our dreams.

Melville got into the huge space literally by sailing out into it as a youth. Many of us do, like my oldest daughter conducting rafting trips in Alaska as I write this. Most of us give it up, to confine ourselves in little spaces to earn a living -- perhaps, with an occasional vacation to bring it back fleetingly. A few regard the usual adjustment as a disaster, like Bulkington, the silent common man of the Pequod, of whom Melville writes:

> . . . this six-inch chapter is the stoneless grave of Bulkington. Let me only say that it fared with him as with the storm-tossed ship, that miserably drives along the leeward land. The port would fain give succor; the port is pitiful; in the port is safety, comfort, hearthstone, supper, warm blankets, friends, all that's kind to our mortalities. But in that gale, the port, the land, is that ship's direst jeopardy; she must fly all hospitality; one touch of land, though it but graze the keel, would make her shudder through and through. (p. 98)

Melville, like his character Bulkington, and like his character Ishmael, has to be out there in the big space, or his soul-ship is in the direst jeopardy. Therefore, when he gives up going there literally, he will go here figuratively in his imagination:

> this mysterious divine Pacific zones the world's whole bulk about; makes all coasts one bay to it; seems the tide-beating heart of earth. Lifted by these eternal swells, you needs must own the seductive god . . . (Olson, p. 115).

or in the terms of <u>Moby-Dick</u>, speaking of

> ocean's utmost bones . . . To have one's hands among the unspeakable foundations, ribs, and very pelvis of the world; this is a fearful thing (Olson, p. 115).

Alfred Kazin, in his considerable introduction to <u>Moby-Dick</u>, calls

This view of reality, this ability to side with nature rather than with man (p. xiii) . . . What Melville does is speak for the whirlwind, for the watery waste, for the sharks . . (p. xii) . . . comparing man with the great thing he is trying to understand . . . Melville has no doubt that man is puny and presumptuous and easily overwhelmed -- in short, drowned -- in the great storm of reality he tries to encompass. (p. xiii)

Given this puniness against this vastness, the only thing to do is evoke it in writing:

The greatest single metaphor in the book is that of bigness . . . he feels grave; mighty waters are rolling around him. This compelling sense of magnitude, however, gets him to organize the book brilliantly, in a great flood of chapters -- some of them very small, one or two only a paragraph long, in the descriptive method which is the great homage he pays to his subject, and which so provides him with an inexhaustible delight in devoting himself to every conceivable detail about the whale . . . it is this sense of a limitless subject that gives the style its peculiarly loping quality, as if it were constantly looking for connectives, since on the subject of the whale no single word or statement is enough. (p. xiii)

The thing is to

admit human beings into its tremendous scale. (p. xiii)

Now I say this is there for us every night, if we could but admit ourselves. Space is paradise (p. 82, Olson):

This once he had his answer -- how man acquires the lost dimension of space. There is a way to disclose paternity, declare yourself the rival of earth, air, fire and water. (Olson, p. 85)

Melville's answer to the common man is for him to go before the mast, and literally go into the Pacific:

Extracts
(supplied by a sub-sub-librarian)

Give it up, Sub-Subs! For by how much the more pains ye take to please the world, by so much more shall ye forever go thankless! Would that I could clear out Hampton Court and the Tuileries for ye! But gulp down your tears and hie aloft to the royal-mast with your hearts; for your friends who have gone before are clearing out the seven-storied heavens, and making refugees of long-pampered Gabriel, Michael, and Raphael, against your coming. (p 11, 1851)

But Melville is no naif. He knows that such men are at the mercy of their captains in democracy:

> A whaleship reminded Melville of two things: (1) democracy had not rid itself of overlords; (2) the common man, however free, leans on a leader, the leader, however dedicated, leans on a straw. He pitched his tragedy right there. (Olson, p. 64)

I would have men set sail in their own dreams, for these leaders we have are not worth sailing under. They'll show up in our dreams, as for Alice (Carroll, 1865) going underground and finding the same old fuddy-duddy's of Oxford, mixed up with the animals.

Melville had the great mistaken idea that Shakespeare ought to have been more frank with more of

> . . . those short, quick probings at the very axis of reality (Olson, p. 43)

Hence he underlined the Fool's answer to Lear's threat of the angry threat of the whip:

> . . . Truth's a dog must to kennel; he must be whipp'd out, when Lady the brach may stand by th'fire and stink. (Olson, p. 42)

Melville loves this Fool and would bring him out more, as

> Nay, an thou canst not smile as the wind sits, thou'lt catch cold shortly. (Olson, p. 48)

Still, Melville knows very well that our rulers will not allow it, and that the best he can do is render them in counterpoint in his own Globe:

> The long ease and sea swell of Ishmael's narrative prose contrasts this short, rent language of Ahab. The opposition of cadence is part of the counterpoint of the book. (p. 68)

So it is that our dreams in America are of this counterpoint. Look at Twain's Huck Finn (1885) and Faulkner's "The Bear" (1942). Did I leave out Thoreau's Walden (1854) of the same period as Moby-Dick (1851)? I will show you in the dreams of my patients next, and then in my own.

So why did Melville give up his paradise? and its counterpoint with the men who would destroy it? Olson's account seems full of gaps to me. It is clear what he surrendered to, and less of why. After an exhilarating trip to Istanbul, and to the Pyramids, both evoking the huge space of the ocean, he fell back into the New Testament of Christianity. I'd rather leave it alone, by him, and figure out why and how we surrender ourselves. It will be enough for us to stay out in the big space ourselves.

For us, Melville's probing of the fastnesses of nature can remain the place where we are reborn in our voyages there -- literally, in going to the sea, or symbolically, by dream navigation. It is the ancient path into the vortex of the cold engine. But we always have to come back to land, at least for supplies. And that means we have to trade in something, for exchange value.

Herein lies a very great difficulty, for Shakespeare in 1600 and Melville in 1850 and us near to the year 2000. Commerce is ruled increasingly by bottom lines. If the thing is profitable, it lives. If the thing is unprofitable, it dies. It is all a matter of numbers, that is, of quantity.

In such a dire world, quality is difficult to defend. What is quality? It is as Bateson would put it

the pattern that connects (p. 8, 1979).

It is how the total biological world is put together, as in the pattern of the claw of a crab:

The anatomy of a crab is repetitive and rhythmical. It is, like music, repetitive with modulation. Indeed, the direction from head toward tail corresponds to a sequence in time: In embryology, the head is older than the tail. A flow of information is possible, from front to rear. (p. 10)

If you need to eat the meat of a crab, you will destroy this architecture by one blow after another. If you are respectful of nature, you will not do it any more than is absolutely necessary, leaving the great reserve in its wild state.

But modern man is in a very big hurry for turning everything to a profit. He builds enormous machinery which uses up quality to end up with quantity (Marx, 1843-1844). The whaling industry was a little thing, a forerunner. They only turned the most amazing and hugest creature of the world into oil for the lamps of men. Their modern brethren can do this to any creature at all, to any field, to any subject. For example, they have been able to turn education in psychiatry into a program for how to dampen anxiety, or elevate depression, or both simultaneously.

Break the pattern which connects the items of learning and you necessarily destroy all quality. (p. 8)

Simply to ask a patient what he is looking for, and to map out with him how he might find it or find trouble, is to breathe life back into the field. For a pattern now emerges which is a recurrent story in the patient's life, and this, in turn, becomes a variant in the set of stories constrained by the family burden, and the cultural burden. If the patient is searching for something -- assuming he has not given up like so many -- then we can go searching with him.

Of course, the main line of the architecture of this book is that dreaming is searching. Thus, going with a patient by day in search of what he is looking for is the very equivalent of dreaming. The day search is complemented by the night search, which knows how to look for what is overlooked in the glare of day, by going into the realm of shadows, and night.

If the armature of my musical score is accurate, then the search to be reborn in dreams is going to be a set of mixed forms, or modulations between the rebirth itself in the forces of nature -- the cold engine of air, earth, fire and water -- and re-entry into the forces of man -- the hot engine that transforms quality into the quantity of symbolic or literal capital (Marx, 1843-1844).

I need to say further that the hot engine's transformation of quality into quantity results not only in capital but in a tremendous amount of discarded shapeless material (Charbonnier, 1969). Its energy has been taken from it, its shape destroyed, and it is now waste material. The lost quality is not only the biosphere, but also the mineral sphere, and it is the laboring force itself. This is the entropy production of the hot engine, and its result is wasteland and its denizens.

Few consider how this wasteland production has speeded up tremendously in the last twenty-five years. The third world has been turned into huge factories of impoverished people making all the basic goods of the Western World. It makes the old slavery look amateurish. Now, there are Chinese middlemen and Sri Lanka middlemen and Bolivian middlemen getting contracts to put in harness millions of their country men. It is slavery on a world scale, to feed the consumption of the West. This slavery works by the threat or vulnerability to have absolutely nothing, rather than literally by the gun.

You can see huge pockets of it in the United States, in the big cities, in the abandoned countryside, in the blank suburbs everywhere. Wherever people are so depleted that the television is their chief resource is wasteland from the point of view of entropy. Shapeless, rhythmless, and pointless.

The essential roles in the wasteland are the worn-out Puritan man, Dr. Jekyll, or his female equivalent, the worn-out Puritan lady who is swamped with problems, and the enraged Mr. Hyde who comes out at night (Stevenson, 1886). Thus, a crude shape emerges out of the worn shapelessness, and it is nightmarish (Yeats, 1928). On television, it is the only energy left.

Our dreams are going to be suspended between the poles of the world, between the cold engine vortex of nature // and the hot engine spewing capital out the top and wasteland out the bottom. These poles are not exactly heaven and hell, but more like space and time as in Figure 12.1.

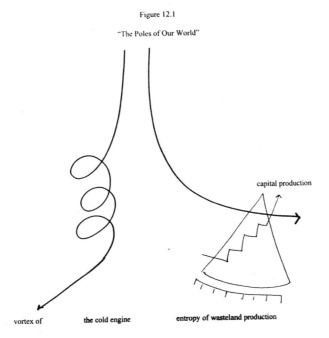

Figure 12.1

"The Poles of Our World"

capital production

vortex of   the cold engine   entropy of wasteland production

The great space is great in its beauty and in its renewal, but it also swallows man up. It is thus very dangerous. But so is time when it speeds up in its Puritan urgency. Olson suggested that Melville was in the great space in Moby-Dick, and surrendered to the time of Christianity:

> It is space, and its feeding on man, that is the essence of his vision, bred in him here in America, and it is time which is at the heart of Christianity. (Olson, p. 100)

Our dreams are going to modulate between the great forces of nature // and the great forces of man. This will be the potential score, but gaps will usually be punched out. Some dreams will be way over into the terrors of huge nature, and some will be way over into the time-urgency of man as in examination dreams. A dream can search any particular sector of this map, or over its entirety.

They will go into regions like Dante's Inferno, which will look like our wastelands with their ruined people, and they will ascend into the heights and depths of a hazardous paradise, and often they will have the two mixed up in a kind of surrealism like that of Bosch. In such a world, rebirth of nature always has to descend again and navigate among the dead.

This brings me back in my mind to Hillman's perspective, discussed in Chapter 6, of the dream as pure space, seen from upside down, from the timeless realm of the House of the Dead:

> The underworld itself is a topography: the House of Hades, the Halls of Valhalla, the rivers, islands, ever descending levels (p. 188, Hillman, 1979) . . . Death is the scrap dealer, stripping the world for spare parts, separating, destroying connections . . . which love -- continuing Freud's metaphor -- fuses into new entities. The imagination at night takes events out of life, and the bricoleur (potterer, jack-of-all-trades, my translation) in the service of the death instinct scavenges and forages for day residues, removing more

and more empirical trash of the personal world out of life and into psyche for the sake of its love (p. 128, Hillman, 1979)

Certainly, space is the great devourer as Hillman says, but why so little emphasis on space as the great creation? Hillman's perspective is hyper-developed on space as destroyer, a strange variant of the armature, which is driven by what? I think it is one possible response to the wasteland, which has been very common among artists. I might say:

Surrealism (collage) is the great scrap dealer, stripping the world for spare parts, separating, destroying connections.

When so much of the world is dead at its very inception, in its pledge to being practico-inert, then there is a very great deal of garbage indeed that will swamp us unless we can recycle it. I find Hillman is quite helpful, for sighting this terrible problem of getting free of and rid of dead things which will otherwise drag us down in their toxicity.

An Array of Attempts at Rebirth in My Patients

Let us go now like J. Alfred Prufrock (Eliot, 1917 originally; 1958) and pay our visit to man and woman in the late twentieth century struggling to be reborn in a deadly repetitious world of worn out ideas, things and people. Eliot foresaw the main difficulty, and how the hero is ruined by fitting in, trying to please, and dreading to offend. Remember Melville's call to Sub-sub! In a toxic world, this is a deadly marriage. Read Prufrock here, and take it as the first dream in this series, which ends at the bottom of the sea, and drowning by having to wake up again to the deadly upper world. It is an upside down dream, in which vitality is in the depths of the sea, and is surrendered when Prufrock wakes, hat in hand to serve like Polonius for another day in rotten Denmark. Let's go and have a look at a little series.

The Simplest Counterpoint

When everything has already been formulated as in our manuals of everything (viz., Pies, 1994), how is man to dare speak at all? He surrenders his sovereignty (Percy, 1975), and the clever doctor asks him questions about his symptoms, his eating, his sleeping, his suicidality, and prescribes him the official treatment. He leaves like Prufrock, never having been there. The usual suspects have been rounded up, and Algiers is secure for another night (Fanon, 1961 originally; 1968). This is Marcuse's (1964) world of total administration of lives.

It is so simple to breathe life back into these patients, when I am attending with our residents in the Clinic. All I have to do is to ask what the patient is looking for now? or summarize from what I have heard that he seems to be looking for _____. The face which has been a mask begins to move, as well as the body which has been encased by the folded arms, and rebirth is underway in the House of the Dead. The patient begins to search about, and we are essentially in the realm of dreams, even if a dream is not specifically mentioned. Often, one will come right up, like a fish suddenly surfacing out of the deep.

Here are five put simply in a row, taken out of the last week or two of my practice. I think of them as I do of baseball in America, the body roaming in the field, anxious about the score. If the ancient rhythm can come through, the modern contest (Gustafson & Cooper, 1990) is breached for a moment, as in Figure 12.2.

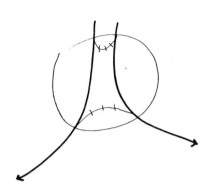

Figure 12.2

"Baseball as the Simplest Counterpoint in America"

A Dream of the Church Bazaar. My patient's hour is filled with thefts (Porter, 1935) by her son, old lover, doctor, ex-, friend, etc., and she drops into this series a dream of:

> I am at a church bazaar, and turn my back on my purse. When I turn around it's been stolen from. I look and see it's only $60, and my license and credit cards are still there.

Taken in the series of thefts, she is surprisingly upset by the dream, awakened to the bodily fact that she minds very much having her life pilfered.

A Dream of a Bear-Hug. This man is considering whether to return to classroom teaching, finish his Ph.D., go with his girlfriend and get married. He dreams

> I am in a bathroom. Somebody grabs me from behind, harder than he needed to be, and the hurt is excruciating. I think it is a monster dream.

He feels himself to be playing both parts. Somebody playing the lot of Jekyll trying to do the right thing, and somebody tempted like Hyde to crush others for trapping him (Stevenson, 1886). Here, he is in excruciating pain, like Christ on the Cross.

A Dream of a Dead Body in a Cave. This single mother has surprised herself with being able to stop getting fried, by taking on the toxic needs of everybody around her. On a Sunday night, heading into another work week, she dreams (somewhat abridged here):

> I am walking in a field with three men on a sunny, soft day. One runs off, and comes back about a dead body in a dark cave. I follow him down into a dark valley, and come to a cave sealed by flat rock. It has lots of markings, drawings on it. I have to wait for a thumbprint to appear on it, and put my thumb up on to match it, and the door moves open. I feel real sick with the smell of the dead. I quickly run out to the sun, and can't look back.

Several more scenes occur in which she seeks help, and the help is creepy. In all of them, there is her refrain, "What did I do to deserve this?" In her naive innocence, still, she is conducted out of green fields // into the House of Death. Her education never got her ready for a rotten world, but we are underway.

A Dream of Trying to Stop the Water. This patient has had a long long struggle to let go into her spontaneity, from having been in complete control (on top of things). She dreams, perhaps, the latest in a series of a hundred and fifty dreams:

> It is all water again, like the lake coming at me, on a strong east wind, closer and closer in waves, exciting, and then making me concerned. I have those old clothes-poles in different sizes, and I use them to measure (the depth of the water) inside the house. I am aiming and shooting to stop the water. I dance to stop the water. I hold up different sizes of the poles. I must prove it won't work. A man is in the house trying to help stop it also. I get hit (by the water). I am at the diningroom table. I keep using regular towels or poles, instead of the big ones.

This one reaches to "playing in the sheets" innocently using the clothes-poles to put the clothes up higher in the wind as a girl // and to a betrayal by a family member who took sexual advantage of her innocence. Her letting go with the water carries us to letting go of tears and rage about him. She can't have the free flow, without the grief that comes with it. (See Plath, 1992, "Dream with Clam Diggers")

A Dream of a Three-Decker Bus. This man is going to visit his very worn-out parents, with a story he has just written about which he is very high. He dreams

> My wife and I are driving back into my old town in a triple-decker bus on the top. It is as high as a two-story building. As we come around a corner, it tips over. The old people won't help.

My patient readies himself for a big come down, in a comic spirit which is more and more prepared for the dead of this world. He is no longer as deferent as Prufrock, and his daring can come down off the green field into the dugout.

More Depth

As the patient becomes more capable of penetrating the layers of the dream superimposed upon one another, I can wander with her through entire worlds. We can use the same dream text for delving further for several hours. The patient who dreamt "A Variant on Lord of the Flies" was so capable at the outset of such journeys of the imagination that we could do this with her very first dream.

A Variant on Lord of the Flies, Second Hour. Two weeks after the first hour presented in Chapter 11, she returned full of further leads on this dream:

A) I remembered that I not only watched the dream as in a movie, but I became the father and so I rolled my eyes at the boy in fun at swallowing the knife, and then I read of my death in the newspaper on the table in front of me as the blood gushed out.
B) The fair man across from me is my husband, who brings in all these dark men who weigh us down. I feel how terrible it is that he lets this happen to me, just because he wants to save these guys.
C) The weapon is a kind of cross we swallow in our family (the sacrament), the tragic flaw we have been taking so lightly.

It is remarkable how these tremendous findings were out of focus in the first hour, and came into focus in the second. In Vicki Hearne's (1986) metaphor, I had been able to ask something of the horse, and she had responded with a brave ride into the very tragedy of her family's version of Christianity.

She is able to see herself as a version of her father, making light of being sacrificed. She is very upset that he allowed this to happen to himself, and that she is allowing the same thing to happen to her. She is able to see her husband's failing to see her plight, and be very upset with him. In this story of English Puritan tragedy, her husband is another Puritan variation, like the lawyer, Mr. Utterson, who tries to save Dr. Henry Jekyll from being totally swallowed up by Mr. Hyde:

> Mr. Utterson the lawyer was a man of rugged countenance, that was never lighted by a smile; cold, scanty and embarrassed in discourse; backward in sentiment; lean, long, dusty, dreary, and yet somehow lovable. . . . In this character it was frequently his fortune to be the last reputable acquaintance and the last good influence in the lives of down-going men. (Stevenson, p. 9, 1886)

Because it is her husband's mission like Utterson to bring in the down-going men, she is lost from his sight even though he is sitting right across the table from her in the dream. Very upsetting, as well.

Depth From a Series of Dreams

This patient I have mentioned before usually brings in a painting of a dream every week, often from the night after our last session. To illustrate the power of a series, let me present three recent dreams, which will fall into the very series starting from Prufrock.

<u>Dream of a Dangling Telephone in the Middle of a Soccer Field</u>. My patient is distressed as usual by her boss's high-handed intrusions, and her children being difficult. She dreams:

> I am at a soccer field. There is a door frame standing alone in the center of the field, from which a dangling telephone hangs, which she needs to use. Woman standing next to her says: "Anyone can change with enough black claws."

The field is where she watches one of her children, and the telephone in the door frame is her department's door to its meeting room. The claws are bear claws, and the woman is a dog trainer. The dream alludes to all the main figures in her life, whom she tolerates taking advantage of her. She wants to play as on a green field // but the center of power is superimposed on the playing field (figure on ground, a mixed form of the cold engine of play and the hot engine of command). The dog trainer recommends summoning up some bear power.

<u>The Dream of Being a Photographer in a 5' X 5' X 5' Black Box</u>. Three weeks later, she reports this dream after a terrible picnic in which she must suffer again her husband's cold rudeness to friends and family of the children:

> I am in a box too small, trying to take a picture of a toy, a stuffed toy. I couldn't get in the animal's ear, because I was too close. I try to watch the flickering shadows of the two candles in the box, as shows on the wall.

This reverses the logic of the previous dream, for now the ground is the trap of power, and the figure is her trying to utilize her art to bear her confinement (another kind of bear, so to speak). It won't work. This reminds her of a story she just heard of a woman who had a fifty-year anniversary party with all the extended family, and the day after announced her divorce, saying, "I can't stand another day with the bastard." For fifteen years, she, herself, has been looking to her husband to get better, making one excuse after another for the delay.

<u>The Dream of Making Up Her Face Upside Down</u>. She is very distressed about her girls being drawn into the role of being sex objects for men. She dreams

> I am putting on a <u>lot</u> of make-up. Lips on forehead. Mascara on mouth. Rouge up high. Seriously. Carefully.

Upside down reminds her of being a child playing on the bars upside down, until a boy saw her panties, and she stopped. She had no friends, until one girl held her hand, and then stopped. Here she has resumed playing, in dead seriousness. We had been talking about Lear's Fool and how he is the only one who can tell Lear how cracked he is. She plays the fool in this dream.

"Il Postino" and Seven Dreams of the Author

I end this book with a discussion of a current Italian film, and of the progression of dreams in myself over the last several years. Rebirth in a wasteland is a hazardous thing, and I mean to map out as well as I can. If the young people that come after me can catch on sooner than I did, it may be because I can provide the maps for those interested to look at them. My teachers all faltered, after some promise, because they could not cope with the forces I am discussing here. I mean to be some kind of Virgil (Alighieri, 1300) of dreams, and I offer this last music for my own children, and students, and patients. I would that I had been so taught.

Il Postino

The translation of "Il Postino" is the postman, a drab word for a man that begins drably but ascends into heaven. He is the son of a poor fisherman in a poor village off the coast of Italy, consigned to a meager existence. All is transformed for him by the arrival of the famous socialist poet, Pablo Neruda, in exile from Chile with his wife in a villa high up above the poor town. Mario gets the job of delivering the mail, voluminous, solely to Neruda, and gradually gets an ear for his poems. Mario is particularly transformed by metaphors, by which one thing can stand for another. Copying Neruda, quite literally, he woos Beatrice Russo, and wins her over, against the fierce protest of her grandmother whose little tavern she works in. Neruda and his wife preside over the wedding, movingly, with a poem and with a dance with the bride. All is well, and about to come down.

Mario has pedaled up the purgatorial mountain out of the petty and rural wasteland of the wasted fisherman. Mario keeps muttering "Pescadore, pescadore . . ." in the gloom of following such footsteps. Ascending he blooms. Beatrice, entranced by this Dante, is conjoined to him.

The tragedy is in the descent back into town for its prosaic and deadly life. Neruda disappears back to Chile, and forgets Mario. De Cosimo (meaning, of the world) promises the town a water supply, and reneges when he is elected. Mario reads a poem at a socialist rally, and is trampled to death by the police.

So it goes on the western circuit (Hardy, 1891) with rebirth, so often built up too high in extravagance as Binswanger put it and as we discussed in Chapter 3 on the existentialists. When it comes down, it crashes. It was built on a conjunction of circumstances, which will not recur again. Mario is so transported by metaphor, that he is badly defended on earth.

The key to this movie for me is the terrible oversight of Neruda, to elevate this man, and to leave him undefended for the forces of hell to take him. He is a seductive father to Mario, only half right in his map. Mario pays with his life, crucified to his father's lack of discernment. In the end Neruda and his wife return to the town to discover the disaster, and the final scene is of Neruda standing on the beach in gloomy meditation, while the camera backs off until he is a speck in the massif of the island. As if to say, look, grand poet, you do not count for much here.

That is the key to the following series of dreams, where I have to modulate back and forth, on my bicycle as it were, between epiphany and the dead weight of the culture. Every rebirth is another immersion in meaningless quantity. Out of non-productive formlessness, I rise up again. D. H. Lawrence got it right by me about this back and forth in his poem, "The Ship of Death" (1930 originally; 1959) which begins

> Now it is autumn and the falling fruit
> and the long journey towards oblivion.

And later

> O build your ship of death, your little ark
> and furnish it with food, with little cakes, and wine
> for the dark flight down oblivion.

We all need our little ship of death, for the night of the waste of waters is forever coming back. We have to survive it, until the morning comes.

<u>Dream of May 6, 1994: Pioneer Park</u>. I had just read a review of two of my teachers, the clever engineers, and a novel which began high and low and ended up in dead flats with all low. I dreamt

> I am trying to play a game like golf in a park in Billings, Montana, actually called Pioneer Park, down the block from which we lived 1971-1973. I have an impossible shot up a volcano, through a dark wood (as of Dante), while my rivals have a simple straight shot right across the top. I decide not to make the attempt. A pioneer has no chance of coming up from the depths, in this **cheap modern** game, as the topography illustrates in Figure 12.3.

Figure 12.3

"Pioneer Park"

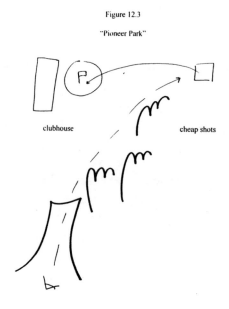

<u>Dream of May 28, 1994: Tolstoy's Elementary School</u>. I was too hot at work, caught up in the Puritan urgency of time, when I got a cooling letter from a friend about the powers of the sea in Yeats. I dreamt

I circle a barren square counter-clockwise, and begin a huge, slow curve through Afghanistan with my wife on two luge sleds. We wake up in the rain, which I can hear on the canvas over our heads, and feel on my forehand when I push the canvas back. A baptism. I look out from the watery beach we are on -- surely Lake Baikal, the greatest fresh water lake in the world, whose photograph is on my wall -- and see a magnificent rock fortress shining in gold from the rising sun. It looks like the elementary school my children all went to, and I know it is Tolstoy's. This is all illustrated in Figure 12.4.

Figure 12.4

"Tolstoy's Elementary School"

I have quit the game of Pioneer Park, to go counterclockwise into the ancient powers with Tolstoy.

<u>Dream of July 17, 1994: The Queen's Whirling Palace</u>. About a week before one of my yearly workshops in the Door County Summer Institute, after writing about complexity, and watching one of our magnificent July thunderstorms, I dreamt (as reported in Chapter 2)

I am in a hotel in Door County which looks like Mont Saint Michel in France, and escape with two guys down three chutes as in mountain-climbing. I sight a huge cloud, while lying on the highway, of a Queen's Palace. It is rotating counter-clockwise with tremendous force, causing the waters of the coast to rise with huge waves. A gonzo truck is going downhill backwards making more chutes, as illustrated in Figure 12.5. The palace is for sale.

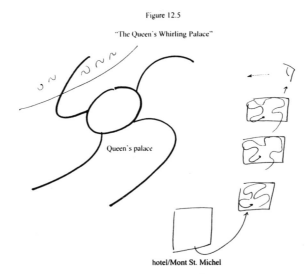

Figure 12.5

"The Queen's Whirling Palace"

Queen's palace

hotel/Mont St. Michel

If I go backwards out of time into the vortex of space, I am in a tremendous place, counter-clockwise. Here I am with Melville, having given up on the modern game in Pioneer Park.

Dream of June 22, 1996: My Cycling Team. On a day of considerable alienation from my department, I dream

> I am riding down a freeway amidst cars in a brown sleet with a team in the center lane which is only for cyclists. The cars are at a crawl, while we fly. We reach a stairway as in an airport, and put our bikes down a chute (again, a chute) which takes us (as in Alice) to the Wisconsin Union. I apologize to my team for not having packed the hors d'oevres.

I have brought my friends, Tolstoy, Melville, and so forth, back into the modern contest, and borrow a chute from Lewis Carroll to take a little banquet. I am bringing the beautiful and renewing cold engine back onto the field of the hot engine. I seem to know how to get around, and make the necessary transitions.

Dream of July 9, 1996: The Puritan Lady Doctor Has Hepatitis. Like Il Postino, I have had a day of ruined people. I dream

> A woman who is a doctor, whom I also know to be The Goddess of Complete Being, has hepatitis. But she hasn't time to be tested, nor to be treated. She just wants it fixed.

In other words, her liver is flooded with too much garbage. In her hurry, she cannot slow down. This dream alludes to Jung's Liverpool Dream discussed in Chapter 2. Jung was also flooded by modern garbage, and dreamt of a pool of light in which a beautiful red magnolia stood. All the streets radiated from this pool. That became his Chinese castle in 1928, for the circumambulation of the self as mandala. Flight into the cold engine.

<u>Dream of July 2, 1996: A Political Couple in San Francisco Divorced</u>. After another day in the Clinic of ruined lives, and a beautiful evening of tennis amidst mounting thunderstorms, I dream

A well-known political couple in San Francisco is getting divorced.

This dream harkens back thirty years to my internship and residency in that city, and to the marriage of Joan Baez and David Harris. My youthful belief in the combination of beauty and politics is divorcing, like that of Yeats in Ireland. It is a bogus conjunctio.

<u>Dreams of July 13 and 14, 1996: Humpty Dumpty's Sonata</u>. I finished a hard week of work playing the Western Hard Court Championships of Tennis here in Madison as the sun went down through another huge thunderstorm. I felt like competing only for the first set, which I won, and thereafter only when a fresh wind came up. Otherwise, it seemed like a lot of foolish old soldiers, battling as Hamlet says, over an eggshell. I dreamt

A fellow I knew in college on the Harvard tennis team, but two years younger, was taking my wife and I on a tour of a small state college in eastern Massachusetts. It was boarded up like my old junior high school, and the canyon he took us up (between two wings) was a dead end of asphalt. This is illustrated in Figure 12.6.

Figure 12.6

"Humpty-Dumpty's Sonata"

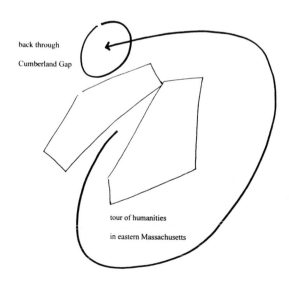

back through

Cumberland Gap

tour of humanities

in eastern Massachusetts

The fellow was one behind me on the ladder of Harvard tennis, whom I had feared would come up and pass me. Now I see what has become of him, on the great staircase of history. As I drew out the dream, I saw a setting sun with the warriors at Troy, and the same warriors at Powless Flats here, and the same warriors at Harvard, and I saw it was pointless (Ecclesiastes). All the king's men (Warren, 1946) were cracked, and like Humpty Dumpty could not be put back together again. Fragments dry up, once broken off from the great body of Nature.

The next night of July 14 brought me another variation in this sonata of Humpty Dumpty. I had been at a department party. It was like all the others, and I could not stand it more than an hour. I could not say exactly why, but I dreamt

> I am a medical student, and I am called by the O.R. (operating room) to come saw off the cranium of a man and sear his brain. I talk to some people about this, trying to buy time, when a scrub nurse (like Juliet's nurse in Romeo and Juliet) passing by, overhears my predicament, and says briskly, "Tell him you don't know how to do it." I go to the chairman of surgery and say this, and he frowns with displeasure, and says he'll think about it.

This dream links up society, business, vulnerability, sham, decapitation and Puritan will. Now, I am called upon to make a Humpty Dumpty out of a man who will not smile at his station in life and offends the King. It refers to my vulnerability to this business of psychiatry when I was a youth, and to the shams I was called upon to participate in as one of the king's men bringing another of the king's men in line.

When I looked again at the drawing of Figure 12.6, I saw that time led forward into All the King's Men (Warren, 1946), clockwise, but that I could also go counterclockwise, back through Cumberland Gap, to the court of the Virgin. I ride the vortex, out of time and into space. I also know how to get back.

Afterword

Having followed my own book all the way through, I have one more thing to say as a kind of warning. If the dream is essentially the imagination, the history of the imagination teaches a grave lesson. The good news is as Wallace Stevens wrote, and I quoted earlier:

> It is a violence from within that protects us from a violence without. It is the imagination pressing back against the pressure of reality. (p. 36, 1965)

The bad news is that while imagination helps in creating beautiful maps, it hinders if it confuses the map with the territory. If the territory of our time is Puritan history (McNeil, originally 1963; 1991), flattening itself out into a dead wasteland, then the map-makers had better refrain from the romantic error I discussed in Chapter 8 of imagining they are going to do much of anything about where mankind is going. It will be enough to enjoy our own art.

Three dreams I had illustrate this better than any prose I might compose.

Dream of July 1, 1994, on The Quantitative Tide of Mud.

I am trying to get from the Chicago Art Institute to the Drake Hotel, across a sand bar. Unfortunately, a tide of mud is inundating the passage, and the graduation circus tent of the Harvard Medical School which had been over the passage is flapping in the wind, its poles dashing madly about, as illustrated in Figure 13.1.

Figure 13.1

"The Quantitative Tide of Mud"

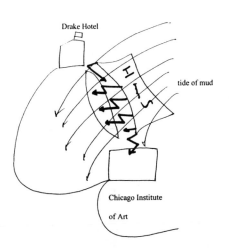

This dream pictures my attempt to bring art (from the museum) to the world (of the hotel) under the auspices of my pretentious medical school. It is drowned in the quantitative tide of mud which is the Puritan history of our time.

Dream of August 8, 1996, on The Flotilla of the Imagination Trying to Take Back Poughkeepsie.

I am standing like one of the French explorers in a war canoe, with an Indian guide in front of me, as we move in a vast flotilla, from left to right, towards Poughkeepsie, as illustrated in Figure 13.2.

Figure 13.2

"The Flotilla of the Imagination Trying to Take Back Poughkeepsie"

As the illustration shows in but diagrammatic form, the dream is classical in that it is all in a foreground plane, yet it is baroque in that there is a diagonal from the front war canoe to those in the depths, and yet it is impressionistic in that the horizon is above our gaze, and yet it is surreal in that it is a kind of verbal joke (see Chapter 6 on the perspectives of painting): towit, that all of the imagination of man, classical, baroque, impressionistic, or surreal, assembled in a great flotilla led by myself, is not going to take back Poughkeepsie (see the last dream in my last book departing from Poughkeepsie, Gustafson, 1995a) from the white man. He is aboard a train for New York City, as compartmentalized man on his way to a profit from his Puritanical discipline.

Dream of August 10, 1996, of The Author Studying the Origin of Time.

I am in Italy with my wife who is ordering lunch at an Italian ristorante at 9 in the morning. The waiter is only half-complying, so it is very frustrating, and I have a fit. (//)

I am in European train stations, studying the origin of time. I sit inadvertently on my baseball cap, waiting for a train, and then go off leaving it behind. I decide to leave off being a Clockwise Puritan.

This dream close on the heels of the previous one mentioned reminded me that nature, art, and play cannot be fit into the program of compartmentalized man. He is total administration, and he will get everything to work like clockwork.

For myself, I plan to enjoy dreams like that of my great flotilla of the imagination of man as the play of art, as an orchestral score, as pure map-making -- and leave the world to go wherever it has to go.

Rabelais Gets the Final Word

Several months later on the occasion of a departmental retreat, I realized that I had to change the ending of this book concerning the relationship of imagination and the world of force.

The Author's Dream of Rabelais's Laughter Dissolving History: The night before this retreat, I had a dream in preparation for it: I dreamt

> I was getting a patient of mine to laugh very heartily, as in Rabelais. I was wearing surgical covers over my shoes, as big as pillow cases. I took our little (fox-like) dog to visit a very serious colleague in his office to play with his little dog, in a corridor that looked like my junior high school.

In other words, my unconscious was plotting a correction against taking this thing seriously.

In the retreat itself, there was a great deal of anxiety about loss of revenue. Our chairman, an expert monkey doctor, replied with a "State of the Union" addressed to us as an ailing troop of monkeys. He showed slides of his research monkeys on an island, in varying states of distress at being threatened. For consolation, he showed the troop of young males on Monkey Rock where they took refuge together. He suggested that we could all survive on such a rock with him.

I had taken along my Portable Rabelais (Gargantua and Pantagruel, 1542, 1946) in my briefcase, but I did not take it out until the evening after the retreat. I opened it at random, or so I thought, to "Pantagruel Advises Panurge to Try to Forecast the Happiness or Unhappiness of His Marriage Through Dreams" (p. 429). If I had ever known that Rabelais discusses the divine import of dreams, I had forgotten. In any event, here I was in the situation of having my own dream of Rabelais's laughter, in response to history, getting me to discover Rabelais's view of dreaming:

> . . . our soul . . seeks its recreation by revisiting its fatherland, which is heaven. There it is intimately initiated into its divine origin . . . – at that mystic center, where nothing happens, nothing passes, nothing falls away, and all time is at the present – there the soul not only notes those things that have come to pass, but also things that are to come (pp. 429-430)

This view is tested in the next section of the book called "Panurge's Dream and Its Interpretation." The reader is left to read this droll passage for him or herself, while I merely summarize the final remark of Pantagruel:

> And at this point, I recall what the Cabalists and Masoretes, the interpreters of the Sacred Scriptures, have to say, in explaining how one may, with discernment, test the veracity of angelic apparitions; since it sometimes happens that the Angel of Satan is transformed into the Angel of Light. They state that the difference between the two visitations lies in the fact that when the benign and consoling Angel appears to man, he begins by

frightening his host and ends up comforting him; whereas the malign and seducing Angel begins by gladdening man, but ends by leaving him perturbed, annoyed and perplexed (p. 442)

The Author's Dream of the Black Shoes and of the White Shoes: If Rabelais can speak to my condition 544 years after he wrote, then I dare to speak to my reader 544 years after I write, in the year 2540. Both of us speak via dreams.

I dreamt I was playing in a divine game resembling basketball. On one court, I was wearing heavy black workingman's shoes, and needed to go get the light, white, fast ones. On another court, I was wearing the fast ones, and realized I had to go get the slow ones. While the fast ones got things done, the slow ones were needed to perceive accurately the pattern that connects things – and vice versa. I awoke perturbed, to use Rabelais's word, that I had to depart from this divine balance, of black and white, of heavy and light, of fast and slow, back to the game of monkeys in psychiatry.

Is this not our condition? History will still be running on in the year 2540, with juvenile monkeys playing king on the hill, imitating each other, quarreling, just like Agamemnon and Achilles in the year 1000 B.C. at the outset of The Iliad. As Simone Weil puts it in "The Poem of Force,"

Battles are . . . decided . . . between men stripped of these abilities, transformed, fallen to the level either of inert matter (which is nothing but passivity) or of blind forces (which are nothing but momentum). That is the final secret of war (1940, p. 109)

It is also the final secret of business, which is nothing but war by other means. So, yes, my chairman is entirely right that our business is little more than monkeys falling over each other on the grand staircase of history (Kott, 1974). Yet, they will do nothing but hold and lose power, being made into things by imitating each other, and ending up as worn out old monkeys.

Dreams remain our access to the divine balance, that place where creation works like counterpoint between opposites. If we want to be reborn, eternally, we have to know how to go there, as with Rabelais himself searching out the place. If we want to survive on a raw frontier, we have to know how to come back to the crudity of group life in its endless posturing.

References

Abrams, D. M. (1992). The dream's mirror of reality. *Contemporary Psychoanalysis* 28:50-71.

Adams, H. (1904). *Mont Saint-Michel and Chartres*. New York: Penguin, 1986.

_____ (1907). *The Education of Henry Adams*. Boston: Houghton Mifflin, 1961.

Alexander, F. (1925). Dreams in pairs and series. *International Journal of Psychoanalysis* 6:446-450.

Alighieri, Dante (1300). *Inferno*, trans. Robert Pinsky. New York: Farrar, Straus, and Giroux, 1994.

Altman, L. (1969). *The Dream in Psychoanalysis*. New York: International Universities Press.

Aristotle (336-322 B.C.). *Art of Rhetoric*. New York: Penguin, 1991.

Bachelard, G. (1964). *The Psychoanalysis of Fire,* trans. Alan C. M. Ross. Boston: Beacon Press, originally published in French, 1930.

_____ (1971a). *On Poetic Imagination and Reverie,* trans. Colette Gaudin. Dallas: Spring.

_____ (1971b). *The Poetics of Reverie,* trans. Daniel Russell. Boston: Beacon Press. Originally published in French, 1960.

_____ (1983). *Water and Dreams,* trans. E. R. Farrell. Dallas: Dallas Institute of Humanities and Culture. Original, 1942.

Balint, M. (1968). *The Basic Fault, Therapeutic Aspects of Regression*. London: Tavistock.

Barfield, O. (1977). *The Rediscovery of Meaning and Other Essays*. Middletown, Connecticut: Wesleyan University Press.

Bateson, G. (1971). The cybernetics of "self:" A theory of alcoholism. *Psychiatry* 34:1-17.

_____ (1972). Steps Toward An Ecology of Mind. New York: Ballentine.

_____ (1979). *Mind and Nature. A Necessary Unity*. New York: Bantam Books.

Bayley, J. (1981). *Shakespeare and Tragedy*. London: Routledge and Kegan Paul.

Beebe, J. (1993). A Jungian approach to working with dreams. In *New Directions in Dream Interpretation*, ed. G. Delaney. Albany: SUNY Press.

Bergson, H. (1900). Laughter. In *Comedy*, ed. W. Sypher. Baltimore: Johns Hopkins University Press, 1980.

Bergson, H. (1901). *Dreams*. London: T. Fisher Unwin, 1914.

Berry, P. (1974). An approach to the dream. *Spring* 58-79.

The Bhagavad Gita (3rd century BCE), trans. W. J. Johnson. New York: Oxford University Press.

Binswanger, L. (1963). Dream and existence. In *Being-in-the-World, Selected Papers of Ludwig Binswanger*, ed. J. Needleman. New York: Harper and Row, 1967.

_____ (1963). Extravagance (Verstiegenheit). In *Being-in-the-World, Selected Papers of Ludwig Binswanger*, ed. L. Binswanger. New York: Harper and Row, 1967.

Blake, W. (1987). *The Essential Blake*. Selected by Stanley Kunitz. New York: Ecco Press.

Bion, W. (1959). *Experiences in Groups*. New York: Basic Books.

Borges, J. L. (1971). The congress. In *The Book of Sand*, ed. J. L. Borges. London: Penguin.

_____ (1984). Nightmares. In *Seven Nights*, trans. Eliot Weinberger. New York: New Directions. Originally published 1980.

Boss, M. (1963). *Psychoanalysis and Daseinanalysis*, trans. L. B. Lefebre. New York: Basic.

_____ (1977). I Dreamt Last Night, trans. S. Conway. New York: Gardner Press.

Bradlow, P. A. (1987). On prediction and the manifest content of the initial dream reported in psychoanalysis. In *The Interpretations of Dreams in Clinical Work*, ed. A. Rothstein, pp. 155-178. Madison, Connecticut: International Universities Press.

Brecht, B. (1930). *The Rise and Fall of the City of Mahagonny*, trans. W. R. Auden. Boston: David R. Godine, 1976.

Breuer, J., and Freud, S. (1895). *Studies on Hysteria. Standard Edition 2*. New York: W.W. Norton.

Callahan, J., and Sashin, J. I. (1986). Models of affect-response and anorexia nervosa. *Annals of the New York Academy of Sciences* 504:241-259.

_____ (1990). Predictive models in psychoanalysis. *Behavioral Science* 35:60-76.

Campbell, J. (1949). *The Hero With a Thousand Faces.* Princeton, New Jersey: Princeton University Press.

_____ (1959). *The Masks of God: Primitive Mythology.* New York: Penguin.

_____ (1964). *The Masks of God: Occidental Mythology.* New York: Penguin.

_____ (1971). *The Portable Jung.* New York: Penguin.

Canetti, E. (1960). *Crowds and Power*, trans. Carol Stewart. New York: Continuum.

Carroll, L. (1865). *Alice in Wonderland.* Illustrated by Michael Hague. New York: Henry Holt and Company, 1985.

Carskadon, M. A. (1993). *Encyclopedia of Sleep and Dreaming.* New York: MacMillan.

Charbonnier, G. (1969). *Conversations with Claude Levi-Strauss.* Trans. by John and Doreen Weightman. London: Jonathan Cape.

Chen, E. Y. H. (1994). A neural network model of cortical information processing in schizophrenia. *Canadian Journal of Psychiatry* 39:362-367.

Craig, P. E., and Walsh, S. J. (1993). Phenomenological challenges for the clinical use of dreams. In *New Directions in Dream Interpretation*, ed. G. Delaney. Albany: SUNY Press.

Davenport, G. (1981). Charles Ives. In *The Geography of the Imagination*, ed. G. Davenport. San Francisco: North Point Press.

Delaney, G. (1993). *New Directions in Dream Interpretation.* Albany: State University of New York Press.

Densmore, F. (1979). *Chippewa Customs.* St. Paul: Minnesota Historical Society Press.

Deutsch, A. T. (1949). *The Mentally Ill in America.* New York: Colombia University Press.

Deutsch, F. (1957). A footnote to Freud's "Fragment of an analysis of a case of hysteria." *Psychoanalytic Quarterly* 26:159-167.

Devereux, G. (1969). *Reality and Dream. Psychotherapy of a Plains Indian.* New York: New York University Press.

Dickens, C. (1850). *David Copperfield.* New York: Oxford University Press, 1981.

Dickinson, E. (1960). *The Complete Poems of Emily Dickinson*, ed. T. H. Johnson. Boston: Little Brown.

Durrenmatt, F. (1956). *The Visit*. New York: Grove Press.

Durrenmatt, F. (1962). *The Physicists*. Trans. James Kirkup. New York: Grove Press, 1964.

Edelman, G. M. (1979). Group selection and phasic reentrant signaling: a theory of higher brain function. In *The Mindful Brain*, ed. G. M. Edelman and V. B. Mountcastle, pp. 51-100. Cambridge, MA: MIT Press.

Eliade, M. (1963). *Myth and Reality*. New York: Harper.

Eliot, T. S. (1915). The love-song of J. Alfred Prufrock. In *The Waste Land and Other Poems*. New York: Harcourt, Brace, Jovanovich, 1958.

Emerson, R. W. (1841, 1844). *The Essays of Ralph Waldo Emerson*. Cambridge: Harvard University Press, 1987.

Erasmus (1511). *Praise of Folly and Letter to Maarten VanDorp*. New York: Penguin, 1971.

Erikson, E. H. (1954). The dream specimen of psychoanalysis. *Journal of the American Psychoanalytical Association* 2:5-56.

_____ (1963). *Childhood and Society*. New York: W. W. Norton. First edition, 1950.

Ernst, M. (1952). Inspiration to order. In *The Creative Process*, ed. B. Ghiselin. Berkeley, California: University of California Press, 1985.

_____ (1973). *Inside the Sight*. Houston, Texas: Institute for the Arts, Rice University.

Fanon, F. (1963). *The Wretched of the Earth*, trans. Constance Farrington. New York: Grove Press.

Farber, L. (1966). *The Ways of the Will*. New York: Basic Books.

Faulkner, W. (1942). The bear. In *The Norton Anthology of Short Fiction*, ed. R. V. Cassill. New York: W.W. Norton, 1986.

Foucault, M. (1975). *Discipline and Punish: The Birth of the Prison*, trans. Alan Sheridan. New York: Vintage, 1979.

Franz von, Marie-Louise (1975). *C. G. Jung, His Myth in Our Time*. New York: G. P. Putnam's Sons.

Freeman, W. J. (1990). Non-linear dynamics in olfaction as a model for cognition. In *Chaos in Brain Function*, ed. E. Basar. Berlin: Springer Verlag, pp. 19-29.

Freire, P. (1970). *Pedagogy of the Oppressed.* New York: Herder and Herder.

French, T. M. (1970). *Psychoanalytic Interpretations. The Selected Papers of Thomas M. French.* Chicago: Quadrangle Books.

Freud, S. (1900). The interpretation of dreams. *Standard Edition 4.* London: Hogarth Press. New York: Avon Books, 1965 (pagination from).

_____ (1905). Fragment of an analysis of a case of hysteria. *Standard Edition* 7:3-122.

_____ (1913). The occurrence in dreams of material from fairy tales. *Standard Edition 12.* Reprinted in *Character and Culture*, ed. P. Rieff. New York: Collier, 1963.

_____ (1917). Mourning and melancholia. *Standard Edition 14.*

_____ (1920). Beyond the pleasure principle. *Standard Edition 18.*

_____ (1930). *Civilization and its Discontents. Standard Edition* 21.

_____ (1989). *The Freud Reader*, ed. P. Gay. New York: W. W. Norton.

Frost, R. (1969). Build soil. A political pastoral. In *The Poetry of Robert Frost*, ed. E. C. Latham. New York: Henry Holt.

_____ (1874-1963). Departmental. In *The New Oxford Book of American Verse*, ed. R. Ellman. New York: Oxford University Press, 1976.

_____ (1874-1963). Neither out far nor in deep. In *The New Oxford Book of American Verse*, ed. R. Ellman. New York: Oxford University Press, 1976.

_____ (1874-1963). *The Poetry of Robert Frost.* New York: Henry Holt, 1969.

Frye, N. (1957). *Anatomy of Criticism. Four Essays.* Princeton, New Jersey: Princeton University Press.

Gabbard, G.O. (1994). *Psychodynamic Psychiatry in Clinical Practice.* Washington, D.C.: American Psychiatric Press.

Garcia Marquez, G. (1982). *One Hundred Years of Solitude*, ed. G. Rabassa. New York: Limited Editions Club.

Gardner, H. (1971). *Religion and Literature.* London: Faber and Faber.

Gardner, M. (1971). *The Wolf Man By The Wolf Man*. New York: Basic Books.

Gedo, J. (1979). *Beyond Interpretation, Towards a Revised Theory for Psychoanalysis*. New York: International Universities Press.

Genet, J. (1958). *The Balcony*. New York: Grove Press, Inc.

Genova, P. (1995a). Dream rebuts therapist in a case of unresolved grief. *Psychiatric Times*, February, pp. 4-5.

_____ (1995b). Catfish on the bottom: Inverting a patient's imagery in analytic therapy. *Psychiatric Times*, December, pp. 9-10.

Ghiselin, B. (1986). *The Creative Process*. Berkeley, California: University of California Press. Originally published, 1952.

Goethe, J. W. von (1832). *Faust*. Trans. L. MacNeice. New York: Oxford, 1951.

Golding, W. (1954). *Lord of the Flies*. New York: Putnam.

Grant, M., & Hazel (1993). *Who's Who in Classical Mythology*. New York: Oxford University Press.

Greenberg, R. (1987). Self-psychology and dreams: The merging of different perspectives. *Psychiatric Journal of the University of Ottawa* 12:98-102.

Greenberg, R., and Pearlman, C. (1980). The private language of the dream. In *The Dream in Clinical Practice*, ed. J. Natterson. New York: Jason Aronson. Reprinted in paperback Masterwork Series, 1993.

Greenberg, R., Katz, H., Schwartz, W., and Pearlman, C. (1992). A research-based reconsideration of the psychoanalytic theory of dreaming. *Journal of the American Psychoanalytic Association* 40:531-550.

Greenson, R. R. (1967). *The Technique and Practice of Psychoanalysis*, Volume 1. New York: International Universities Press.

_____ (1970). The exceptional position of the dream in psychoanalytic practice. *Psychoanalytic Quarterly* 39:519-549.

Grinnell, R. (1970). Reflections on the archetype of consciousness: Personality and psychological faith. *Spring* 15-39.

Grinstein, A. (1968). *Sigmund Freud's Dreams*. New York: International Universities Press.

_____ (1992). Basic technical suggestions for dream interpretation. In *The Technique and Practice of Psychoanalysis, Volume II: A Memorial Volume to Ralph R. Greenson*, ed. A. Sugarman, R. A. Nemiroff, and D. P. Greenson. Madison, Connecticut: International Universities Press.

Guntrip, H. (1968). *Schizoid Phenomena, Object-Relations and the Self.* New York: International Universities Press.

Gustafson, J. P. (1967). *Hallucinoia.* Thesis, Harvard Medical School, unpublished.

_____ (1976). The mirror transference in the psychoanalytic psychotherapy of alcoholism. *International Journal of Psychoanalytic Psychotherapy* 5:65-85.

_____ (1986). *The Complex Secret of Brief Psychotherapy.* New York: Norton & Co. Reprinted in paperback, 1997, with new preface. New York: Jason Aronson.

_____ (1989). A scientific journey of twenty years. *Journal of Strategic and Systemic Therapies*, July, 1989.

_____ (1992). *Self-Delight in a Harsh World. The Main Stories of Individual, Marital and Family Psychotherapy.* New York: W. W. Norton.

_____ (1995a). *Brief Versus Long Psychotherapy.* New York: Jason Aronson.

_____ (1995b). *The Dilemmas of Brief Psychotherapy, and Taking Care of the Patient.* New York: Plenum.

_____ (in preparation). *American Character.*

Gustafson, J. P., and Cooper, L. W. (1990). *The Modern Contest. A Systemic Guide to the Pattern That Connects Individual Psychotherapy, Family Therapy, Group Work, Teaching, Organizational Life, and Large-Scale Social Problems.* New York: W. W. Norton.

Gustafson, K. (1996). Two centuries of insanity in America. Unpublished.

Hardy, T. (1891). On the western circuit. In *Collected Short Stories*, ed. T. Hardy. London: MacMillan, 1988.

Havens, L. (1965). Anatomy of a suicide. *New England Journal of Medicine* 272:401-406.

Hayles, K. (1994). *Chaos Bound: Orderly Disorder in Contemporary Literature and Science.* Ithaca, New York: Cornell University Press.

Heaney, S. (1980). *Preoccupations, Selected Prose, 1968-1978*. New York: Noonday Press, Farrar, Straus and Giroux.

_____ (1988). *The Government of the Tongue. Selected Prose 1978-1987*. New York: The Noonday Press, Farrar, Straus and Giroux.

_____ (1995). *The Redress of Poetry*. New York: Farrar, Straus and Giroux.

Hearne, V. (1986). Reflections. Questions about language. I. Horses. *The New Yorker*, August 18, 33-57.

Heidegger, M. (1959). *An Introduction to Metaphysics*, trans. Ralph Manheim. New Haven: Yale University Press. Originally given as a lecture in 1935.

_____ (1962). *Being and Time*, trans. John Macquarrie and Edward Robinson. New York: Harper and Row. Originally published in German in 1927.

Henry, J. (1973). *On Sham, Vulnerability, and Other Forms of Self-destruction*. New York: Random House.

Herbert, Z. (1985). *Barbarian in the Garden*, trans. Michael March and Jaroslaw Anders. Manchester, England: Carcanet. Original, in Polish, 1962.

Herbert, Z. (1986). *Selected Poems*. New York: Ecco Press. Originally published, 1968.

Hillman, J. (1977). An inquiry into image. *Spring* 62-88.

_____ (1988). Further notes on images. *Spring* 152-182.

_____ (1979a). *Puer Papers*. Dallas, Texas: Spring Publications.

_____ (1979b). *The Dream and the Underworld*. New York: Harper and Row.

Hilts, P. J. (1997). Listening to the conversation of neurons. *Psychiatric Times*, 32, July.

Hobson, J. A. (1995). *Sleep*. New York: Scientific American Library.

Homer (1000 B.C.). *The Iliad*, trans. Robert Fitzgerald. Garden City, New York: Anchor Books, 1974.

_____ (1000 B.C.). *The Odyssey*, trans. Robert Fitzgerald. New York: Anchor Books, 1963.

Hopkins, G. M. (1966). *A Hopkins Reader*, ed. J. Pick. New York: Doubleday.

Hughes, T. (1971). *A Choice of Shakespeare's Verse*. London: Faber and Faber.

_____ (1991). *The Essential Shakespeare*. New York: Ecco Press.

_____ (1992). *Shakespeare and the Goddess of Complete Being*. New York: Farrar, Straus and Giroux.

Ibsen, H. (1890). *Hedda Gabler*. In *Seven Famous Plays*, ed. W. Archer. London: Duckworth, 1961.

Isakower, O. (1938). A contribution to the patho-psychology of phenomena associated with falling asleep. *International Journal of Psychoanalysis* 19:331-345.

James, W. (1902). *The Varieties of Religious Experience*. New York: Mentor, 1958.

Joyce, J. (1914). *Ulysses*. New York: Modern Library, 1961.

Jung, C. G. (1911). *The Psychology of the Unconscious*. New York: Dodd, Mead and Company, 1949.

_____ (1916, 1935). The relations between the ego and the unconscious. In *Two Essays on Analytical Psychology*, second edition. Bollingen series. Princeton, New Jersey: Princeton University Press, 1972. Also in *The Portable Jung*, ed. J. Campbell. New York: Penguin, 1971.

_____ (1916, 1958). The transcendent function. In *The Portable Jung*, ed. J. Campbell. New York: Penguin, 1971.

_____ (1917, 1943). On the psychology of the unconscious. In *Two Essays on Analytical Psychology*, second edition, Bollinger Series. Princeton, New Jersey: Princeton University Press, 1972.

_____ (1928-1930). *Dream Analysis, Notes of a Seminar*. Bollingen Series, XCIX. Princeton: Princeton University Press, 1984.

_____ (1933). Dream-analysis in its practical application. In *Modern Man in Search of a Soul*, trans. W. S. Dell and Cary F. Baynes. New York: Harcourt, Brace and Company.

_____ (1944, 1952). Dream symbolism in relation to alchemy. In Jung, *Dreams*. Princeton, New Jersey: Princeton Unviersity Press, 1974.

_____ (1946). The psychology of the transference. In *The Practice of Psychotherapy*. Princeton: Princeton University Press, 1966.

_____ (1950). A study in the process of individuation. In *The Archetypes and the Collective Unconscious*. Princeton: Princeton University Press, 1968.

_____ (1955-1956). *Mysterium Conjunctionis*, trans. R. F. C. Hull. Princeton: Princeton University Press, 1963.

_____ (1963). *Memories, Dreams and Reflections*, ed. A. Jaffe, trans. R. and C. Winston. New York: Vintage Books, 1989.

Kafka, F. (1946). My neighbor. In *The Great Wall of China*. New York: Schocken.

_____ (1948). A report to an academy. In *The Metamorphosis, The Penal Colony and Other Stories*, trans. W. and E. Muir. New York: Schocken.

_____ (1971). My neighbor. In F. Kafka, *The Complete Stories*. New York: Shocken Books.

Kaku, M. (1994). *Hyperspace*. New York: Oxford University Press.

Khan, M. (1974b). The use and abuse of dream in psychic experience. In *The Privacy of the Self*. New York: International Universities Press.

Kinsella, W. P. (1987). Apartheid. In *Red Wolf, Red Wolf*. Toronto: Collins.

Kohut, H. (1971). *The Analysis of the Self*. New York: International Universities Press.

_____ (1979). The two analyses of Mr. Z. *International Journal of Psychoanalysis* 60:3-27.

Kott, J. (1974). *Shakespeare, Our Contemporary*, trans. Boleslaw Taborski. New York: W.W. Norton. Originally published in Polish, 1964.

_____ (1987). *The Eating of the Gods. An Interpretation of Greek Tragedy*, trans. Boleslaw Taborski and Edward J. Czerwinski. Evanston, Illinois: Northwestern University Press. Original, 1974.

Kundera, M. (1984). *The Unbearable Lightness of Being*. Trans. Michael Henry Heim. New York: Harper.

_____ (1990). *Immortality*. Trans. Peter Kuss. New York: Harper.

Kunert, G. (1979). Why I Write. In *The Poet's Work. 29 Masters of 20th Century Poetry on the Origins and Practice of Their Art*, ed. R. Gibbons. Boston: Houghton Mifflin.

Kuper, A. (1989). Symbols in myths and dreams: Freud vs. Levi-Strauss. *Encounter*, March, 26-31.

Kuper, A. and Stone, A. A. (1982). The dream of Irma's injection: A structural analysis. *American Journal of Psychiatry* 139:1225-1234.

Lacan, J. (1991). *The Seminar of Jacques Lacan. Book II. The Ego in Freud's Theory and in the Technique of Psychoanalysis 1954-1955*, trans. Sylvana Tomaselli, ed. Jacques-Alain Miller. New York: Norton. Original in French, 1978.

Laing, R. D. (1959). *The Divided Self. An Existential Study in Sanity and Madness*. London: Tavistock Press.

Laing, R. D. and Cooper, D. G. (1964). *Reason and Violence. A Decade of Sartre's Philosophy 1950-1960*. New York: Vintage Books.

Lawrence, D. H. (1929-1930). The ship of death. In *Selected Poems*. New York: Viking Press, 1959.

Leach, E. (1970). *Claude Levi-Strauss*. New York: Penguin.

Leopold, A. (1949). *A Sand County Almanac*. New York: Ballantine, 1966.

Levi-Strauss, C. (1963). *Structural Anthropology*, trans. C. Jacobson and B. G. Schoepf. New York: Basic. Originally published, 1958.

_____ (1977). *Tristes Tropiques*, trans. J. and D. Weightman. New York: Pocket Books. Originally published, 1955.

_____ (1983). *The Raw and the Cooked. Mythologiques, Volume I*, trans. John and Doreen Weightman. Chicago: University of Chicago Press. Originally published, 1964.

Lewin, B. (1973). *Selected Writings of Bertram D. Lewin*. New York: Psychoanalytic Quarterly Press.

Lopez-Pedraza, R. (1977). *Hermes and His Children*. Einsiedeln, Switzerland: Daimon Verlag, 1989.

Main, T. (1957). The ailment. *British Journal of Medical Psychology* 30:129-145.

Malan, D. (1979). *Individual Psychotherapy and the Science of Psychodynamics*. London: Butterworths.

Mann, T. (1929). Mario and the magician. In *Death in Venice and Seven Other Stories*. New York: Vintage, 1954.

Marcuse, H. (1964). *One-Dimensional Man*. Boston: Beacon.

Margulies, A. (1989). *The Empathic Imagination*. New York: W. W. Norton.

_____ (1993). Contemplating the mirror of the other. Empathy and self-analysis. In *Self-Analysis: Critical Inquiries*, ed. J. W. Barron. New York: The Analytic Press.

_____ (in preparation). *To The Edge of Awareness*.

Marquez, G. G. (1968). The handsomest drowned man in the world. In *The Norton Anthology of Short Fiction*, ed. R. V. Cassill. New York: W. W. Norton, 1986.

Marx, K. (1843-1844). *Early Writings*. Trans. R. Livingstone, G. Benton. New York: Vintage Press, 1975.

Maturana, H., and Varela F. J. (1980). *Autopoesis and Cognition*. Boston: D. Reidel.

May, R., Angel, E., and Ellenberger, H. F (1958). *Existence. A New Dimension in Psychiatry and Psychology*. New York: Simon and Schuster.

McNeill, W. H. (1963). *The Rise of the West*. Chicago: University of Chicago Press. Reprinted 1991.

Melville, H. (1851). *Moby-Dick or, the Whale. Edited with an introduction by* Alfred Kazin. Boston: Houghton Mifflin, 1956.

_____ (1853). Bartleby the scrivener. In *The Norton Anthology of Short Fiction*, ed. R. V. Cassill. New York: W. W. Norton, 1986.

Michnik, A. (1986). *Letters From Prison*. Berkeley: University of California Press.

Miller, A. (1949). *Death of a Salesman*. New York: Penguin, 1976.

Mills, C. W. (1959). *The Sociological Imagination*. New York: Oxford University Press.

Minkowski, E. (1933). *Lived Time. Phenomenological and Psychopathological Studies*, trans. N. Metzel. Evanston, IL: Northwestern University Press, 1970.

Moliere, J. B. P. (1666). A doctor in spite of himself. In *The Misanthrope and Other Plays*. New York: Penguin, 1959.

_____ (1666, 1669). *The Misanthrope and Tartuffe*. Trans. R. Wilbur. New York: Harcourt, Brace, Jovanovitch, 1965.

Moran, J. M., and Morgan, M. D. (1986). *Meteorology. The Atmosphere and the Science of Weather*. New York: Macmillan.

Mumford, L. (1970). The first megamachine. In *The Lewis Mumford Reader*, ed. D. L. Miller. Athens: University of Georgia Press.

Natterson, J. (1980). *The Dream in Clinical Practice*. New York: Jason Aronson. Reprinted in paperback Masterwork Series, 1993.

_____ (1993). Dreams: The gateway to consciousness. In *New Directions in Dream Interpretation*, ed. G. Delaney. Albany: SUNY Press.

Nietzsche, F. (1954). *The Portable Nietzsche*. New York: Viking Press.

Noll, R. (1994). *The Jung Cult. Origins of a Charismatic Movement*. Princeton, New Jersey: Princeton University Press.

O'Connor, F. (1955). A good man is hard to find. In *The Norton Anthology of Short Fiction*, ed. R. V. Cassill. New York: W. W. Norton, 1986.

Ollman, B. (1971). *Alienation. Marx's Conception of Man in Capitalist Society*. Cambridge: Cambridge University Press.

Olson, C. (1947). *Call Me Ishmael*. San Francisco: City Lights.

Oremlund, J. (1987a). A specific dream in the termination phase of successful treatment. In *The Interpretation of Dreams in Clinical Work*, ed. A. Rothstein. Madison, Connecticut: International Universities Press.

_____ (1987b). Dreams in the borderline and schizophrenic personality. In *The Interpretation of Dreams in Clinical Work*, ed. A. Rothstein. Madison, Connecticut: International Universities Press.

Ornstein, A. (1974). The dread to repeat and the new beginning: a contribution to the psychoanalytic psychotherapy of narcissistic personality disorders. *Annual of Psychoanalysis* 2:231-248.

Ornstein, P. H. (1987). On self-state dreams in the psychoanalytic treatment process. In *The Interpretation of Dreams in Clinical Work*, ed. A. Rothstein. Madison, Connecticut: International Universities Press.

Otto, R. (1923). *The Idea of the Holy*, trans. John W. Harvey. New York: Oxford University Press, 1958.

Paris, G. (1990). *Pagan Grace*. Woodstock, Connecticut: Spring Publications.

Percy, W. (1975). Metaphor as mistake. In *The Message in the Bottle*. New York: Farrar, Straus and Giroux.

Perls, F., Hefferline, R. F., and Goodman, P. (1951). *Gestalt Therapy*. New York: Dell Publishing.

Pies, R. W. (1994). *Clinical Manual of Psychiatric Diagnosis and Treatment*. Washington, D.C.: American Psychiatric Press.

Plath, S. (1992). *Collected Poems*, ed. T. Hughes. New York: Harper Collins.

Poirier, R. (1966). *A World Elsewhere. The Place of Style in American Literature*. Madison, Wisconsin: University of Wisconsin Press.

Porter, K. (1935). Theft. In *The Norton Anthology of Short Fiction*, ed. R.V. Cassill. New York: W. W. Norton, 1986.

Proust, M. (1913). *Swann's Way*, trans. C. K. Scott Moncrieff. New York: Vintage Books, Random House, 1970.

Raban, J. (1996). The unlamented west. *The New Yorker*, May 20, pp. 60-81.

Rabelais, F. (1542). Gargantua and Pantagruel. In *The Portable Rabelais*, trans. S. Putnam. New York: Viking, 1946.

Rafferty, T. (1994). True west. *The New Yorker*, January 10, pp. 81-83.

Rapoport, D. and Gill, M. M. (1959). The points of view and assumptions of metapsychology. *International Journal of Psychoanalysis* 40:153-162.

Reich, W. (1931). Character formation and the phobias of childhood. *International Journal of Psychoanalysis* 12:219.

_____ (1933). *Character Analysis*. New York: Farrar, Straus and Giroux, 1949.

Rilke, R. M. (1907). The panther. In *Translations From the Poetry of Rainier Maria Rilke*, trans. M. D. Herder Norton. New York: W.W. Norton, 1938.

_____ (1993). *Letters To a Young Poet*, trans. M.D. Herter Norton. Originally written, 1903-1908. New York: W. W. Norton.

Roethke, T. (1948). My papa's waltz. In *The Collected Poems of Theodore Roethke*. New York: Anchor Doubleday, 1966.

_____ (1965). *On the Poet and His Craft. Selected Prose of Theodore Roethke*, ed. R.J. Mills, Jr. Seattle: University of Washington Press.

Rotenberg, V. S. (1992a). Sleep and memory. I. The influence of different sleep stages on memory. *Neuroscience and Biobehavioral Review* 16:497-502.

_____ (1992b). Sleep and memory. II. Investigations on humans. *Neuroscience and Biobehavioral Review* 16:503-505.

Rothstein, A. (1987). *The Interpretations of Dreams in Clinical Work*. Madison, Connecticut: International Universities Press.

Rushdie, S. (1994). *East, West Stories*. New York: Pantheon Press.

Ryle, A. (1994). Introduction to cognitive analytic therapy. *International Journal of Short-Term Psychotherapy* 9:93-110.

St. Exupery, A. de (1939). *Wind, Sand and Stars*, trans. Lewis Galantiere. New York: Harcourt, Brace, Jovanovich.

_____ (1943). *The Little Prince*, trans. Katherine Woods. New York: Harcourt, Brace, Jovanovich.

Sartre, Jean-Paul (1966). *Being and Nothingness*, trans. Hazel Barnes. New York: Washington Square Press. Original in French in 1953.

Sashin, J. I. (1985). Affect tolerance: A model of affect-response using catastrophe theory. *Journal of Social and Biological Structure* 8:175-202.

Sashin, J. I., and Callahan, J. (1990). A model of affect using dynamical systems. *The Annual of Psychoanalysis* 18:213-231.

Schmid, G. B. (1991). Chaos theory and schizophrenia: elementary aspects. *Psychopathology* 24:185-198.

Schmidt, G. L. (unpublished). The chaotic brain, A unifying theory for psychiatry.

Schorske, C. E. (1981). *Fin-De-Siecle Vienna, Politics and Culture*. New York: Vintage Books. Original, 1980.

Schumacher, E. F. (1977). *A Guide for the Perplexed*. New York: Harper and Row.

Schur, M. (1966). Some additional "day residues" of "the specimen dream of psychoanalysis." In *Psychoanalysis -- A General Psychology*, eds. R. M. Loewenstein, L. M. Newman, M. Schur, and A. J. Solnit. New York: International Universities Press.

Seager, A. (1991). *The Glass House. The Life of Theodore Roethke.* Ann Arbor, Michigan: University of Michigan Press. Originally published, 1968.

Sekida, K. (1977). *Two Zen Classics. Mumankan and Hekiganroku.* New York: Weatherhill.

Sendak, M. (1963). *Where the Wild Things Are.* New York: Harper and Row.

Shakespeare, William (1597a). The tragedy of King Richard the Second. In *William Shakespeare, The Complete Works*, ed. Alfred Harbage. Baltimore: Penguin, 1969, revised edition.

_____ (1597b). The tragedy of King Richard the Third. In *William Shakespeare, The Complete Works*, ed. Alfred Harbage. Baltimore: Penguin, 1969, revised edition.

_____ (1600). Hamlet, Prince of Denmark. In *William Shakespeare, The Complete Works*, ed. Alfred Harbage. Baltimore: Penguin, 1969, revised edition.

_____ (1604). Measure for measure. In *William Shakespeare, The Complete Works*, ed. Alfred Harbage. Baltimore: Penguin, 1969, revised edition.

_____ (1605-1606). King Lear. In *William Shakespeare, The Complete Works*, ed. Alfred Harbage. Baltimore, Maryland: Penguin, 1969, revised edition.

_____ (1611). The tempest. In *William Shakespeare, The Complete Works*, ed. Alfred Harbage. Baltimore, Maryland: Penguin, 1969, revised edition.

Sharaf, M. (1983). *Fury on Earth.* New York: St. Martin's Press.

Sharpe, E. F. (1951). *Dream Analysis.* London: Hogarth.

Shields, P. (1990). Dreaming and interpretation: A treatment of *The Interpretation of Dreams* as a dream. *Psychoanalysis and Contemporary Thought* 13:79-106.

Shorris, E. (1994). A nation of salesmen. *Harper's*, October, pp. 39-54.

Snyder, G. (1990). *The Practice of the Wild.* San Francisco: North Point Press.

Spies, W. (1991). *Max Ernst, A Retrospective.* Munich: Prestel-Verlag.

Stendhal (1830). *The Red and the Black*, trans. Charles Tergie. New York: Collier, 1961.

Stevens, W. (1965). *The Necessary Angel. Essays on Reality and the Imagination.* New York: Vintage Books.

Stevenson, R. L. (1886). *The Strange Case of Dr. Jekyll and Mr. Hyde*. New York: Puffin Books, 1985.

_____ (1888). A chapter on dreams. In *Across the Plains*. London: Chatto and Windus, Piccadilly.

_____ (1892). The lantern-bearers. In *Across the Plains*. London: Chatto and Windus, Piccadilly.

Sullivan, H. S. (1946). *Conceptions of Modern Psychiatry*. New York: Norton.

_____ (1953). Sleep, dream and myths. In *The Interpersonal Theory of Psychiatry*. New York: W. W. Norton.

_____ (1954). *The Psychiatric Interview*. New York: W. W. Norton & Co.

_____ (1956). *Clinical Studies in Psychiatry*. New York: W. W. Norton.

Tate, A. (1948). *On The Limits of Poetry*. New York: Swallow Press and William Morrow, Inc. Reprinted in 1970 by Books for Libraries Press, Freeport, New York.

Terkel, S. (1972). *Working*. New York: Avon.

Thomas, D. (1934-1952). *The Collected Poems of Dylan Thomas*. New York: New Directions, 1971.

Thoreau, H. D. (1854). Walden. In *The Portable Thoreau*. New York: Penguin, 1947.

Thurber, J. (1942). The secret life of Walter Mitty. In *The Norton Anthology of Short Fiction*, ed. R. V. Cassill. New York: W. W. Norton, 1986.

Tolstoy, L. (1869). *War and Peace*. New York: Modern Library, 1966.

_____ (1875-1877). *Anna Karenina*. New York: W. W. Norton, 1970.

_____ (1903). *Esarhaddon and Other Tales*, trans. L. and A. Maude. New York: Funk and Wagnalls.

Travis, D. (1994). Mathematics and photography. *Bulletin of the American Academy of Arts and Sciences* 47:23-45.

Turner, A. K. (1993). *The History of Hell*. New York: Harcourt, Brace.

Turner, F. J. (1920). *The Frontier in American History*. Tucson, Arizona: University of Arizona Press, 1994.

Twain, M. (1876). The pinch-bug and his prey. From *Tom Sawyer*. In *The World Treasury of Children's Literature*, ed. C. Fadiman. Boston: Little Brown, 1985.

_____ (1885). *The Adventures of Huckleberry Finn*. New York: Collier, 1962.

Ullman, M. (1993). Dreams, the dreamer and society. In *New Directions in Dream Interpretation*, ed. G. Delaney. Albany: SUNY Press.

Varnedoe, K. (1990). *A Fine Disregard. What Makes Modern Art Modern*. New York: Harry N. Abrams.

Warren, R. P. (1946). *All The King's Men*. New York: Harcourt, Brace and Company.

Weber, M. (1904-1905). *The Protestant Ethic and The Spirit of Capitalism*, trans. Talcott Parsons. New York: Charles Scribner's Sons, 1958.

Weil, S. (1940). *The Iliad*, or the poem of force, trans. Richard Ringler. In *Dilemmas of War and Peace: A Source Book*, ed. R. Ringler. London: Routledge, 1993.

_____ (1952). *Gravity and Grace*, trans. Arthur Wills. New York: G.P. Putnam's Sons.

Weiss, J. (1993). *How Psychotherapy Works: Process and Technique*. New York: Guilford.

Weiss, J. and Sampson, H. (1986). *The Psychoanalytic Process*. New York: Guilford.

Williams, W. C. (1934). The American background: America and Alfred Stieglitz. In *Selected Essays*. New York: New Directions, 1969.

_____ (1956). *In the American Grain*. New York: New Directions. Originally published, 1926.

Wilson, Z. V. (1986). *The Quick and the Dead*. New York: Arbor House.

Winnicott, D. W. (1947). Hate in the countertransference. In D. W. Winnicott, *Through Pediatrics to Psychoanalysis*. New York: Basic Books, 1958.

Winnicott, D. W. (1971a). *Playing and Reality*. London: Tavistock Publications.

_____ (1971b). *Therapeutic Consultations in Child Psychiatry*. New York: Basic Books.

Wolff, J. (1994). The Portneuf Gap, a Zen nocturne. In *Where the Morning Light's Still Blue*, ed. W. Studebaker and R. Ardinger. Moscow, Idaho: University of Idaho Press.

Wölfflin, H. (1950). *Principles of Art History. The Problem of The Development of Style in Later Art*, trans. M. D. Hottinger. New York: Dover. Originally published, 1915.

Wooldridge, D. (1974). *From the Steeples and Mountains, A Study of Charles Ives*. New York: Alfred A. Knopf.

Yates, F. A. (1966). *The Art of Memory*. Chicago: University of Chicago Press.

Yeats, W. B. (1919). The fisherman. In *Selected Poems and Two Plays of William Butler Yeats*, ed. M.L. Rosenthal. New York: MacMillan, 1962.

_____ (1928). Sailing to Byzantium. In *Selected Poems and Two Plays of William Butler Yeats*, ed. M.L. Rosenthal. New York: MacMillan, 1962.

_____ (1986). The thinking of the body. In *The Creative Process*, ed. B. Ghiselin. Berkeley: University of California Press. Originally published, 1952.

Index of Dreams Dreamt by Author

Index of Dreams Dreamt by Others

Index of Dreams Dreamt by Author

Index of Dreams Dreamt by Others

Index

Credits

The author gratefully acknowledges permission to reprint the following:

Excerpts from *Shakespeare, Our Contemporary*, by J. Kott, translated by Boleslaw Taborski. Published by W. W. Norton, 1974; originally published in Polish, 1964. Reprinted by permission of Bantam Doubleday Dell Publishing Group.

Excerpts from *To The Edge of Awareness*, by A. Margulies. Reprinted by permission of the author.

Excerpts from *A Sand County Almanac*, by Aldo Leopold. Copyright © 1949, 1953, 1966, renewed 1977, 1981 by Oxford University Press, Inc. Used by permission of Oxford University Press, Inc.

Excerpts from *The Interpersonal Theory of Psychiatry*, by Henry Stack Sullivan. Copyright © 1953 by the William Alanson White Psychiatric Foundation. Reprinted by permission of W. W. Norton & Company, Inc.

Excerpts from *On Poetic Imagination and Reverie*, by G. Bachelard, translated by Colette Gaudin. Published by Spring Publications, Inc.. Reprinted by permission of Spring Publications, Inc.

Excerpts from *Fin-De-Siecle Vienna, Politics and Culture*, by Carl E. Schorske. Copyright © 1979 by Carl E. Schorske. Reprinted by permission of Alfred A. Knopf, Inc.

Excerpts from *The Dream and the Underworld*, by J. Hillman. Published by Harper and Row, 1979. Reprinted by permission of HarperCollins Publishers.

Excerpts from *New Directions in Dream Interpretation*, edited by G. Delaney. Published by State University of New York Press, 1993. Reprinted by permission of State University of New York Press.

Excerpts from *The Divided Self. An Existential Study in Sanity and Madness*, by R. D. Laing. Published by Tavistock Publications, 1959. Reprinted by permission of Tavistock Publications.

Excerpts from *The Basic Fault, Therapeutic Aspects of Regression*, by M. Balint. Published by Tavistock Publications, 1968. Reprinted by permission of Tavistock Publications.

Excerpts from *Therapeutic Consultations in Child Psychiatry*, by D. W. Winnicott. Published by Basic Books, 1971. Copyright © by the Executors of the Estate of D. W. Winnicott. Reprinted by permission of BasicBooks, a division of HarperCollins Publishers, Inc.

Excerpts from *Structural Anthropology*, by C. Levi-Strauss, translated by C. Jacobson and B. G. Schoepf. Published by Basic Books, 1963, originally published 1958. Reprinted by permission of BasicBooks, a division of HarperCollins Publishers, Inc.

Excerpts from *Psychoanalysis and Daseinanalysis*, by M. Boss, translated by L. B. Lefebre. Published by Basic Books, 1963. Reprinted by permission of BasicBooks, a division of HarperCollins Publishers, Inc.

Excerpts from "The Dream Specimen of Psychoanalysis," by E. H. Erikson, published in *Journal of the American Psychoanalytic Association*, 2(1):5-56, 1954. Reprinted by permission of International Universities Press, Inc.

Excerpts from *Moby-Dick or, the Whale*, by H. Melville (1851), edited with an introduction by Alfred Kazin. Published by Houghton Mifflin, 1956. Reprinted by permission of Houghton Mifflin.